COOKING
with FIRE

COOKING
WITH
FIRE

FROM ROASTING ON A SPIT TO BAKING IN A TANNUR, Rediscovered Techniques and Recipes That Capture the Flavors of Wood-Fired Cooking

PAULA MARCOUX

PHOTOGRAPHY BY KELLER + KELLER

Storey Publishing

The mission of Storey Publishing is to serve our customers by
publishing practical information that encourages
personal independence in harmony with the environment.

Edited by Carleen Madigan
Art direction, book design, and photo styling by Alethea Morrison

Cover, jacket, and interior photography by © Keller + Keller Photography, except © Anagramm/iStockphoto.com, jacket (front flap, background), 93; © Chris Cheadle/All Canada Photos/Superstock, 196; © da-kuk/iStockphoto.com, front cover (title, background), 1 and throughout; © Jenny Matthews/Alamy, 165; © RusN/iStockphoto.com, jacket (back flap, background), 93

Indexed by Christine R. Lindemer, Boston Road Communications

The information in this book is true and complete to the best of our knowledge. All recommendations are made without guarantee on the part of the author or Storey Publishing. The author and publisher disclaim any liability in connection with the use of this information.

Storey books are available for special premium and promotional uses and for customized editions. For further information, please call 1-800-793-9396.

Read all instructions thoroughly, and be sure that you know how to safely operate your equipment, before using the techniques or making the recipes in this book. Always take appropriate safety precautions and remain alert and vigilant when working with fire.

Storey Publishing
210 MASS MoCA Way
North Adams, MA 01247
www.storey.com

Printed in China by Print Plus
10 9 8 7 6 5 4 3 2 1

Storey Publishing is committed to making environmentally responsible manufacturing decisions. This book was printed on paper made from sustainably harvested fiber.

Library of Congress Cataloging-in-Publication Data

Marcoux, Paula, 1960-
  Cooking with fire / by Paula Marcoux.
     pages cm
  Includes bibliographical references and index.
  ISBN 978-1-61212-158-1 (pbk. : alk. paper)
  ISBN 978-1-60342-912-2 (ebook) 1. Fireplace cooking. I. Title.
TX840.F5M37 2014
641.5'8--dc23
                    2013040132

CONTENTS

A FIRE AND A STICK

It all starts with the fire.

Humans have been at this cooking business for a very long time — as long as 1.9 million years, according to a recent and brilliant reinterpretation of hominid development that positions cooked food at the crux of a major evolutionary watershed. Thanks to our capability of controlling fire and applying it to food, we developed a smaller digestive tract, and smaller mouths and teeth. More importantly, we saved hours a day in chewing time, freeing us up to do things like invent bread, pottery, beer, kebabs, bellows, tamales, accounting, and cheese.

One million, nine hundred thousand years. That's hundreds of millennia we've been cooking, while adapting our understanding of fire and its interactions with food to all kinds of changing conditions. We humans have cooked our way into and through ice ages, deforestation and desertification, falling seas and rising seas, global migrations, mass extinctions of megafauna, the domestication of plants and animals, wars, displacements, and enslavement. And that's all before written history began.

Archaeology hints at some of the rich culinary traditions and ingenious foodways practices of bygone cultures over the millennia. Among some living cultures, a strong oral tradition still preserves food techniques and knowledge a century or more old. But our earliest written recipes are only a few thousand years old, which means that most of the vast spectrum of past human cooking traditions is unknowable to us.

BACK TO BASICS

In the first section of this book, we'll consider using fire for cooking at its most elemental level, without the intermediaries of pots and pans, spits and grills, griddles and ovens. Just live fire and a stick.

Why cook without pottery and metal? First, it's a great way to reintroduce yourself to fire. Spending some quality time with fire, while observing and manipulating it and its relationship with food without any technological barriers, is a great way to understand this primordial element. Regardless of what you cook, you pay attention differently when it's just the fire and the food.

Plus, it's fun; there's a reason we liked to cook things on sticks when we were kids. Oddly, in our culture, it's unusual for grownups to continue the practice. But, with the right group, it's a very social experience. Everyone around the fire is involved in producing their own meal, often at a leisurely pace.

And last, it develops respect for the millions of cooks who have gone before: parching grains on hearths, cooking roots or eggs in hot ashes, roasting bits of meat on sticks. All of these techniques require skill and attention to perfect; once you can cook without tools, the rest is cake.

Ultimately, nothing beats taking on a fun cooking project with a bunch of friends or launching some crazy food production as an entertainment at a social event. But to nurture the relationship that makes all this possible, I recommend spending some quality time alone with fire first. Observe how it behaves in different settings with different fuels, and how it reacts to small changes you make to its arrangement, and then, how it works to cook your food. If you've done a lot of grilling, or are already really good at building fires, you may feel like this exercise doesn't apply to you. But I feel that there's always something new to understand and there's never anything to be lost from the quiet, active contemplation of fire.

Making a Fire — Before You Start

This first series of exercises may be undertaken indoors at a fireplace, or better yet, outdoors on the ground.

Assemble everything you need at arm's reach before you strike a match. For the fire I have in mind, that would be kindling (an armload of dry sticks and twigs of varying sizes), in an amount you can gather in a basket or box or bucket in five minutes' time while wandering around the yard. If that doesn't describe where you live, you may want to get in the habit of traveling with such a receptacle so that you can snag kindling as you cross its path. For the purpose of today's exercise, pick up both hardwood and softwood materials; both have their place in firemaking and cooking. Later on in the exercise, you'll need three or four pieces of split hardwood. You will find a sturdy, sharp knife handy. And, of course, you will need an igniter: matches, lighter, ember from another fire, magnifying lens, bow drill, or flint and steel.

MAKING A FIRE: MATERIALS

Hardwoods like these burn down to great coals for cooking, regardless of size. Material for kindling a fire may be produced from larger wood by carving or splitting off shavings or splints with a sharp, sturdy knife.

HARDWOODS VERSUS SOFTWOODS

Softwoods, like pine, are generally more volatile than hardwoods, which is why they are usually preferable for fire starting. Hardwoods, like oak, maple, and hickory, are a denser source of carbon, the primary component of the coals that will be left on your hearth when the flames have died down. (Smokeless, very hot-burning natural charcoal is the almost-pure carbon material that remains when the volatiles are burned out of hardwood in an oxygen-poor environment.)

Thus, hardwood is preferred for most hearth cooking. It is the deep and even heat emanating from a pile of coals that roasts and grills, maintains a steady simmer in a pot, and blasts one thousand degrees of searing heat at your pizza. Even frying, which favors the quick heat from thinly split pine, benefits from the steadying effect of a bed of hardwood coals underlying the whole operation.

However, pine has its place and one unassailable advantage in that, due to its undesirability as fuel for woodstoves and other heating, it is often given away freely. I am quick to snag it and salt it away for kindling, for boiling and frying in cast iron, for recreational burning, and most of all for heating wood-fired bread ovens, a task at which it excels.

Kindling Your Fire

If you're at an indoor fireplace, open the damper in the flue, and shove any andirons or any other unnecessary appurtenances out of the way. Indoors or out, have a quick look to make sure that flammable things are not contiguous to your fire zone. Dried-flower arrangements, the Christmas tree, a pile of leaves, your double-knit leisure suit . . . all these should be moved away from the fire area. I have seen each one of these items burn, and you don't want to be surprised by that kind of sudden ignition.

There is no need to be dogmatic about a fire-making approach, except that you should expect to adapt your strategy to the materials at hand. This is a way that works for me, given the type of materials described above.

Bearing in mind that fire is composed of just as much oxygen as fuel, lay one softwood stick in the middle of the hearth and set another so that one end sits across the end of the first one. Where they cross, lean a number of very small sticks or twigs.

Take a sturdy knife and pare off some fine strips of softwood; or, shred up the inner bark from a cedar tree, or pull apart a chunk of white birch bark, or drop in a handful of dry pine needles. Top this puffy pile with a few more medium sticks to anchor it and give the fire something to catch on to.

KINDLING A FIRE

1. Lean one piece of small, dry wood on another to establish an open foundation through which oxygen will be drawn to nourish the fire.

2. Provide an airy, puffy nest of wood fiber — here just shavings pared from the same oak scraps we intend to cook with — and stick a match or other igniter in it.

3. Have more small stuff at hand, both to stabilize and fuel the fire. Maintain the open structure so that air continues to flow from beneath.

4. Gradually, without collapsing the fire's structure, add more and larger fuel to help it gain strength. Keep an eye on its progress while resisting the urge to overtend.

Have a bunch of broken-up dry sticks handy to feed the fire, as well as the next size of fuel you plan to burn, in this case, just larger sticks, broken or sawn or chopped to a manageable length. If you have the proper tool — a big sturdy knife works — splitting dry sticks into smaller splints really increases the likelihood of their igniting easily.

Look at your fire setup. At its nexus should be something that looks like a little bird's nest of puffy wood fibers; touch your match there to kindle your fire. When it appears to have caught, add a few more small pieces without collapsing your structure. Visualize oxygen coming up from beneath your little nest of fire, driving the flames into the fuel. Be patient and allow each addition to truly catch; introduce slightly larger pieces gradually and precisely. As this arrangement burns and collapses, it will ignite the foundation sticks below.

FIREWOOD STORAGE

Whether hardwood or softwood, the most desirable characteristic in any of your fuel is *dryness*. Unless you live in a very arid environment, keeping firewood under cover is a must. Use an airy woodshed, a lean-to, a sheet of plywood over a stack — find some manner of keeping water from getting into your woodstack, while letting air circulate.

It pays to sort your fuels, too, as you store them. Short chunks of oak for roasting, long straight pine that splits easily for firing the oven or frying, nice dry apple for smoking — the uses of these woods are so specific that it's silly to store them in a jumble. They are rarely interchangeable.

Be sure to have a separate and accessible pile of less-wonderful wood that's just for non-culinary burning. When late-night enthusiasm takes hold of your guests, make sure the pyros have something expendable to burn.

Making a Coal Bed

If you have begun to add some hardwood sticks to your little fire, you've already taken the first step in getting a real cooking fire going — creating some coals. As inconsequential as these first tiny coals may seem, the success of most hearth cooking operations basically comes down to having the right volume of those glowing lumps of smoldering carbon in the right place at the right time. So let's make some more. When you have an actively burning small fire composed of sticks that are large enough to support them, place a couple of pieces of split hardwood on the structure. They should be more or less parallel, and nearly touching, over the center of the fire, so that the flames and oxygen from below are forced to pass between them, hastening ignition of the new wood.

MAKING A COAL BED

1. Start the transition from softwood to hardwood with twigs and sticks, or small split material.

2. Coals will form from hardwood of any size. A big pile of small wood is a quicker route to a roasting fire than a small pile of big wood.

3. As you add more hardwood, be sure to maintain an open structure to the fire, so that air can whoosh up through the fuel and feed the flames.

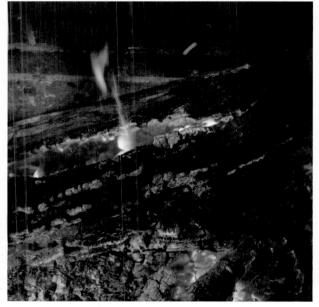

4. New fuel goes to the back of the fire, coals come out from the front. Also, you can just push a well-established fire aside to access the coals that have formed beneath.

Experiment with this proximity phenomenon as you add more fuel and adjust the fire with a stick or poker. Notice what happens when you push things closer together or pull them further apart. You'll find that there is an optimal distance, determined by a great many variables and worthy of an honors physics project, which provides for the most efficient combustion of fuel in any particular fire. No two fires will be exactly the same in this regard. Fortunately, you don't have to resort to some sort of algorithm to calculate this factor. In fact, the knowledge is almost intuitive; some folks make absolutely perfect fires all their lives without even thinking about it for a second. I describe the phenomenon because it is the first thing to look at when a fire is *not* behaving to your liking. Wood piled too close together on an uncertain fire will tend to smother it, especially if the air flow from below is choked off. On the other hand, fuel scattered too widely deprives the fire of the intensity it should have; it's as if you are nursing several small fires rather than enabling one focused act of combustion. When the wood is just the right distance apart, and oxygen is whooshing into it from beneath, your fire is burning optimally.

FIRE-POKING CAVEATS AND THE SACRIFICIAL FIRE

One thing you may discover in experimentally poking your test-fire is that the wrong kind of poking can just about extinguish a healthy blaze. In fact, more than once a certain dear friend has, in the course of telling an especially engrossing story, reduced a virtual bonfire to a scatter of smoldering logs before we wrestled her poking stick away. Now she surrenders it voluntarily when the narrative starts to get good.

Would that all guests had such self-knowledge. Once you have developed a sense of purpose about fire, you may find that you need to restrain well-meaning people from destroying your handiwork. Worse, still, than the accidental extinguisher is the zealot on the other end of the spectrum — the pyromaniac. The cook comes back from an errand in the house to find that an inferno has singed the roast, scorched the soup, and even cracked the pot. Sometimes the powers of these, usually macho, interlopers may be deflected toward the good — turning a roast on a spit, for instance. In the case of children, fearful parents are often allies ("Stop waving that firebrand before you put someone's eye out!"). But I have found that the most effective and least painful way of preserving the integrity of a cooking fire at a large party is to set up a more attractive, purely recreational fire a little distance away. Everyone gets to have fun, and dinner gets cooked, too.

GETTING STARTED: ROASTING ON A STICK

Artfully add a few more pieces of hardwood, and you have a cooking fire underway. It's just a matter of time until a small coal bed forms beneath the logs, all ready to perform its alchemy on a dish of food. However, before we get to the sublime, let's start with the ridiculous: the marshmallow. That's right, the lowest common denominator of campfire cooking.

Well, the marshmallow, silly as it is, is a great learning tool. Its sugary ingredients make it highly responsive to heat, so that to toast one is like roasting real food on fast-forward. Yet it is rare to observe a marshmallow-cook, adult or child, who takes the task seriously. Most marshmallows go down in flames, an inevitable end for a ball of aerated sugars suspended thoughtlessly over a pine inferno. But every now and again I see a crafty and patient individual who firmly plants the confection on a greenwood stick, who scopes out the fire for a perfect little hearth of coals at its base, and who turns and turns the rigid gummy cylinder into a perfectly molten blob encased in a crisp, even, golden-brown skin. Meanwhile a dozen others nearby have been immolated over the fire with protests of, "*This* is how I like to do it!"

So, give it a try, if you're not already one of the patient and crafty ones. Even if you *do* like marshmallows charred on the exterior and cold and hard at the core (and I am skeptical), accept the challenge of observing what you are doing when you cook them perfectly. Experiencing that process attentively will allow you to approach roasting anything — a chicken, a hog, an eggplant, a fish (things you really don't want carbonized on the outside and raw in the middle) — with a refreshed understanding of the task.

Correct Heat, Sufficient Support

Here are a few technical aspects to consider when roasting the marshmallow, applicable also to more involved roasting projects:

THE FIRE. People don't make high-quality roasting fires to cook marshmallows, but that's okay. Even the lamest campfire will have a spot that can cook the perfect marshmallow. Look around the base of any fire that has been burning for an hour or so. Even if the fuel is the nastiest green pine logs, eventually something like a coal bed, sufficient for marshmallows anyway, will appear.

The fire you just made for the foregoing exercise, though, is a high-quality affair. You may use some coals that spill out from it, or you may push the fire over a little to expose a nice coal bed for you to use easily, or you may take a fire shovel and scoop out a glowing heap of coals to put in a convenient place for your slow marshmallow-roasting pleasure. All of these approaches will serve you well in

Sometimes the fire naturally furnishes a small cave of perfectly even heat.

your future hearth cooking. And if you were setting about cooking some real food, a rabbit, say, you would make the same demand on your fire: coals, coals, coals.

THE SPIT. When roasting marshmallows, use a greenwood stick. Make sure it's long enough for your comfort and stout enough that the marshmallow won't droop down into the fire. Whether or not it's necessary, the time-honored Girl Scout way is to use a knife to skin the bark off of the thin end of the stick and put a bit of a point on it.

Cooking foods on sticks has a very deep, broad, and mostly unknowable prehistory. European visitors to the Atlantic coast of North America described skillful native cooks roasting whole fish, reptiles, and small mammals propped on sticks before a fire. Pre-modern and modern stick cookery in the European tradition has usually been of the do-it-yourself snack category; cheese, sausage, bacon, toast — recreational treats functionally not unlike the marshmallow, but made of actual food.

The greenwood stick is appropriate technology for the marshmallow, simple and disposable. A half-ounce confection doesn't put a lot of strain on a device, so there is no need for anything more robust. And even if the flimsy tool should fail, the marshmallow's expendability means its loss is not a culinary or economic tragedy. All of which points to the converse, that the roasting tools you select for any job should be able to support the weight of the food in both raw and cooked form. The size, thickness, shape, and density of the foods will help determine the hardware necessary.

THE SWEET SPOT. Sometimes the fire naturally furnishes a small cave of perfectly even heat, a tiny inferno that seems just made to toast a marshmallow in jig time. One false move, though, or a second too long, can bring your exercise to a flaming conclusion. Or you may find that that little oven is *just too hot*, leaving a cold, hard marshmallow heart within a perfectly toasted exterior. Try these solutions: find a prop like a brick or chunk of wood to place several inches in front of the sweet spot. Use that fulcrum to keep your roasting stick still while you slowly spin it for the seconds it takes to crisp and brown. If the inside is "raw," try a preliminary roasting over a few coals in a much cooler location, then finish it in the hot box.

If all this seems like a lot of mental effort for a lousy marshmallow, consider how helpful these skills will be when the stakes are higher. When you are setting up and troubleshooting a suckling pig or an heirloom turkey, you will want to have the resources and confidence to make small changes to get the effect you are after — the crispy delicious exterior and the perfectly done interior.

Peel and sharpen the end of a greenwood stick, long enough for your comfort and stout enough that the marshmallow will not droop down into the fire.

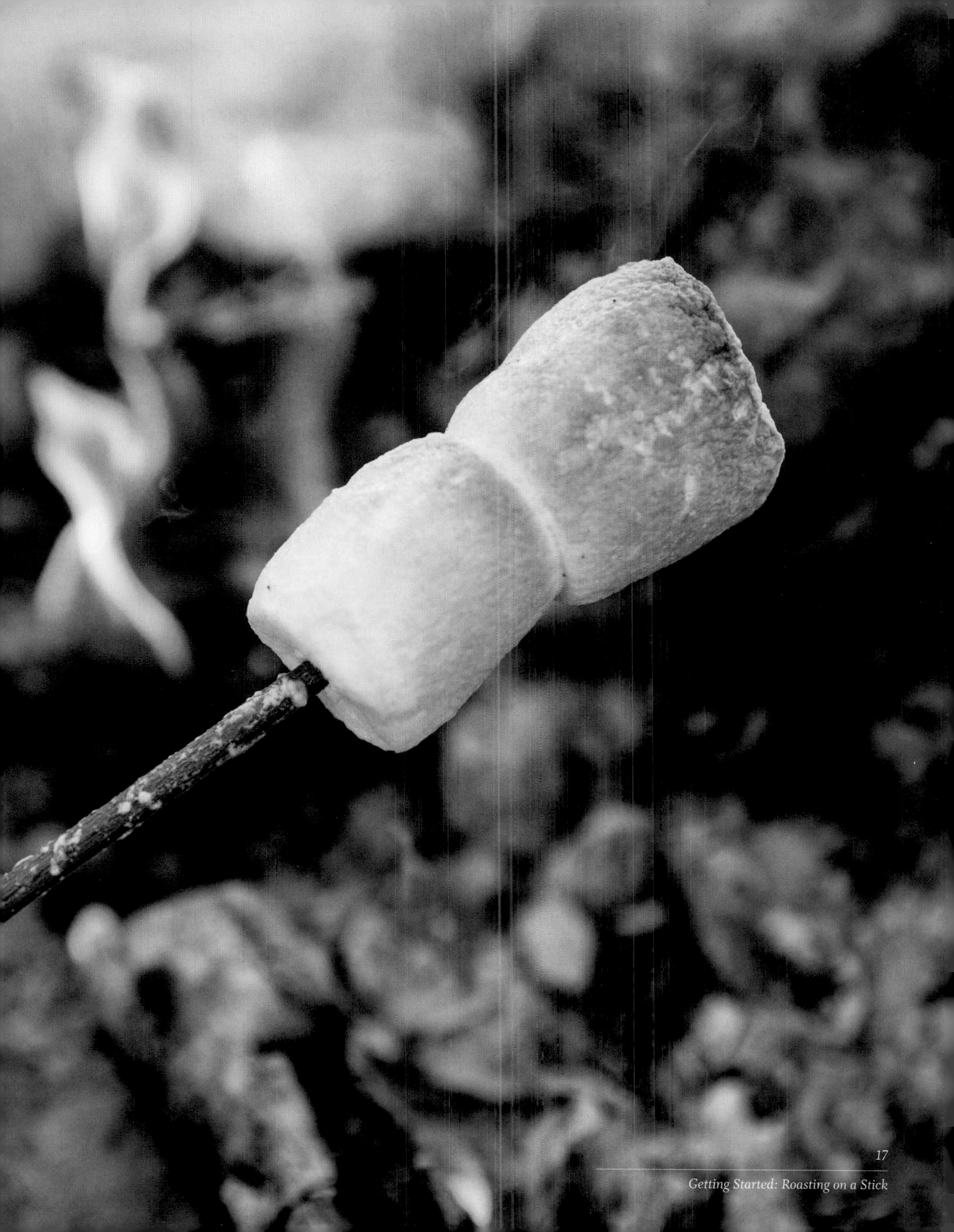

FOCUS ON FUELS

Cut and split cordwood is the typical commercially available firewood in America today, and it can be convenient and effective for cooking. But, like so many other things that have become standardized by industrialization, it is not the only way to go, especially if you are willing to take a hand in things yourself.

For example, I live in a reforested area of New England, surrounded by trees. When a subdivision goes in or an ice storm strikes or the power company trims around the lines, a massive pile of carbon-bearing biomass comes down around our heads. Sometimes it's possible to divert the flow of all that useful wood from an ignominious end in the brush chipper to a useful afterlife cooking our food.

A hardwood treetop has tremendous cooking potential bottled up in it. Larger branch stock can be dealt with like cordwood, but the smaller stuff, the unruly small branches, merit different tools and skills — quiet, humane tools and practical, contemplative skills. Once tamed, wood of small diameter or quirky shape dries down rather quickly when stacked under cover. And it's surprising how serious and effective a fuel the stuff can be. An armload burns down to make a decent bed of coals in no time.

Cooking on small wood like this connects us to many generations of pre-industrial cooks worldwide. Along with drawing water, gathering wood has ever been a precursor labor to actual cooking, drudgery for most of the people who did (or still do) it every day. Branches, deadfall, twigs, gorse, and straw were forms of fuel traditionally gathered in rural areas of pre-industrial Europe.

But commercial firewood also has a long history. Large establishments, like estates and monasteries, maintained woodlots, places where biomass was managed by coppicing, strategically pruning growth from standard trees on a set schedule. Town and city cooks relied on purchasing bundles of such wood, or professionally made charcoal in some places, to fuel their kitchens. As regulated commercial products, these loads of bavins or faggots (bundles of sticks) and billets (arm-size pieces) were ancestors to our modern American cordwood. But as the maple or hazel tree from which they were harvested lived to grow another batch of fuel to be pruned in another seven years, this system valued sustainability in a way that makes our current approach to our forests seem quite random, crude, and benighted.

Coppiced wood provided cooking fuel for densely settled Europe for centuries; getting in the habit of gathering branch stock is an easy way to experiment with a traditional and excellent fuel.

THE STUMP. Cutting wood with any tool is safer and easier with a stable platform, such as a stump.

THE HEAVY KNIFE, KUKRI, BILLHOOK, KOA. These tools are used for splitting small wood smaller, whittling cooking equipment, knocking branches off, and cutting small-diameter wood to length.

MACHETE AND HATCHET. These two tools have similar uses as the ones above, but they are larger. Adept handlers will use them for every job (depending on their cultural background), but that takes much caution and practice. I've seen a Costa Rican guy cut a lawn with a machete, and I've seen my husband cut the joinery for a house frame with a hatchet.

AXE. Different versions are used for cutting medium wood to length, felling trees, or splitting cordwood.

CROSSCUT SAW. This saw is used for cutting wood of all sorts to length.

LOPPERS AND PRUNERS. Underappreciated tools, these can be used for reducing a treetop to quickly usable fuel.

FROE AND CLUB. These are used for splitting wood along the grain. (Useful for the occasional cooking task.)

TOOLS FOR FUELS

Having a range of tools at your disposal makes it easy to accommodate all sorts of wood in a variety of sizes. Some implements excel at one task — pruners and loppers at snipping up brush, the combos of club/ froe and maul/wedge at splitting along the grain. Others are generalists; if I could only have one tool, I'd choose a small hatchet.

Kukri

Knife

Pruners

Club

Froe

Wedge

Loppers

Crosscut saw

Machete

Hatchet

Pruning saw

Maul

TOASTING CHEESE

Toasting cheese is good, low-maintenance, self-service, indoor/outdoor fun, and a smart step up for both adults and children who have mastered the marshmallow. The equipment requirements are flexible; pretty much any fire with a few coals will do for the heat source, whether in a hearth or campfire, a front-loading woodstove, or a chiminea. Cheese weighs considerably more than a marshmallow; if you are fashioning greenwood sticks for cheese-toasting, make sure they are sturdy and not too springy (lest you invent the hot-cheese-trebuchet). Small diameter skewers and long iron forks have also served us well; historic sources mention that both swords and knitting needles served as cheese toasters.

Warning: making the transition from marshmallows to Double Gloucester is like removing the training wheels from your stick-roasting practice. Danger can strike just as the cheese reaches perfection. When cheese is molten, it doesn't have the gluey traction of a hot marshmallow; instead it greasily drops into the fire and is an utter heartbreaking loss. So be ready with your toast at the first sign of slippage.

Yes, Double Gloucester is a cheese mentioned by nineteenth-century authors as being an English favorite for a toasted cheese supper, but there are many other options. In terms of successful toasting, the texture of the cheese is actually more important than the flavor, so that latter part's up to you. Any cheese that is moist enough to be impaled without cracking, and that has a melting quality, should work. These characteristics do happen to describe most of the greater cheddar family of cheeses, but there are many other cheeses from other lands (Havarti, fontina, young Gouda) that are also splendid in this application.

Oh, and toast. Thin slices of bread may be toasted on the same implements before the same fire and kept warm and dry until the cheese beckons. Alternatively, if you can set up a little grill over some coals ahead and make a bunch of toast, your guests can concentrate on their cheese, for which they may be grateful.

Toasting Cheese

TOASTED CHEESE, OLD-SCHOOL

Today "toasted cheese" is British English for what Americans call "a grilled cheese sandwich." But in the days before sandwiches were formally known and named as such, "toasted cheese" existed in a variety of guises. The earliest manner consisted of simply a chunk of cheese, impaled on the end of a stick or skewer (or sword, according to Shakespeare), and roasted, marshmallow fashion. The golden molten glob would be applied to a thin slice of crispy toast, if available.

8 ounces cheese, cut into 1- by 1- by 1-inch cubes, preferably at room temperature

1 half loaf of favorite bread, sliced thinly, and toasted crisp

OPTIONAL ADORNMENTS
mustard or chutney, thinly sliced onion

4 servings, barring accidents

I. Have ready a medium fire with a bed of coals.

2. Each cheese-toasting individual should carefully impale a cube of cheese upon an implement. Try not to run it all the way through. Unless the cheese is very elastic and forgiving, this abuse will tend to split it in half.

3. Use a fire shovel to pull some coals forward. Each guest may toast cheese to the degree favored by extending t over the coals. Turn it slowly for even exposure to the heat. No quick motions. Be attentive to slumping, and be ready with the toast.

4. Spread out the cheese on the toast, applying optional adornments to taste, and perhaps washing down with a glass of pale ale.

RACLETTE SUPPER

If you were to use an Appenzeller cheese or other semi-hard Swiss cheese for your toasted-cheese project, you would be approaching the delicious Alpen idea of *raclette*, another leisurely combination of cheese and fire. Preparing *raclette* is a bit more formalized than the toasted-cheese free-for-all, at least in its classic form.

Not every American grocery store stocks Valais cheese for *raclette*, although some that employ a caring cheese manager may stock it during the winter holidays, especially if loyal customers talk it up. So be on the lookout for it, or buy it online, where both French and Swiss varieties are available. Alternatively, you might experiment with other types of cheese — semi-hard and a bit pungent, preferably — to see if you can get it to melt and brown *à la raclette*. It may not be 100 percent authentic, but how bad could it be?

¼ wheel (about 2½ pounds) raclette cheese
4 pounds fingerling potatoes, scrubbed
1 teaspoon salt
1 jar of *cornichons*

OPTIONAL ADORNMENTS
a green salad, cured meats

---

8 to 12 servings

---

1. Allow the cheese to come to room temperature.

2. Make a medium hardwood fire on a clean level hearth. Find a few clean bricks that can be used to support the cheese before the fire. If you happen to have a durable ceramic tile around, see if you can set that on the bricks under the cheese to make it easy to slide closer to and further from the fire. Set the cheese aside in a safe place until you are ready to start broiling it.

3. Cover the fingerlings with water in an iron pot; add salt and cover. Hang the pot up over the fire. When the potatoes begin to simmer, move to a cooler spot on the fire so that they cook without boiling over. When they are tender, drain them and return them to the still hot pot, setting them well to the side of the hearth to keep warm. Also put the diners' plates in a good place to warm up.

4. Poke the fire a bit and drag some coals out to the front toward where you intend to make the *raclette*. Feed the fire from the back to make sure you'll still have plenty of heat coming up. Set up the cheese on the tile or directly on the brick pedestal. Let it broil in the heat of the coals and flames until the cheese is molten with a crisp golden brown exterior. Pick up the cheese and use a long knife to scrape off only the melted, crisped crust onto one of the plates. Let the diners help themselves to a potato or two and some *cornichons* to accompany the cheesy glob.

5. Continue broiling and scraping onto your guests' plates, making adjustments to the cheese's position as necessary.

ROMANI BACON

I am indebted to my friend Gabe Selak for introducing me to this elemental dish, which featured in his Hungarian-American upbringing in Pennsylvania. While its ingredients are few, this food-event requires plenty of slack time and some beverages and select good company. It takes the right kind of guests to want to hang out by the fire and roast their personal bacon slabs in a leisurely fashion. One recent convert describes it as "s'mores for grownups."

2 Italian frying peppers, seeded and chopped
2 Hungarian wax peppers, seeded and chopped
1 large white onion, finely chopped
   Fat pinch salt
1 tablespoon balsamic vinegar
   Freshly ground black pepper
1 loaf rye bread or other rustic bread
1 pound very best quality slab bacon, with rind

---

6 to 8 ultra-casual snack-size servings

1. Kindle a nice campfire with plenty of hardwood. Lots of small sticks are fine.

2. Locate some sturdy greenwood sticks to skewer the bacon — or better, have each guest find his or her own. A nice strong point needs to be whittled on one end. Emphasize to the diners that the safety of their bacon is in their own hands.

3. While your guests are distracted with fire-tending and stick-whittling responsibilities, prepare the accompaniments. Mix the peppers, onion, salt, vinegar, and black pepper in a medium serving bowl. Slice the bread in thick slices. Have all this stuff within arm's reach of the fire.

4. Cut the bacon into oblongs of about 1- by 2-inches. Now you're ready to go.

5. Demonstrate this next part for your guests. Carefully cut crosswise repeatedly into the meaty face of your piece of bacon, making parallel cuts about ¼ inch apart; do not cut all the way through. Imagine that this chunk of bacon is a little book, and that the rind is the binding (see page 6).

6. Thread your skewer-stick through the bacon-book. Use a fire shovel or a stick to drag out some nice glowing coals in front of the fire; make a nice coal bed. (Don't forget to keep feeding the fire so that you'll have more coals later.)

7. Now everyone roasts their own bacon over the coals. It's usually a bit slow to get going, and it cannot be rushed. Turn to cook all around. When it starts to sizzle and spit, spread some of the pepper salad on a slice of bread and keep it handy. The idea is to let the bacon drippings fall on the salad as they come. (This is where the patience comes in; lusty singing and wine drinking and stories of derring-do are all helpful during this procedure, as long as there are no sudden clumsy gesticulations.)

8. Some like to nibble on the greasy salad sandwich as the dripping comes along, and then devour neat the eventual crispy bacon nugget that remains, while others prefer to preserve the sandwich and drippings unmolested until the perfectly frizzled bacon may be pulled apart to eat on top.

A Fire and a Stick

ROASTING IN ASHES AND COALS

What can you roast by a fire using no utensils whatsoever? Most ingredients I've had success with in this mode exhibit a few common characteristics. Self-contained, high-density items with moderate internal moisture (sweet potatoes, butternut squash) do well, because cooking by this method is low and slow and steady. It's also good if the foods come equipped with a sacrificial layer that can be stripped away before eating (plantains, corn, garlic) since the cooking is done right down in the ashes, and some exterior charring and ash adhesion come with the territory.

Finally, it's best to select candidates that are abundant and inexpensive (peanuts, potatoes), since there is usually some shrinkage. This sort of minimalist roasting, it must be admitted, is not the easiest to control. Inadvertent and tragic contact is sometimes made between the food and very hot burning coals; it can be tricky to tell if the foods are perfectly situated to cook evenly. And occasionally — especially when it's dark and the party's running into the wee hours — a few things just get lost in the ashes or explode.

All that being said, the technique has a good deal going for it, and not only for the obvious reason that you don't need any tools. Like the traditional on-a-stick projects, it can be a great way to amuse guests around a campfire and let them take a hand in their own hearth-cooking projects. Most of all, with a little effort and attention it can yield very intensely flavored foods.

There are basically two ways to go about roasting with this technique, both requiring a fire that has burned hardwood long enough to accumulate a heap of coals and ashes. In one method, you bury the foods directly in the hot ashes; in the other, you set the foods near enough to the heat of the fire, within the hearth, that they simply roast. Both methods are slow going, which is not necessarily disadvantageous, since other sorts of cooking or merry-making may be carried out on all sides simultaneously.

Sometimes I use this technique as an entertaining way to produce late-night snacks for people who ate a real meal a few hours before. For example, as you transition your cookfire into a campfire after supper, why not bury some treats — chestnuts, say — in the ashes for later?

And done indoors, where often a lot of BTUs are just bouncing around a masonry hearth to no particular end, this type of roasting allows you to take advantage of collateral heat without a lot of fuss — think about a line of roasting onions perched on bricks behind, or to one otherwise idle side of, the fire while you spit-roast, stew, fry, or broil dinner.

A Fire and a Stick

Specific Pointers

POTATOES. Scrub large potatoes clean, and towel dry. Bury them in a pile of hot ashes in a hot cooking hearth. After an hour turn them over and end-for-end, and rebury. From time to time you may lay a shovelful of new coals over the ashes, as long as they don't make direct contact with the spuds. For very large russets, expect two hours' baking. Smaller potatoes will take less time, of course, but are easier to lose.

To test, retrieve one potato from the ashes. Hold it in an old towel, and pinch it cautiously to feel for overall doneness. If it gives nicely, towel it clean, and repeat with the rest. A nineteenth-century cookbook author advises serving with cold butter, salt, and pepper.

ONIONS. Use large unpeeled onions. If you are cooking in an outdoor fire pit, you'll need a fire of moderate size, preferably set down in the ground a bit, and with bricks (or stones) surrounding. Place the onions, pointy end up, so that they have the hot bricks at their backs and the fire in front of them, about 10 to 12 inches away. They may be sitting in a little bed of hot ashes or upon other hot bricks or stones. If you are cooking in a fireplace, set a row of bricks on edge near the fire, but out of the way, as a roasting pedestal for the onions. In both scenarios, rotate all the onions 90 degrees each time they begin to show some color (about every 15 or 20 minutes). If one side of your fire is much hotter than the other, switch them around after 45 minutes. These will take over an hour. One American cookbook of 1840 suggests parboiling the onions first, roasting them thus, and then peeling them to serve whole with just butter and salt, as a side dish. Incidentally, a roasted onion applied to the ear was about the commonest remedy for earache in nineteenth-century America.

GARLIC. Follow the same method as with onions (not the parboiling option).

SWEET POTATOES. You may use the potato method or the onion method. Cook until the potato oozes caramelizing juice. Peel after cooking if necessary for ash-free consumption.

SWEET CORN. Here is an exception to the low-heat/long-cooking rule. Take whole ears of corn (no need to fuss with the husks or silk in any way) and lay directly on a hot coal bed. The outer husks will scorch, but no matter; in fact, it's all to the good. Turn the ears over and end-for-end to get even heating, and in short order you'll end up with perfectly steamed, succulent corn on the cob. Test for desired degree of doneness by pulling the husk back for a look. Optionally, leave them on the coals a bit longer for some smoky caramelization of the kernels themselves.

A Fire and a Stick

For best results, choose foods that have a sacrificial outer layer, since the outside will scorch.

CHESTNUTS. To avoid explosions, use a small knife to make an incision in the shell of each chestnut. Bury in a hot hearth with hot ashes. Roast until nut is tender through, about 30 to 40 minutes.

PEANUTS. Roast raw peanuts in the shell in hot ashes, stirring from time to time and testing occasionally, until the shells are brittle and the nuts crisp and tasty. Senegalese cooks roast peanuts submerged in hot sand for a nice even heat.

WINTER SQUASH. Set a whole butternut, acorn, or other hard squash on a moderately hot bed of coals and ash, turning it to roast evenly. When it is uniformly lightly charred, test it with a skewer or small knife where the flesh is thickest. When the squash is tender through, peel off the burnt exterior, halve it and seed it, mash or chop it, and season to taste or use in your favorite recipe. Or for rough fireside dining, simply halve or quarter the roasted squash, and scrape out seeds and stringy bits. Each diner adds a blob of butter and other seasonings and eats with a spoon.

EGGS. An entirely bygone food going back to at least the days of Rome, the roasted egg is a creature more of poetry than of cookbooks, a trope of Shakespeare, Pope, and Scott that seems meant to convey the idea of reason or skill hidden in an unlikely guise. However, it is, or was, a real food, and one that, homely and simple as it seems, has indeed taken me a few passes to achieve, let alone perfect. Although cookbooks omit coverage, very good egg-roasting instructions may be found in Thomas Boys's memoir from the Napoleonic Wars, in which he describes "a jolly old Spaniard" who took an egg, "cracked it at one end, and stuck it upright in the hot embers." Boys's verdict? "I beg to state that a roast egg — so roasted, i.e., done slowly in the embers — not only is altogether a different sort of thing from a boiled egg, but beats it to sticks: especially if washed down, as mine were on the present occasion, with a cup or two of good sound Spanish wine out of a leathern bag."

The Spaniard's technique of perforating the small end of the egg is essential to successful egg roasting; as I happen to know they have a fatal tendency to explode if left intact. The other needful trick is plain old patience; for even cooking, the egg must be rotated on occasion in its ashen bed. Sir Walter Scott's character Davie, an intellectually challenged innkeeper's boy, was known as the best egg roaster in the highlands; he "lay with his nose almost in the fire, nuzzling among the ashes, kicking his heels, mumbling to himself, turning the eggs as they lay in the hot embers . . ."

A Few Takes on Ash-Roasted Vegetables

- Dress roasted onions with olive oil, balsamic vinegar, currants, mint, or oregano, and salt and pepper.

- Roast potatoes in the fire late at night, rescue from the ashes and set aside to peel for hash browns in the morning.

- Once you've pulled back the charred husks from your roast corn, gild the lily. Try dipping a lime quarter in tequila, rubbing the hot, well-browned corn ears with it, and sprinkling them with flavorful hot powdered red chile and kosher salt. Or for a dessert corn, brush the steamy ears with a mix of heavy cream and maple syrup. Grill over slow coals until golden brown and glazed.

- Serve roasted acorn squash halves with abundant garlic slivers fried in olive oil, chunks of goat cheese, chopped cilantro, and a sprinkle of salt.

BAKING WHOLE FISH AND BIRDS IN RAW CLAY

Kerri Helme, a skilled Wampanoag potter and avid student of past technologies, blew me away with a fabulous striped bass cooked in raw clay. Here's how, in her words:

"I usually start off with a hardwood fire, really hot. Let it turn to a big pile of red hot coals. When you first start the fire, take the fish and wrap it completely in a layer of clay about an inch and a half thick . . . After wrapping the fish, leave it out in the sun to dry while your wood turns to hot coals. Then take a rake and make a space under the coals for the fish, putting the fish in between the coals. After that, you cover the fish with coals completely for about 25 minutes. After you remove the fish, you can crack open the clay with a rock or anything, and it should be fine."

"Fine" is an understatement. Scales and (for birds) feathers just come off with the baked clay, leaving tender, moist, perfectly cooked flesh. And, beyond the knife you need to gut the fish or bird, no utensils are really needed, so this is a great trick to know when you are roughing it. That being said, the results are so delicious that there's no reason not to make this at home in your backyard.

Incidentally, Kerri remarks that upland birds are best cooked in this fashion, duck and goose being too fatty. See Resources, page 305, for more on baking in clay.

BAKING BREAD UNDER THE ASHES

Much like a potato, a disk of stiff unleavened dough may be baked under ashes and coals. Today this technique is still practiced by nomads of the Sahara, Sinai, and Negev deserts, but formerly was in very widespread usage globally among people on the move. In fact, back when "on the move" was the human condition, before agricultural commitments had made settlement profitable, it is quite likely that the first bakers converted their gathered wild or semi-wild grains into bread by this method.

Millennia later, in the sophisticated urban centers of Sumer, soldiers weary of the cushy life — eating professionally baked bread and consorting with concubines — expressed eagerness to return to the romance of *kaman tumri*, literally the "flat loaf in ashes," the emblem of the manly, rough life of the battle campaign (at least in a poem, the *Epic of Erra*; many real soldiers were probably pretty happy to put up their swords, eat bread from a bakery, drink beer, and chill with the family back in Babylon).

The Roman-era version of bread under ashes was named *panis focacius*, after the hearth (*focus*) in which it was baked. In the post-Imperial era, these breads endured all over Europe, thinly veiled by aliases like *fougasse*, *focaccia*, *fouäse*, *foisse*, and others. Interestingly, by the early modern era, many of these names had come to refer to particular breads used by professional bakers to "test the heat of the oven" before clearing out the last of the fire and setting in the bread for customers, i.e., to make snacks for the bakery staff. (See chapter 5.)

Baking a disk of dough under embers at a campfire or in a hearth requires almost no tools and makes a surprisingly tasty, if rather hard, bread. A swift thumping knocks the ashes right off.

HEARTH BANNOCK

The English author of an 1828 baking manual described Scots cottagers using pea, bean, oat, or barley flour to make "hearth bannocks": "A certain quantity of meal is taken and made into a very stiff dough; while the person is making and working the dough, a quantity of dried wood is burning on the hearth . . . As soon as the wood is consumed, so far as not to give forth any smock, the hearth is swept clean, the bannock put on it, and the glowing embers around and over it, and suffered to remain so until the bread is baken. All who have eaten of this bread give it an excellent character; but it is nothing the worse of a piece of good fresh butter to help it."

I followed his directions, but used wheat flour like the Bedouin. If you should get your hands on some really fresh whole-wheat flour — or, better, emmer, einkorn, or spelt — this would be a good way to get in touch with some real antiquity.

12 ounces bread flour
4 ounces whole-wheat flour
2 teaspoons salt
About 1½ cups very warm water

1 manly loaf

I. Make a hardwood fire in a clean hearth (i.e., no residual heavy metals or glass from past fires), or on the desert floor, beach, or forest, for that matter. A large pile of brush or branches works great for fuel, leaving coals that are uniformly small. You'll want to burn it for an hour or so.

2. As soon as your fire's started, mix together all the ingredients, then knead briefly to make a very stiff dough. Keep the dough in an airtight container until your fire is almost ready, at least 30 minutes. Take it out and knead again for a few minutes on a well-floured surface. Round up into a nice ball and cover. Allow to rest another 10 minutes, then pat it out into a disk about ½ inch thick.

3. The Bedouin do all this work on a heavy cloth, and then use that to get the dough into the proximity of the fire; you can do the same or use a peel, a cookie sheet, or a cutting board. Use a stick or a shovel to push all the coals and ashes to one side. Lay the dough into the center of the hearth, and push the ashes and coals back over, completely covering the dough.

4. After 15 to 20 minutes, poke a stick alongside to find the disc. If it is rigid, pry it out, flip it over and re-cover. If not, try again in a few minutes. Bake 15 to 25 minutes longer, until pretty hard. Pry it out again and thump it briskly to jar loose any extraneous bits.

5. We enjoy it with olive oil and salt, in the mode of focaccia: ancient Sumerians loved rich broth and beer, if you'd like to reach further back in time for accompaniment ideas.

PINE-NEEDLE MUSSELS

In October, the pitch pines and white pines around our house drop a beautiful puffy mat of russet needles. It takes but a few minutes to gather up the pile needed to have this kind of fun. This is an irresistible introduction for newbies of any age to both cooking with fire and eating shellfish.

About 4 or 5 pounds of fresh mussels in the shell

6 to 10 servings, as an appetizer

1. Gather ½ to 1 bushel nice dry pine needles.

2. We like to set this up directly on an outdoor wooden table, but you can use a large board (say 3 by 3 feet) or a very flat large stone. Be aware that you will leave a pretty good scorching on whatever surface you select. Also look around before you start to make sure that you will not inadvertently set something else on fire; have a bucket of water handy just in case.

3. Place something small and stable in the middle of the board; a quarter of a brick, a small oblong stone, a half of a potato, cut side down, a small cube of stale bread . . . Arrange the mussels around it, leaning against the supporting object, with their pointy ends sticking upward. Continue arranging all the mussels in a concentric manner. Many hands make quick work and add to the fun.

4. Now let everyone scatter the pine needles evenly, and as deeply as possible, over the top of the mussels. Give a brief safety lecture, then take a single coal from whatever fire you have burning nearby and deposit it deep in the mountain of pine needles, directly on top of the little support in the middle. (If for some reason you don't have a fire already burning somewhere, just use a match.) Stand back; these babies really go up.

5. That's it. When the fire dies down, within the smoking ruins lies a tasty appetizer. Resiny-smoky, briny, delicious. I once tried offering toast and remoulade sauce as accompaniments, but was soundly rebuffed with cries of "they're too good alone!"

6. If for some reason there's a cool spot in the fire and some of the mussels don't open, gather them up and rearrange them with new pine needles for a quick encore pyre.

A Fire and a Stick

Baking Bread under the Ashes

A FEW SIMPLE TOOLS

So far, we've done quite a bit with very little gear. A modicum of additional equipment, though, will help to manage larger items by the fire, which will really increase our culinary range. These simple tools are mostly just take-offs on The Stick, but they confer on the cook the latitude to walk off and do something else rather than hold a lump of meat over coals from the beginning to the end of the cooking process. The tools in question — the spit, the piece of twine, the metal grate — safely suspend the foods above the coals and ashes on the hearth, in the process known as roasting (which includes its subset, grilling). The job of these tools is to hold the food at just the right distance from hot coals, keeping it clean as it cooks through to the desired degree, so that the delicious crispy glistening crust — one of the joys of carnivorism — may be enjoyed grit-free by the diner.

The skills and equipment required to produce a perfect roast do vary as you scale up from a quail to an ox, but the understanding and judgment you develop working with small foods are utterly applicable to the larger ones. So, I recommend starting with lighter and more manageable items, and using cheap or free gear at the outset. Then, when you decide that you'd like to graduate to a whole lamb or pig, you'll understand deep down the advantages of very secure purpose-made equipment that provides easy manipulation before the fire. Until that day, I honestly think that well-thought-out jury-rigged equipment serves quite as well. In fact, in some cases the lowest-tech solution is actually the best. For example, a leg of lamb roasted over coals while suspended from a five-cent piece of string bests one roasted on an expensive electric rotisserie-driven spit; the meat may be perfectly cooked inside and out by both methods, but one of those legs will inevitably suffer the demerit of having had a metal rod shoved through it.

SPIT ROASTING

The archaeological record of the earliest horizon of spit-roasting is murky to non-existent, the basic tools being minimal and, before the relatively recent days of iron spits, biodegradable. A low-tech rotisserie requires only a well-formed stick of the proper weight and gauge for the item to be roasted, perhaps some smaller sticks for secure fastening, and a couple of props to act as andirons — no more than small stumps or crotchets of wood driven into the ground. Most hearths found by archaeologists dating from before the Neolithic period, therefore, don't reveal many specifics about the cooking techniques used in them: a scatter of fire-cracked rocks, some carbonized bones with butchering marks, a shell midden, a greasy ash-stain in the soil. Even if an archaeologist can determine that a bone sample came from roasted meat, it is impossible to say whether that roast was on a spit or not.

But more recently, in the last eight thousand years, as people began depending much more upon domesticated plants and animals for their diets, they also started leaving us evidence of their cooking practices in the form of some pretty interesting, functionally differentiated hearths. Compellingly, all over the world, the complex of cultural changes that accompanied the shift toward domestication of animals and plants seems to have included considerable innovation in cooking. Whether its effects took place over the course of decades or centuries, the adoption of agriculture has to have introduced an era of culinary novelty, as new or at least newly reliable ingredients became part of the diet, and some part of the population settled in permanent villages.

The early adopters of agriculture — cultures from Mesopotamia to the Levant and through the Balkans to Greece — left some archaeological evidence of the effects of these sweeping cultural changes. Bone and other animal remains show a shift from gazelle and ibex to sheep and goat, for example. Genetic changes to grains and legumes reveal the effects of human selection and improvement.

Settling down brought greater complexity to the built environment of the kitchen, too, as these Neolithic cooks invested in lovely hearths with platforms and enclosures and built-in containers, all out of mudbrick and plaster and pebbles. Some of these installations are worthwhile models to improve our wood-fired cooking today.

HOW TO MAKE AN EFFICIENT AND PLEASANT ROASTING HEARTH

I've adopted as a model for most of my outdoor roasting a simple Neolithic hearth type I came across in an archaeological site report. It's a saucer-shaped depression, neatly lined with like-sized pebbles. These hearths were rather large at the original site, but can be made any size. Although you can spit-roast over bare ground with very little ceremony, this improvement is worth considering if you expect to roast in the same place more than once, whatever the scale of your outdoor cooking, at least if you live in a region where stones abound. The result is both visually pleasing and quite functional.

Tools and Materials

You need a shovel and a good pile of smallish stones. A mason's trowel, a rubber mallet, and a small broom are optional but helpful. If you plan to use crochets — forked sticks — as spit supports, supply yourself with a few short stakes or sticks about an inch and a half in diameter to use as placeholders for them.

About the stones: have on hand more than you think you could possibly use. Egg-shaped or oblong rocks about the size of a grapefruit or large orange are ideal. Lemon-size stones make a very elegant hearth, but it just takes a lot of them. Some sand, for bedding the stones, is helpful if your soil is very heavy.

This hearth, built of materials at hand, uses the natural terrain to create a subtle heat-reflecting effect.

A Few Simple Tools

It's good to get in the habit of "grading" rocks as you come across them in your yard or garden; these projects go easiest when you have plenty of the right sort of material at hand. Accordingly, whenever I dig a hole I chuck the rocks in different piles for my various future projects. I am also not above cannibalizing an old project to make a new one. Or filling up my car with stones from an obvious rubble pile at a construction site or along the power lines . . .

Choose Your Site

Wind can be a negative factor in your cooking. Look at the terrain when selecting a place to work. Is there a masonry wall near which you might situate your fire pit? Working in the lee of even a sandbank or boulder can be very helpful.

If nothing suggests itself as a windbreak, consider depressing your entire hearth below grade by a few inches or berming around it a bit. But be careful not to overdo the effect because draft can be difficult if the fire becomes too subterranean, especially in a small fire pit. Also, it's not comfortable to have to reach continually to a level below one's feet when tending a fire, let alone a roast.

Determine the Shape, Size, and Lining

Eyeball the size of the hearth you'll need, based on your cooking plans, and scratch it on the ground. Think about the length of the food you're most likely to roast. As well as the size of the overall pit, this factor will decide how far apart you'll want the spit supports. For example, if you are preparing to roast a rabbit, the supports for the spit may be installed no closer than the length of the animal fully drawn out, plus at least a few inches clearance on either side. Think ahead to make your pit easy to modify for the next use. Say you want to roast a young kid or lamb, about twice the length of the rabbit you roasted last week. If the pit is already broad enough, you'll just need to use new supports, further apart (and probably taller) for the lamb.

Dig out a shallow, shapely pit a few inches deeper than your intention for the finished specimen. The size of the stones you use to line the hearth will determine how much extra depth is necessary. Rough it out with the shovel, and use a trowel or your hand to smooth out the saucer.

If your soil is light and sandy like mine, the following step may not be necessary, but if it is unyielding clay, you might want to spread out about an inch of sand in the pit. Start lining the pit with stone from the center. Select one of your longer stones, hold it lengthwise, and tap it into the center of the pit using the butt of your trowel, another stone, or, better, a rubber mallet.

Work, spiral-wise, out from your anchor stone, nestling the stones as close as possible together, minimizing gaps and trying to achieve a pleasant overall shape.

BUILDING A FIRE PIT

1. A rough lumpy depression in the lawn is the perfect site for a new fire pit.

2. The homeowner has removed the turf and is exaggerating the natural terrain by digging a shallow dishlike pit.

3. After the center of the hearth is established, he works against the slope at the rear to build a subtle fire-back, intended to bounce heat back at future roasting projects.

4. Not long after, he's ready to roast. This simple fire pit can be easily enlarged or modified with spit supports or a tripod, to support a great range of cooking projects.

A Few Simple Tools

Don't obsess; this isn't Stonehenge. (But it may help to remember that Stonehenge, too, was a Neolithic project.) Just work around the stakes if you're using them.

When you have lined up to the lip of the pit with the stones, sprinkle sand or light soil over the whole thing and use a small broom or handbrush to sweep it around, allowing it to infiltrate down through the cracks. Just sweep away any excess.

THE SPIT

You have a few choices, depending on your aesthetic and technological leanings, and whether or not you want to invest a few bucks.

Greenwood

Counterintuitive as it may seem, wooden cooking tools can be serviceable and fairly durable, holding up many a roast before finally succumbing to the flames (and that end is usually an accident late at night and unrelated to cooking, when someone fails to recognize a stick as a tool and tosses it on the fire).

What wood ultimately lacks in permanence, it more than makes up for in other ways. Crafting your own spits and skewers is cheap and fun. And in at least one respect, using wooden tools makes roasting much more trouble-free. One of the trickiest parts of spit-roasting a whole animal is keeping the meat turning with the spit, especially when that spit is made of smooth, terribly thin metal. A wooden spit that is many times the thickness of a metal one will still be light enough to easily wield around the fire, and the meat will cling to a wooden spit much more readily. Fashion your custom-made spit of larger-gauge stock and leave it fat enough that its girth is almost wedged through the carcass. Along with a few skewers deployed crosswise, this practice helps keep the animal fastened smartly.

Using the shape and size of the food you plan to roast as your guide, select a green branch or sprout from a hardwood tree, certainly a nontoxic species and preferably one without an aggressive smell. Maple, blueberry, and basswood are my favorites, since they have a neutral or even pleasant aroma, are locally abundant, and tend to grow obligingly into spit-shaped forms. Search out what makes sense in your region.

Look for a natural "crank" at the heavy end of the stick, and otherwise considerable straightness. Consider the length, weight, and conformation of the item to be cooked. Is the stick fat enough to bore holes in for some skewer attachment points without fatally weakening it? For the rabbit example, look for something with nearly an inch diameter on average; for the kid or lamb, over an inch and a half.

Gather a few as you find them, so you have fallback in case of hidden flaws. Using pruners, a knife, machete, or small hatchet, trim off all the side branches

MAKING A GREENWOOD SPIT

I. Lop off any branches and irregularities that won't be helpful to your roasting task.

2. Pare off the bark.

3. Cut the spit to length and sharpen the point.

4. Perforate the spit to accommodate skewers for securing the roast.

5. Split, pare, and whittle a straight section of branch or sapling stock for skewers.

6. Locate the fastening points strategically for the roast.

A Few Simple Tools

and twigs that will be in the way. Cut any excess length away and sharpen it to a point. Pare off the bark.

For fastening the meat to the spit, you may use short metal or bamboo skewers if you already have them. Or to continue with the woodland theme, you may prepare some from a similar branch stock. For very small roasts, you may get away with using small, flexible sticks in the round, but they tend to be weak for their size. A much stronger skewer may be made by splitting a length of a larger branch in quarters using a heavy bladed knife, and whittling the quarters until they are small and sharp enough to do the job. Willow sprouts are great for this purpose.

Again, using the meat that is to be roasted as a guide, bore holes in strategic points in the wooden spit. If we continue with the rabbit example, that will mean in the vicinity of the hips and the shoulders. For a fowl, three holes are helpful: one for fastening through the carcass along the spine near the wing and thigh joints and two for tying the drumsticks. You may use any sort of drill, from a cordless power model to a brace-and-bit to a gimlet to a stone awl, depending on how archaic you're feeling; we usually have success with some of those otherwise inexplicable blades on a pocket knife. Keep the holes as small as possible to accommodate the skewers. If the skewers have a flat profile, poke two or more small holes near each other to open up a slot lengthwise in the spit.

Metal

One simple, functional spit design — a long pointy piece of metal with an offset handle — was long in favor in cultures where blacksmithing skill was widespread and cooking large joints of meat was considered desirable (cultures in which the device that turned the spit was the human hand, at any rate). When the spit was geared to mechanical means of turning, the crank at the end was transformed into a wheel, or other form, designed to interface with the driver, whether canine, mechanical, or electrical.

A basic spit can be easily reproduced in iron or steel by a blacksmith or fabricator. One helpful refinement is to flatten the spit where the meat will be held, as an encouragement to its staying put. (The areas of the spit that will rest on supports must be kept in the round, of course.) Flattish skewers of metal or wood are pierced through the meat and engaged against the flat of the spit, to keep the meat rotating properly with it. This technique is very helpful in roasting a joint or loin of meat, and even a whole animal.

Another refinement to the metal spit is to cut a few slots within it to receive skewers, like we did with the wooden spit. Or you can make yourself a nice adaptable steel spit inexpensively with just a few tools. I bought a 3-foot piece of ⅜-inch square stock from a regular big-box home improvement emporium. I ordered gadgets called "meat forks" from an online specialty supplier (See Resources, page 305.)

A homemade spit equipped with commercial "meat forks" secures a pork roast over a dripping pan.

An outdoor spit can be supported by simple crochets made from branches.

This indoor roasting setup is hand-forged. The fireplace andirons have built-in supports that allow the spit to be raised and lowered.

These are made for commercial electric-driven rotisseries, but adapt nicely to our purpose. The four-tined attachments clamp on to a spit with thumbscrews and secure the roast so that it spins with the spit. These are especially good for boxy roasts like pork loins and mid-sized poultry.

To round off the corners of the steel and to make a point on one end, you need a grinder with a general-purpose metal grinding wheel. If you are using a handheld model, clamp it securely to a workbench. Wear safety glasses and hearing protection and gloves. Grind off the corners of the square stock, and taper one end to a point over about 1½ inches.

Rather than bend the spit to make an offset handle (which would take more tools and skill, and would make the spit pretty short), just use vice-grip pliers (if they're not already in your toolbox, that's $12) or a C-clamp ($5) as a detachable handle. This whole arrangement, while not classic, has its own charm, once you've given it all a good scrub with hot soapy water.

Supporting the Spit

If you are enjoying the greenwood theme, crochets, forked sticks driven into the ground, are a simple and attractive way of supporting your spitted roast. Find two robust (1½-inch diameter, or larger for something heavy) branch forms containing the necessary Y-shape, and trim away the superfluous top with a saw or hatchet. Leave plenty of wood at the bottom so that it will stand securely upright when driven into the ground. Rest the base on a stump and, cutting downward in short chops with a hatchet, put a point on it. Drive the crochets into the soil in or at the perimeter of the hearth, far enough apart so that there are a few inches to spare on either end of the roast.

Perhaps less elegant, but just as effective, is to use something solid and stable, such as small stumps of wood with grooves in the top surface to keep the spit from creeping, or as we see in seventeenth-century Dutch genre paintings, an upside-down three-legged kettle.

Whichever course you take, make a trial run of putting the spit across the supports before you make a fire to make sure that the height is right and that it's more or less level. Imagine the same scenario with coals and meat to get an idea of whether the height of the supports will work. Remember that you can always move coals around to intensify or buffer heat.

The traditional indoor method of supporting a spitted roast is with andirons that have been furnished with hooks at various heights. Today's enterprising metalworker can forge or fabricate such equipment in the traditional L-shaped hearth-cooking format, or even adapt the design for outdoor cooking so that the andirons terminate in long stakes that may be driven into the ground — like a more durable version of the wooden crochets.

Turning the Spit

Historically, a good deal of inventiveness has gone into keeping the roast spinning. For centuries, a viable low-tech option favored by the keepers of larger establishments was the "turnspit," an underling — servant or slave — whose job was exactly that, turning the spit. It was probably not a Tudor concern for child welfare that brought in the "turnspit dog," a poor little wiener dog that ran on a caged treadmill cunningly geared to a spit. Similarly, it was probably not a concern for animal welfare that brought in an array of mechanical and even smoke- and steam-driven inventions for spit-turning. These devices were at their most popular in the seventeenth through nineteenth centuries, not coincidentally the heyday of both spit-roasting and clockwork tinkering in Europe and North America.

All of this fuss tends to hide the fact that it is not essential to keep spitted foods rotating continually to produce a very fine result. Many very good home cooks through history have had neither the equipment nor manpower in their kitchens to keep their spits in constant motion, yet have not shied from roasting. I have occasionally had the fun and ease of using an electric rotisserie of high caliber to cook largish whole animals, but most of the roasting I have done has been without that refinement, and the quality of the final product has not been impaired.

That's not to say that roasting sans turnspit will not demand considerable attention from the busy cook. Especially in the first quarter-hour or so of cooking, I like to keep my hand on the spit, so that I can closely observe the fire and its interaction with the food. Once all is proceeding as it ought, then it's more a matter of propping the spit's handle this way and that to achieve even roasting, and manipulating the coals to radiate upon the places that need it most. But, what with feeding the fire, shoveling coals about, and basting — tasks occasioned by roasting even when spit-turning has been knocked out of the equation — the cook's attendance must be frequent regardless.

To my mind, the idea of using fossil fuels in the form of electricity for a rotisserie detracts from the pleasure of roasting (although, I suppose I'm open to solar- or wind-generated spit-turning). On the occasions when electrified efficiency has triumphed over aesthetic scruples, I have managed to enjoy myself nonetheless, and used my freed-up hands to get in other culinary trouble. ("Oh, let's make anchovy toast!") To me the most sensible and fun course, though, would be to return to the idea of using the very fire that roasts the meat to also turn the spit — it's high time for the inventive among us to reengineer the smoke jack and the steam jack for today's green-minded outdoor cooks.

MASTER RECIPE AND TECHNIQUE: ROASTING A SMALL WHOLE ANIMAL

A rabbit, chicken, or duck is a manageable — and delicious — introductory project to the world of whole-animal spit-roasting.

1 rabbit, duck, or chicken (2 to 5 pounds)
1 clove garlic, minced
1 teaspoon kosher or sea salt
   Abundant freshly ground black pepper
1 sprig fresh sage or rosemary, chopped
2 tablespoons extra-virgin olive oil
1 quarter of a lemon

4 to 6 servings

I. Make ready a spit setup in one of the ways discussed previously, allowing the meat to be suspended about 6 to 8 inches above the coals. At least an hour before you intend to start roasting, make a fire of split hardwood behind the space that will be occupied by the meat. You will draw coals forward under the roast when the time comes. The blazing part of the fire should be around 18 inches away from the roast.

2. Meanwhile, rinse and pat dry the animal, and set aside any innards for another use. (The liver, if present, could be subjected to the same marinade, cooked on a skewer like a marshmallow, and then minced as garnish. Offer it to guests in some clever amuse-bouche, or pop it into your mouth when no one is looking.)

3. Mince together the garlic and salt on a cutting board. Add the pepper and sage or rosemary and work it all together. Rub all over the meat. Drizzle over the olive oil, squeeze on the lemon, and massage the whole mess together.

4. Check on the fire. Make sure lots of coals will be forthcoming. Place new fuel on the back of the fire; this habit makes it easier to access the coals at the front and keeps the blaze closest to the roast bright and clear.

5. Wrangle your victim onto the spit, locating the thighs and wings or upper arms where they can be pinned to the spit with skewers. Use a fire shovel to drag coals out from beneath the fire and lay out a nice little coal bed in between the spit supports. Set up the roast over the coals. You may reserve the marinade for basting later.

6. Turn the spit slowly for a few minutes and watch carefully to get a notion of the degree of heat from the coals and the fire, and their effect on the meat. Nothing very dramatic should happen for a little while unless your fire is way too hot or you fail to turn the spit enough.

7. If you have nothing else to do and would like to experience the life of a seventeenth-century kitchen drudge, you may turn the spit slowly and continually. However, your roast will come out just as well if you carefully observe the cooking as it progresses and turn the spit a little at a time, propping the crank end at the proper angles to facilitate even cooking. Strategically shaped sticks or a couple of bricks usually suffice for this purpose.

8. Gradually you may notice that the meat is steaming or sizzling a bit and becoming paler in color, as cooking begins. Observe areas that are lagging behind the rest, and take steps to correct. Replenish the coal bed strategically. Quadrupeds, such as rabbits, are thickest at the hip and shoulder areas. Keeping steady heat on those areas is key. Much less heat is necessary through the midsection; in fact it's desirable to avoid overcooking the loin meat. So, essentially, your coal bed should be hourglass shaped — good heat at either end of the carcass and very little in the middle. In cooking much larger animals, I find that by halfway through the cooking process, it appears that I am essentially maintaining two separate fires, replenishing coals at either end of the animal.

9. When the roast begins to put forth drippings, set up a dripping pan directly under the roast. Use a heavy or expendable pan that can tolerate heat shock and other abuse, and nestle the coals along its edge closest to the fire. Do your best to keep coals and ashes out. Baste with the reserved marinade and the drippings, if you like, periodically through the first 60 minutes of cooking. Stir the contents of the dripping pan and add a splash of wine or water to prevent scorching.

10. Depending on the size of the roast, and your fire, and whether you are inside a brick chimney or out in a wintery wind, the process may take 75 minutes to 2 hours. Observe closely and learn before reaching for your instant-read thermometer: Are there places that could use a little more crisping? Or is it nice and golden-brown all over, with the meat clearly pulling back a bit from the leg bones? This sounds stupid, but most times when meat really *looks* cooked it *is* cooked.

11. Rabbit and poultry ought not be served rare, but neither should you dry it out. When internal temperature, taken near the thigh joint, reads 150°F for rabbit or 165°F for poultry, remove it from the fire, and allow it to rest for 15 minutes in a warm place on a preheated dish, before carving and serving.

THE DRIPPING PAN

When meat that is fattier or juicier than rabbit is on the spit, it's advisable to deploy a dripping pan of some kind. In the heyday of European spit-roasting, consumers could choose among a range of purpose-built options for every budget, from lovely huge cast-iron affairs to funky highly tempered hand-built earthenware models. Now familiarity with this utensil is generally limited to archaeologists and connoisseurs of Dutch genre paintings, so most hearth cooks have to punt.

A Few Simple Tools

MAKING A SAUCE IN THE DRIPPING PAN

    The leftover marinade
 1 tablespoon olive oil, if needed
 2 onions or 4 shallots, slivered
 ½ cup dry red or white wine or ⅓ cup stock
 2 tablespoons wine vinegar
    Freshly ground black pepper
 ½ cup minced parsley
 4 tablespoons cold butter, cut in bits

1. Stick a 10-inch cast-iron pan under the meat as a dripping pan after it's been roasting a little while. Baste with the marinade occasionally for 20 to 30 minutes.

2. The next time you replenish the coals near the roast, pick up the pan and put some coals under there as well. Unless there's a coating of drippings in the pan, add the olive oil; then toss in the onions. Let them cook very slowly until soft and translucent, catching the drippings for the remainder of the roasting time. Stir and look out for burning, moving the pan to a cooler place if necessary for a while.

3. When the cooked roast has been moved away from the fire for its rest period, attend to the sauce. Put the pan on a fresh bed of coals and bring to a sizzle. Add the wine, vinegar, and pepper, and simmer down to almost nothing. When the liquid is reduced and syrupy, pick the pan up and move it to a cooler spot. Meanwhile, carve the roast into serving pieces and arrange on a warm platter.

4. When the iron pan feels warm, rather than hot, it's ready to finish. Stir in the parsley, and then half the cold butter bits. Stir and swirl until the butter softens and amalgamates. Repeat with the other half of the butter; taste the sauce for seasoning and serve immediately with the meat.

TIPS FOR A STUFFED ROAST

Use the stuffing on page 54, or 2 to 3 cups of any favorite dressing. Perform the surgery while your fire is burning and making coals.

1. Rinse the animal and pat it dry. Lay it on a flat surface. For poultry, simply stuff lightly and skewer closed, or sew, as described below, if you'd prefer.

2. For a small quadruped: Thread a needle with about four feet of white or natural cotton thread; double it and knot the end with a big ugly knot. Sew the animal's body cavity about ⅓ closed. Try to make your stitches even and keep a bit of slack in them; don't pull hard on the thread at all. Gently fill the cavity with the stuffing without packing tightly, then finish the suture, neatly tying it off at the end.

3. Carefully, without destroying your handiwork, thread the roast on the spit and fasten with skewers. Roast as previously desribed.

4. Before serving, simply pull on the thread and the whole suture should come out in one piece before carving.

ROAST PORK LOIN (CORMARYE)

Hailing from 14th-century England, this simple recipe is the once-and-future champ of pork roasts in my book. The pork may be seasoned anywhere from two hours to two days ahead. Let the roast come to room temperature before spitting it and laying it down to the fire.

1 tablespoon coriander seeds
1 tablespoon caraway seeds
1 teaspoon black peppercorns
2–4 cloves garlic
1 teaspoon kosher or coarse sea salt
2 tablespoons red wine
1 bone-in pork roast, 3 to 4 pounds
½ cup stock or water

6 to 8 servings

1. Grind the coriander and caraway seeds and the peppercorns with a mortar and pestle. When they are mostly pulverized, toss in the garlic and salt. Crush to a paste, and then work in the wine. Slather the mixture all over the pork roast. Let stand, sealed in a nonreactive container, for two hours at a cool room temperature, or up to two days, in the fridge.

2. Set up your hardwood fire and roasting apparatus much as for the roast rabbit, except that the pork loin will want to be 7 to 9 inches from the coals. (See page 45.) Plan to use either a flat-bladed spit, a spit with a slot that a skewer can pass through, or a spit with adjustable meat forks to secure the roast.

3. There's a bit of a dilemma in spitting a roast like this. You want to avoid impaling the best part of the meat, the center, but at the same time you want the roast to be perfectly balanced on the spit, which is achieved by centering it in the meat. An inevitable contradiction. But when I have a bone-in roast, I find that my mind is made up by the prospect of running the spit flat against the ribs to help secure the rotation. If the lopsided spitting results in one section of the roast being less done because of greater distance from the heat, I can always pay special attention to that area later and compensate by moving coals toward it. If you can only get a boneless roast, then you may as well spit it dead center. Clamp-on meat forks are handy here, especially if you have a thin metal spit.

4. When your fire has produced plenty of coals, use a fire shovel to create a lovely coal bed beneath where the roast will be suspended. Feed the main fire with new hardwood from the back. Lay the roast down over the coals on the spit supports.

5. Turn frequently over the hot coals until it begins to sizzle and make some drippings. Then deploy a dripping pan directly under the roast, and refresh the coal supply between it and the main fire. Don't forget to feed the fire from the back again.

6. If the drippings begin to scorch at all, add a little hot water to the dripping pan. Baste the roast from time to time with the drippings, if you like.

7. Observe the meat as it goes from pinkish-red to creamy to golden brown; and as it shrinks and tightens. These are all signs of cooking. In the best hearth conditions, it may not take too much more than an hour to cook a roast like this. Looking carefully at the roast, turning it to advantage, and taking steps to advance cooking in any places which have fallen behind — these are really all you have to do to roast this loin perfectly. When it looks all crispy and sizzling like a pork roast you'd like to eat, take its internal temperature. At 145°F, you may remove it to a heated platter, and keep warm for a 10 to 15 minute rest. If you find that the center is still too cool, just pull the coals further away to slacken the heat and allow it to continue to roast without much more browning.

8. When the roast is resting, have a look at the drippings. Spoon excess fat from the top of them, and then put the pan back on a little coal bed. Add the stock (and another splash of red wine if you like) and bring to a simmer scraping up the bottom of the pan and stirring. Simmer a few minutes, correct the seasoning, and then just keep warm while you carve the roast in thin slices.

9. Not very period-appropriate, but this pork loin is great with polenta and flavorful garlicky braised greens. It's also tremendous in sandwiches with almost any accompaniments you can think of.

TROUBLESHOOTING: ROASTING
What happens if the meat looks all brown on the outside, yet the thermometer reads 115°F, not 150°F? This situation indicates that your roast has been too close to the coals or to the blaze of the fire. Make a note of that for next time, and then take remedial action right away. Push the fire further away, and just keep roasting over a diminished pile of coals. All is not lost. Just do all you can to sloooow things down until the internal temperature rises.

SPIT-ROASTED STUFFED STRIPED BASS

This is a 17th-century English idea, handed down in an 18th-century Virginia manuscript. I include it here not just to challenge and advance your rigging skills but also because it's a great treat to eat. The original recipe called for carp, but any whole fish with strong body integrity should work.

You'll need a strong, sharp spit, as well as — and this is the most interesting part of the recipe — two pieces of "lath" to support the fish while it cooks. Lath, in the early period, was fabricated by splitting the straight-grained heartwood of appropriate trees thinly with a froe. A drawknife was used to further thin and smooth it. In this case, the laths are fastened along either side of the spitted fish, as insurance against catastrophic structural collapse midroasting.

Because there's so much to do more-or-less simultaneously before you even start cooking — fish-cleaning, lath-splitting, stuffing-making — this is a great team project. And once the spit is turning, all the heavy lifting is done, and it's time to kick back and hang out by the fire.

1 loaf stale good French bread, crust cut off, pulled into shreds or coarsely grated

6 ounces melted butter

2 tablespoons fresh thyme leaves, minced

1 whole striped bass or other large (over 18 inches) firm-fleshed fish, scaled and gutted

Kosher or sea salt

Freshly ground black pepper

1 lemon

3 tablespoons capers

1 knob (about 1 ounce) fresh gingerroot, as young and tender as possible

---

6 to 14 servings, depending on your fish

---

1. Fish at hand, make ready your roasting arrangement — spit, supports, and laths — to suit it. The spit must be fairly robust, since this fish is heavy, but thin and sharp enough to pierce the fish without spoiling it. The laths should be about 2 inches wide, thin and green enough to flex along the fish, and a couple inches longer than the fish. Get a good hardwood fire going a few feet away from the supports.

2. Meanwhile, toss together the breadcrumbs, 4 ounces of the butter, and thyme to make the stuffing. Pat the fish dry inside and out, and season the inside of the cavity with salt and pepper. Double up a length of white cotton thread on a small needle, and neatly sew the cavity about one-half of the way closed. Lightly fill the cavity with as much stuffing as fits easily, and then finish sewing the fish up. Thread the fish very carefully on to the spit, through the mouth, and following the spine.

3. Lay the spitted fish on its side on one of the laths and top it with the other. Secure around the laths about an inch from each end with natural-fiber twine. (It helps to notch the laths where the lashing will pass.)

4. Draw a coal bed out between the spit supports, and hang the fish up about 6 to 8 inches above them. Turn and roast until the fish flakes near the thickest part of the tail, about 45 to 60 minutes. Brush with melted butter from time to time in the first 20 minutes, and replenish the coal bed as necessary.

5. Meanwhile, prepare the garnishes. Trim away the peel and pith from the lemon, and then separate the sections from the membranes, discarding seeds. Chop the lemon sections nicely. If the capers are the large kind, run a knife over them once or twice. Peel the gingerroot and slice it infinitesimally thinly across the grain.

6. When the fish is done, remove it to a preheated platter, carefully extricating it from its gear. Pull out the suture neatly, and use a fork to pull most of the stuffing out onto the platter. Sprinkle with the garnishes and serve. (The original recipe instructs the cook to "rip up the belly" and add more melted butter to the filling, but I leave that up to you.)

VARIATION

If you have a wood-fired oven and find the woodworking portion of this recipe daunting, stuff the fish and bake it (on a sheet of parchment, to make it easy to retrieve) in a medium-hot (say 450°F) oven until just beginning to flake at the thickest part. Garnish and serve as in the roasted version.

ROAST ON A STRING

For many years, I foolishly scoffed at both the historic authenticity and even the actual utility of roasting meat suspended from a twirling length of twine. A little bit of research and a few trials and I stood smartly corrected. While it is not the ideal method in every situation, it is at least a great fallback when you have no other equipment. And it actually *is* the ideal way of cooking a leg of lamb. In fact, even the idea of a leg of lamb can be a helpful guide in deciding whether a particular roast is suited to twine-roasting; the more it has in common with that benchmark cut of meat, the easier it is to cook on a string. Here's why:

A twine-roast leg of lamb can be suspended from a simple tripod such as this one.

- The leg of lamb has a handy, sturdy fastening point pretty well centered in the cut. This means it's a cinch to rig up, and then it spins easily and protractedly with very little attention.

- The overall shape consists of a fat lower end, gradually and smoothly tapering to a slender upper end. (That is, the leg's roasting orientation is opposite to the way in which the leg served the lamb in life.) This form is very convenient when a bed of coals comes into play. The thinnest part is furthest from the heat source and just cooks through by the time the bulk of the meat is done. Also, since any protrusion from the roast tends to block exposure to the heat of the part above it, the leg of lamb's sleek and compact form — no loose bits like wings or flaps of meat — means that it requires zero trussing to achieve that even cooking.

- It is the perfect size to manage easily, yet has enough weight to keep on spinning. Anything much larger calls for another pair of hands, and maybe stouter cordage, to rig up; very light foods require more attention to maintain rotational momentum.

These guidelines are not to utterly discourage the cooking of meats other than the leg of lamb by this method; they are merely to help you anticipate how your roasting plan may differ if you set to cooking a partridge or a haunch of wildebeest on twine.

Considerations for Twine-Roasting, Indoors or Out

SUSPENSION. You will want to hang the roast somewhat off-center from the actual fire, just an inch or two above the level of the coal bed. As the meat spins and cooks, you should be able to tend the coal bed and to move the fire closer and further from the meat as necessary. You will feed the fire from the opposite side, as usual, away from the roast.

If you intend to cook indoors, in a fireplace, inspect along the bottom of the mantelpiece or inside the flue for a place to install a secure fastening point. All you need is a sturdy hook or nail. Situate it off to one side of the hearth, so that you'll have plenty of latitude in moving around your fire and coals next to the roast. If your fireplace is too narrow for that, just hang the roast directly in front of the fire, with the attachment point either on the mantel or the exterior of the chimney or even the ceiling.

If you are cooking out-of-doors, rig up a strong and stable suspension point for your roast, from a tripod or gallows. When I use a tripod. I rig the roast to hang from one of the tripod's legs and maintain the fire dead center.

FIRE. Have on hand plenty of medium-sized dry hardwood, as with any roasting project. Start the fire well ahead to build up a coal bed: an hour or so indoors, twice that outdoors, especially in cold or windy weather. Take precautions against the wind by setting up a windbreak, or performing the whole operation in a shallow depression, which can act as both windbreak and fireback.

CORDAGE. Use sturdy natural fiber twine; cotton butcher's twine is fine. If you are nervous about the weight, just double it up. Make sure there are no rough or sharp edges on either of the twine's attachment points.

THE "DOUBLE STRING MEAT ROASTER"

Getting sufficient heat to play on the top of the roast takes some attention from the cook. This is a Rhode Island solution to the problem, circa 1800, as observed by Thomas Robinson Hazard:

"To obviate this sore imperfection incident to the string roasting, an old sinner by the name of Ephe Hazard, who had a palate inside his mouth, invented what was called the 'double string meat roaster,' whereby the bight of a small cord was passed over a smooth round piece of wood arranged horizontally just below the ceiling above, whilst its two pendant ends were fastened the one to the leg and the other to the neck of the fowl, or to the lower end and upper extremities of the joint of meat. A small stick some three inches in length was tied to one of the strings, so as to make it very convenient for an attendant, with its aid, to put a sharp twist into the machine without much trouble, always preceded by drawing the strings downward and upward alternately so as to reverse the ends of the joint or bird, and thus cause the juices to constantly pass to and fro."

TWINE-ROAST LEG OF LAMB

Unless you have the luxury of butchering your own lamb or buying directly from a slaughterhouse, the leg you purchase will most likely have had the handy string-attachment point known as the "heel" sawn off. Here's your opportunity to get in touch with your inner orthopedic surgeon; see page 61 for instructions on how to prepare the lamb leg for hanging.

How long will it take to cook? Indoors, with a fireplace jamb backing the heat against the roast, it will scarcely take any longer than baking it in a conventional oven — about two hours. Outdoors on a winter night with a cold wind snatching at the heat, plan on around twice that.

The mustard plaster administered to the lamb in its last 45 minutes of roasting reflects the inspired practice of my grandfather, Victor Amédée Brassard, a rôtisseur of high standards.

1 leg of lamb, full bone-in
10 cloves garlic
3½ tablespoons olive oil
2 teaspoons kosher or sea salt
Freshly ground pepper
A bunch of rosemary or thyme, tied together as a basting brush (optional)
2 tablespoons dry mustard
2 tablespoons all-purpose flour
1–2 tablespoons water, as needed
½ cup lamb, chicken, or beef stock or wine or water or some of each

10 to 14 servings

---

1. From 4 to 24 hours ahead, season the lamb: Wipe the meat dry. Sliver 8 of the garlic cloves, and using a very small sharp-pointed knife, make incisions all over the roast and insert the garlic into them. Massage the leg gently with 2 tablespoons of the olive oil, and sprinkle with 1 teaspoon of the salt and plenty of pepper. Cover and chill, but bring to room temperature before roasting.

2. Figure out the logistics for suspending the lamb as described previously and get a nice hardwood fire burning. Remember that you will want the lamb to have room to spin unencumbered a few inches away from, and slightly diagonally above, the coal bed. The fire will continue to burn smartly in a more or less parallel plane to the leg, but a foot or more away.

3. When you have a deep bed of coals under the fire, use a fire shovel to push the actively flaming wood to the opposite side of the hearth from where the roast will hang. Hang the leg of lamb up from the attachment point you have arranged, and double-check to make sure it is entirely secure before you step away. It will probably start spinning slowly of its own accord; encourage it along by twirling the shankbone in the direction it seems to want to go. Place a pan beneath the roast to catch the drippings. Draw some coals closer to the pan, so that you have a lovely steady bed of coals sloping from it up toward the actively burning logs. Look critically at the arrangement. Visualize exactly how the leg is exposed to the heat. What can you do to ensure the most even cooking? Probably one thing is to feed the fire more wood, from the side away from the roast. You are starting the coals that will come into play in 40 minutes or so.

4. That's really all you have to do for the next few hours: keep the leg rotating slowly (which requires very little attention), and provide a nice bed of coals and brisk fire at appropriate distances from the roast. It's fun and picturesque, but scarcely necessary, to brush the roast with the drippings using a bundle of herbs. It pays to be aware of the movements of any dogs or other unrestrained carnivores in the vicinity.

5. As the roast turns, you can mix up the mustard plaster any time you like. Mince together 2 cloves of garlic and 1 teaspoon of salt and plenty of freshly ground pepper. Stir into 1½ tablespoons olive oil. Add the mustard and flour, and as much water as it takes to make a somewhat drippy paste. Set aside until needed.

6. When the roast seems to be about three-quarters done (say, an internal temperature of 120°F or so), apply the mustard plaster. Use a large pastry brush and just lather it on the leg of lamb on all sides. Get a fresh bed of coals set up and continue roasting until the internal temperature of the roast is 145°F, then inspect your handiwork. If the plaster has not firmed up into an irresistible crust, build up your fire to provide one last blast of heat. Ideally, the plaster will be crispy and the lamb will approach 150°F at the same moment.

7. Get someone to help nudge a warm platter under the roast while you snip the string. (Believe me, it is not hard to rustle up helpers at this point.) Place the leg of lamb, loosely tented with some foil, in a warm place to rest for 20 minutes. Strain the drippings into a small nonreactive pot and heat in the remaining coals, adding the stock. Boil for a few minutes, taste, and correct seasoning.

8. Carve the roast and serve with the sauce.

A Few Simple Tools

PREPARING THE LEG FOR ROASTING

1. Drill a clean hole, making sure there are no sharp edges.

2. Thread string through and make a square knot.

3. Suspend using a knot that won't slip, like a bowline.

4. Use a rolling hitch to attach the other end of the string to a tripod.

5. Or use two round turns and two half hitches to attach to a chain.

61

Twine-Roasting Poultry

If you are roasting poultry, truss compactly and, if the bird is larger than a game hen, run at least two lengths of the twine through the body cavity. Join them together above the neck area, and form a hanging loop, experimenting with it to make certain that the fowl will hang securely and as plumb as possible. Even a little slouching or leaning will have a considerable negative effect on the evenness of roasting. (Historic sources indicate that roasting poultry was possibly carried out by merely looping the twine around the legs of the bird. A modern grocery-store chicken rigged up thus would signal doneness by utterly slumping off its drumstick bones, I'm afraid. Attempt this only with a backyard fowl that has the body integrity that comes from supporting its own weight in life and pecking at bugs and so on.)

THE BEST CHICKEN SALAD EVER

String up or spit-roast a midsize chicken to crispy, juicy perfection, and if you can prevent yourself and all around you from just devouring it straight up, try this superlative treatment. The recipe comes from the collection of the culinarily discerning 17th-century English knight, Sir Kenelm Digby.

The meat of a roast chicken, cooled to room temperature and sliced attractively
1 head favorite tender lettuce, broken up and sliced
1 bunch young arugula, chopped
2 or 3 scallions or spring onions, sliced thinly
Several sprigs of tarragon, chopped
2 or 3 sprigs of fresh oregano, chopped (optional)

1 lemon, peel pared away, sliced very thinly and seeded
4 tablespoons best extra-virgin olive oil
1 tablespoon white wine vinegar
Kosher or sea salt
Freshly ground black pepper

3 or 4 servings

Toss the meat, greens, herbs, and lemon flesh. Drizzle with olive oil and vinegar, and sprinkle with salt and pepper. Now devour it.

COOKING ON SKEWERS

Roasting food on skewers — essentially tiny spits — has been popular for millennia for good reason. Cut into uniform pieces, the bits of meat, fish, or vegetables show a lot of surface area to high heat so they cook quickly and develop great seared flavor. All that exposed perimeter also makes for even seasoning and the transfer of complementary flavors between foods.

Prep Work

As you are preparing the ingredients, think about how they will thread on the skewers and how that might translate over coals. For example, I like grilled meat or poultry to have some deeply browned crisp edges and a tender juicy interior. So I cut the meat into little pyramid-shaped pieces to facilitate that result, and grill over very hot coals very quickly. On the other hand, some cooks cut all the pieces so that they can be pressed into a perfect cylinder on the skewer. While traveling in the Middle East, I often saw kebabs so expertly prepped and assembled that their exterior was almost perfectly smooth, plumb, and level, as if the kebab were a stacked sausage without a casing. They were also delicious.

In any event, making kebabs is an opportunity to impose order on otherwise unruly pieces of meat; neatness leads to a better result.

Cooking Arrangements

Most kebabs can be grilled perfectly well on a regular backyard grill. Alternatively, you can very easily rig a kebab setup that obviates the need for the grill, and feel that you are cooking along more traditional lines to boot.

The earliest known complete kebab grill was perfectly preserved under volcanic ash for around 3,700 years at the Greek island site of Akrotiri. This Minoan model consists of a handsome set of clay firedogs, topped with ridges to hold skewers in perfect parallel an appropriate height above hot coals. The base of each clay slab is good and thick for stability, the sides are perforated with large air holes to keep the coals active, and each cool face is furnished with a lug handle for easy manipulation.

Today kebab professionals use a metal box with ridged racks in the same way, burning charcoal or wood below, and keeping the suspended skewers nice and neat and parallel. For many years we mimicked this arrangement when broiling kebabs by setting two steel slats rescued from a junk pile across some level brick supports. Not as elegant, surely, but it takes seconds to set up (and dispose of after cooking) and works fine for those of us who do not need such an arrangement every day. Recently, though, my husband came home with a four-foot-long piece of I-beam. I couldn't help but notice that the flanges were ideal kebab distance apart. We set it up on a base we had hanging around from an old smoker that had disintegrated, making for some convenient table-height entertaining. What it lacks in stowability, it more than makes up for in charm and fun. (It's also great for roasting corn ears very neatly.)

GEARING UP — PROFESSIONAL HELP

Many of the simple tools that are so helpful in hearth cooking are not widely available today — one reason why it's good to get in the habit of repurposing and improvising. Some useful items are available for purchase online. There are many websites, some keyed to historic reenactors and some to outdoor cooking enthusiasts, offering utensils of varying quality and price. (See Resources, page 306.)

But when it comes right down to the nitty-gritty of cooking by a fire, many of us could really use a blacksmith in our corner; someone to whom we can show a picture of a gridiron or pothook or spit or salamander, and stand back while the magic happens. Unless it's important to you to have a true reproduction of an archaic artifact, your metalworker need not be an expert in hand forging iron. If you don't care about historic cachet and are only after the functional equivalent of a bygone implement, the metal fabricator in a nearby industrial park may take on your project and express it in steel with modern welding techniques.

If you do go the post-industrial route, it still pays to respect what went into the original artifact. Think hard about the reasons behind the weight, materials, and proportions of the tools used by past cooks before innovating too much. Consider what your main anticipated use for the utensil will be, and design accordingly. A reproduction of a gridiron is a great example. Do you expect to broil a lot of smallish fish or kidneys? Think about lighter-gauge bars, close together, and a relatively lightweight build. Grilling thick chops or steaks? Maybe the gridiron can be a little sturdier, with the legs made a bit longer, allowing a nice deep coal-bed. And don't neglect a functional handle. It seems simple, but a handle really is a nice design feature that allows the cook to just up and move the gridiron — even with food on it — while you add more coals to the bed, or check for doneness, or whatever.

Any iron or steel may be used to construct cooking tools, as long as they have not been galvanized. Repeat: no galvanized metal in contact with your food.

Accompaniments

In the kebab's Central Asian homeland, every region, every village, it seems, has a signature treatment. Kebabs are sometimes made of finely minced meat applied around a flat sword-like skewer, or sliced from a roasted spitted stack of lamb and lamb fat, or even simmered in a clay pot. I loved the various kebabs I ate in central Turkey. They came to the table on large pebbly-textured flatbread with contrasting sauces involving garlicky yogurt and butter infused with sumac or Aleppo pepper or dried mint.

Of course, kebabs are truly global — from lemon and garlic marinated chicken hearts in Brazil to shallot, chile, and soy inflected mutton satay in Indonesia. Seeing what cooks around the world have made of the idea gave me a few of my own.

Although an unusual application, a chunk of repurposed I-beam makes a great kebab-grill.

BEEF, RED PEPPER, AND MUSHROOM SKEWERS

Flavorful, tender, and evenly marbled, a tri-tip roast is ideal for this treatment.

1 tablespoon black peppercorns

1 tablespoon coriander seeds

1 tablespoon cumin seeds

3 cilantro roots (about ½ tablespoon), minced (if available)

4 cloves garlic or 2 garlic scapes, minced

½ teaspoon flavorful hot red pepper, like New Mexico chile or Aleppo pepper

2 teaspoons kosher salt

2 tablespoons extra-virgin olive oil

½ tablespoon balsamic vinegar

1 tri-tip beef roast (about 2 pounds), cut into 1-inch chunks (see Prep Work, page 63)

1 large red bell pepper, cut in 1-inch bits

12 ounces button mushrooms, halved or quartered (similar size as pepper and beef)

½ cup cilantro leaves and stems, roughly chopped

---

6 to 8 servings, when accompanied by flatbread or a grain dish

---

1. Using a mortar and pestle, crush the pepper, coriander, and cumin to a chunky powder. Add the cilantro roots, garlic, red pepper, and salt, and pound to a rough paste. Work in the oil and vinegar, mashing it all well together. Massage this mixture into the beef chunks and let it come to room temperature, covered. (Alternatively, you may prepare ahead to this point and chill until ready to proceed.)

2. Prepare a medium-hot bed of hardwood coals.

3. Thread meat and vegetables alternately on bamboo or metal skewers. Grill, turning to brown all sides.

4. Slip off skewers and toss with chopped cilantro before serving.

FISH KEBABS WITH FENNEL SALAD

Only firm-fleshed, tight-grained fish take to skewering. This is a nice one-platter meal for a summer supper.

    1   small onion, grated
    ½   cup whole milk plain yogurt
    1   tablespoon fresh oregano, minced
    1   teaspoon cumin seeds
    3   tablespoons extra-virgin olive oil
    1   pound swordfish, halibut, shark, or tuna, cut into
          1-inch cubes
    1   large bulb fennel
    1   small red onion
    ¼   cup parsley, minced
    1   lemon
    ½   teaspoon kosher or sea salt
        Freshly ground black pepper
    ¼   cup pine nuts, toasted golden in a dry pan

3 or 4 servings

1. Mix the grated onion, yogurt, oregano, cumin, and 1 tablespoon of the olive oil. Toss in the fish cubes, and let stand while your fire is prepared.

2. Slice the fennel bulb and red onion as finely as possible. On your serving platter, toss the slices with the parsley, the remaining olive oil, and juice from one-half of the lemon. Season with salt and pepper, and cut the other half lemon into wedges for serving.

3. Thread the fish on skewers and grill over very hot coals for a couple minutes on each side. Peek into a fish cube to see if it is cooked through. Slide the fish off the skewers onto the salad and sprinkle with the toasted pine nuts.

A Few Simple Tools

BEEF HEART KEBAB WRAPS

I initially came up with this recipe because I happened to have one heart in my fridge when a bunch of people, none of whom had previously expressed a lot of excitement about eating heart, incidentally, turned up to stand around the fire and drink beer and eat peanuts. The dish, though, was so well received that I refuse to wait until another heart turns up to make it again. More commonly available meats like pork chops or chicken thighs could do in a pinch.

3 cloves garlic

1 tablespoon sugar

2 tablespoons medium hot or mild ground red chile

1 tablespoon Vietnamese fish sauce

1 tablespoon soy sauce

1 tablespoon vegetable oil

1 beef heart, trimmed of all fascia, fat, and blood vessels, rinsed well, and cut into uniform 1-inch pieces

½ cup cilantro stems and leaves

½ cup fresh mint leaves

1 cup unsalted roasted peanuts, shelled

12 chewy whole-wheat flatbreads

12 servings

1. With a mortar and pestle, crush the garlic cloves with the sugar. Work in the chile, fish sauce, soy sauce, and oil to make a paste. Massage this into the prepared heart bits and thread them onto skewers.

2. Meanwhile prepare a small, very hot hardwood fire, and let it burn down to a nice coal bed.

3. Put the cilantro, mint, and peanuts on a cutting board and run a knife across them a few times so that everything is very coarsely chopped. Place in your serving dish.

4. Grill the skewers over very hot coals. The heart should be brown and crisp on the edges and just about cooked inside. Slide the meat from the skewers into the serving bowl and toss thoroughly to combine with the herbs and peanuts.

5. Set out instantly, rolled in soft thick flatbreads.

THE GRILL

Today, sadly, the deepest most Americans delve into outdoor cooking is doing something they call "grilling," that is, flame-steaming food over gas jets inside an expensive metal box. And that's a shame because true grilling over hardwood coals creates perfectly delicious meals, costs almost nothing, and can be done indoors in your fireplace if outdoor conditions are unsuitable.

Simplest Grilled Chicken (page 74) finishes up over hardwood coals.

In essence, grilling is just another kind of roasting, and the grill itself is little more than another device to support food at a proper distance from coals. Typically, we think of grilling being quick and roasting slow, but that is only because it is much more conventional to cook small or thin foods on the grill.

Historically, the grill itself — the actual grate — started as the production of a blacksmith's forge, and so followed general human accomplishment in iron-working. This is not to discount the single-use, disposable greenwood grill. Visiting Europeans observed native peoples' skillful deployment of such grills in the Caribbean basin, Chesapeake Bay, and coastal New England in the sixteenth and seventeenth centuries, and the Pacific Northwest in the nineteenth century.

The early modern grill was a small portable unit, hand-forged, with short legs and a handle, called by English speakers a gridiron. (See the photo on page 76). Even in iron-heavy northern European cultures, the gridiron mostly played a supporting role in the home-cook's batterie de cuisine; the smaller cuts of meat that could be cooked quickly on it — rashers and chops — being relegated to the breakfast or supper category. For the sake of both tradition and efficiency, the home cook tended to leave better cuts of meat whole — as loins or saddles or haunches — for dinnertime spit-roasting. The grilled-to-order chop or steak was generally regarded as the province of a tavern, cookshop, or eating house.

When cast-iron cookstoves swept the industrializing world in the mid-nineteenth century, gridirons went out the window along with spits and the rest of the equipage of good roasting and grilling. The adoption of a stove into a household did not merely constitute an addition to the cooking arsenal. In most cases, the newfangled gadgets monopolized the entire kitchen by taking over the chimney flue, necessitating the wholesale abandonment of hearth cooking.

By the end of the nineteenth century, stove manufacturers were marketing cast-iron grill attachments for cookstoves, making superior grilling possible indoors again, but the technique does not seem to have been all that widespread in acceptance. The grilled steak or chop remained more in the hands of professionals than home cooks.

Two factors came together in post–World War II America that would spawn a movement impacting generations of cooks and eaters — a cohort of men and women occupationally skilled in metal fabrication, and a new cult of home, leisure, and casual entertainment. Homebuilt backyard grills of every description (and many of dubious usefulness) sprouted all over the land.

A true wood-fired revolution might have been at hand. Unfortunately, it turned out to be more of a giant chemically fueled weenie-roast, as marketing and misinformation lured the public further from the basic idea of cooking — fast or slow, high or low — over hardwood coals. Instead, we got pernicious "labor-saving" innovations like processed charcoal briquettes, the dreaded lighter fluid, and then fossil fueling through propane or electricity.

Equipment for Grilling

Grills of every description and for every budget are available today, and if you have one you like, by all means enjoy it. But to my way of thinking, using salvaged parts and scrounged scraps of iron or steel or bricks creates a more satisfactory cooking experience than using a purchased grill. The cook has almost infinite flexibility about the distance between the hot coals and the food, and the surface area of the grills may expand or contract depending on present need and the number of grates at hand. Because setup takes just a minute or two, I usually custom-build my grilling arrangement every time, then get it out of the way for other cooking or just a recreational fire.

Supporting the Grill

Once you have some grill grates, you only have to figure out how — and how high — to support them. As important as a stable platform is, establishing the height at which the grill is secured over those coals — the distance between meat and heat — is just as critical. At first it may seem burdensome to have to figure this out for yourself each time you set out to cook something. In reality, though, having the flexibility of infinite adjustability is a huge advantage over a one-size-fits-all arrangement pre-ordained for your food by a grill manufacturer.

Calibrating this heat-to-meat distance is an important skill. Consider that a certain coal bed could be used either to flash-grill a fabulous steak in minutes or to start a gnarly pork butt on its ten-hour path to succulent open-pit-style barbeque, depending only on whether the meat is an inch or over a foot away from it. Think about it this way: 1,000 degrees is radiating from the coals. Your steak can use most of that, no problem. Your barbeque pork butt, on the other hand, wants a cooking atmosphere hovering around the boiling point; thus, your distance must be much greater, so much so that the process of cooking is imperceptible in real time. These two examples occupy the ends of the spectrum, but are exemplary of the relationship between intensity-of-heat and distance-from-heat for all those pork chops and chickens in between.

A reclaimed steel grill set on adjustable metal slats or stacks of bricks makes a grill out of any hearth.

THE AFTERLIFE OF THE COMMERCIAL GRILL

A purchased kettle grill is a perfectly fine vehicle for the honorable method of grilling over hardwood charcoal, but be forewarned that such creatures were not designed for the kind of punishment dished out by repeatedly burning hardwood down to coals. That treatment is definitely the high road to premature burnout. But once the base of the kettle is riddled with holes and the legs have just sort of pushed through or fallen off, it pays to salvage anything that's still good. Most of the parts can go on to creative secondary usage.

We maintain a collection of covers of all sizes, occasionally even using them for the purpose for which they were designed, that is, covering food as it cooks on the grill, to create a more oven-like atmosphere. Essentially for the same reason, because it radically reduces draft, you can pop a cover over coals to slow down combustion and save them for a while. And, in the most extreme version of that smothering, you can entirely cover a coal and ash bed, burying the edges of the cover in the ashes. If you have no air leaks, you stand a good chance of not just extinguishing the remains of your fire, but even preserving the coals for another day. (A seventeenth-century tool for this, shaped for all the world like a Weber lid made of earthenware, was charmingly corrupted from the French *couvre-feu* into the English "curfew.")

It goes without saying that any grills or grates you salvage will be useful somehow, someday. Even the little aluminum ash-catching tray that suspends under the Weber kettle's lower vents has been known to find reemployment as a protective shield for bean-hole beans against infiltration by sand.

One happy consequence of the proliferation of gas grills in the modern world is that the drawn steel or cast-iron gratings — the actual grills — are often their sturdiest components and may have plenty of life in them when the defunct monster goes to the scrap heap. Snap them up! Those surviving parts, simply supported on bricks, will go on to cook their best meals ever over hardwood coals in your hearth or campfire. They are usually made very durably, far more so than the grates that come in most kettle grills, and so can be expected to do many years' duty above even the most searing heat.

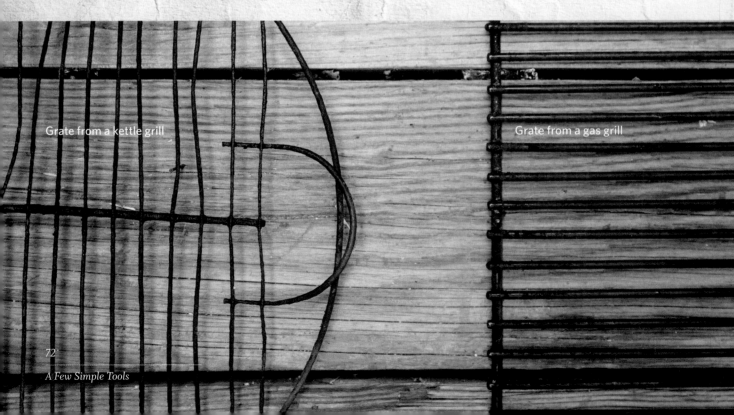

Grate from a kettle grill

Grate from a gas grill

A Few Simple Tools

Once you can visualize where you'd like the grill to be, you have to figure out how to hold it there without slip-ups. One simple method, both indoors and out, consists of stacking a couple of bricks at each end of the grill, leaving plenty of room for air to move around through the coals. Before things get hot, make sure your grill will be supported stably and levelly, and at a reasonable height for your current project. Then either kindle a fire in that setup or shovel in a pile of good coals from a nearby fire, preheat your grate, and have at it.

Once you've given the bricks a few outings, you may perceive possible refinements, based upon your cooking situation and the sort of post-industrial detritus you have on hand. For indoor cooking, you should be aware of a nice little unit expressly made for fireplaces, the so-called Tuscan grill. (See Resources, page 306.)

Outdoors, you usually have plenty of room and the capacity to replace the bricks with scrap metal grill supports driven into the ground right in the firepit. Set up the supports and level the grill before making the fire, remove the grates, burn your hardwood, and reposition the grates to preheat them when the coal bed is right.

Managing an Outdoor Fire Pit for Grilling

If you are like us and deem a recreational fire an important part of any gathering, this idea may be useful to you. It allows you to instantly and easily convert a portion of the fire pit — even one with a blazing fire already underway in it — into a grilling area. In the past, when we had a big recreational fire burning, I used to weigh the advantages of building a separate grilling fire elsewhere — heck, sometimes even in a grill! But since adopting this method, we pretty much quit making a dedicated fire for grilling.

Our fire pits are on rough ground and surrounded by irregular stones. If I think of it before starting a fire, I use those stones, augmented by bricks here and there to stably support two five-foot rails about six or eight inches from the bottom of the pit. The rails, which are really just some light steel angle iron salvaged from someone's scrap heap, must lie in a level plane and the proper distance apart to support your cooking grates. You can then enjoy some relaxing time around a nice fire. When it's time to cook, set up the grates in the section of the rails area most suitable for grilling, depending upon coal accumulation and wind direction. Use a fire shovel to drag coals and flaming wood hither and yon to your advantage before preheating the grates.

A stable cooking area is easy and quick to set up and doesn't even involve messing with bricks in the middle of an inferno. And when cooking is done, the repurposed pit transitions just as quickly back into full recreational mode.

The only downside to this method is the increase in the size of your "useful junk" pile, a lifestyle choice every cook must make.

The Coal Bed

In most cases, the easiest and most sensible way of going about making a coal bed for grilling is to simply burn a nice pile of hardwood (remembering that smaller pieces burn to coal more quickly) and then using a fire shovel to remove coals from under it to the spot where you intend to cook. The other choice is to take the burning wood away to start a secondary fire, leaving only the coals behind in the place where you will grill. (Either way, replenish fuel on the secondary fire, so that more coals will be forthcoming.) When the ashes have settled, set the clean grill grate or grates on the supports to preheat thoroughly before starting to cook.

Coal beds usually have hot and cool spots that occur naturally with the burning of hardwood. The temperature variations can be your allies. Even before it's time to flip the food, the map of warm and cool spots usually becomes obvious; take advantage of them as you move food around the grill. For example, a little judicious maneuvering with the tongs allows you to use the cool spots to cook thick items thoroughly over low heat even after they have plenty of sear on them.

SIMPLEST GRILLED CHICKEN

Vary the seasonings to suit your menu. This version is nice with rice pilaf, seared asparagus, and a sprinkling of toasted almonds.

6 chicken thighs

4 cups cold water

3 tablespoons kosher salt

1 teaspoon coriander seeds

1 teaspoon black peppercorns

1 small dry red chile, crumbled

2 cloves garlic, mashed

2 tablespoons chopped fresh oregano

1 tablespoon sherry vinegar

2 tablespoons extra-virgin olive oil

1 lime

6 servings

I. Place the chicken in a sealable container. Cover with the cold water and salt. Swish around, seal, and chill 1 hour to overnight.

2. While you are burning a hardwood fire to make coals for grilling, make the rub. Crush the coriander, pepper, and chile in a mortar to coarse powder. Add the garlic, herbs, vinegar, and oil. Stir in the juice from half of the lime.

3. Drain the chicken, pat dry a bit, and slather with the rub. Place on a preheated grill over medium coals and cook, turning as needed, until internal temp reaches 165°F. Transfer to a warm platter, and squeeze over the remaining half-lime as you serve.

BUTTERFLIED LEG OF LAMB

Reducing the thickness of foods makes them simple to grill; butterflying a leg of lamb employs this strategy. Get the boning out of the way the day before and marinate overnight for a great, easy party dish. This is lovely with a grain salad full of scallions, mint, and lemon.

1 leg of lamb, butterflied
6 cloves garlic, lightly crushed
4 scallions, chopped
1 teaspoon black peppercorns, crushed in a mortar
1 teaspoon kosher or sea salt
1 bunch fresh mint, chopped
¼ cup extra-virgin olive oil
1 lemon, washed and quartered

8 servings

1. Put the meat in a sealable container. Toss on the garlic, scallions, pepper, salt, mint, and oil. Massage it together for a moment. Squeeze in the lemon and toss in the lemon rinds. Close the container and chill overnight. Bring to room temperature before grilling.

2. Grill 2 to 2½ inches above medium-hot coals, turning once, until crispy and brown on the outside, from 25 to 35 minutes. Insert an instant-read thermometer and look for the 130°F range. Remove the roast to a pan and cover very loosely with foil. Rest at room temperature for 20 minutes, then carve in thin slices.

BUTTERFLYING A LEG OF LAMB

Nowadays it's harder to buy a leg of lamb with the bone still in it than one that has already been boned or butterflied. But if you do start out with a whole leg, you can butterfly it yourself. All you need is a sharp boning knife and a few minutes without interruption. On one side of the shin, you can see the bone. Cut along that toward the knee (which you can feel by bending the leg). Work your knife up and down the shinbone cleanly, freeing the bone on both sides. Then make a clean incision following the thighbone from the knee up. Once you have exposed the entire bone, just trim the meat away from it, keeping the meat in one piece. (When you have freed the bone, set it aside for stock.) Now lay the meat out and cut shallowly along the seams between the muscles, which allows the whole thing to be spread open wider. You may make single lengthwise incisions in each of the two largest muscles (so that you can open them out like a book) if you want the whole thing to cook evenly. (I sometimes skip that step if I'm serving people who enjoy a range of doneness in lamb — the fat muscles remain rare while the thinner bits crisp up.)

While sparing you this work, commercially packed butterflied legs of lamb seem to include only a portion of the musculature that is intrinsic to a lamb's walking apparatus. Likewise boned roasts, especially those sold with a tell-tale netting to hold them together, usually have been deprived of the bodily integrity useful in this recipe; perhaps they would serve for kebabs.

AN OYSTER ROAST

At the inn where I once cooked on an island off the coast of Georgia, every winter Saturday was marked with an early evening oyster roast. Under the broad porch of the big house, an old brick barbeque blazed with gnarly live oak chunks. A bumpy sheet of expanded metal sagged across the coals, supporting hundreds of Apalachicola or Cumberland Island oysters. Cocktails flowed and staff helped guests to oysters cooked just how they liked them, from barely warmed, to steamed plump, to chewy saline jerky.

Accustomed since childhood to consume these bivalves raw and chilly, I was prepared, in my snotty Yankee way, to take a high-handed view of such treatment. Turns out my prejudice was wrong again, probably because I couldn't resist the introduction of fire to the slow collaborative celebratory shellfish-eating process I already loved. It was seductive — oysters are a huge treat we tend to enjoy in winter where I come from, so why not take the chill off? So it was with great pleasure that I recently came across an account of a homey bygone Yankee oyster roast in a letter from the 1870s, describing an impromptu late-winter supper in a coastal Massachusetts parlor, of oysters broiled on a gridiron over a lovely bed of coals. And that's the beauty of the oyster roast — fun indoors or out for a few or a party. Little preparation, little pressure, every oyster cooked to the taste of the diner.

4	ounces butter
3	tablespoons sherry
½	teaspoon cayenne pepper (or to taste)
48	oysters (6 to 12 per person), cleansed of mud

8 servings

I. Prepare a grill setup and burn a hardwood fire to build up some good coals.

2. Round up some tongs, some oyster knives or just small paring knives, and some kitchen towels (the faded, stained, and torn ones, not the hand-embroidered ones).

3. Put the butter, sherry, and cayenne in a small clay pot or saucepan, and place in a nest of coals out of the way to heat. Simmer briefly, then keep warm.

4. Meanwhile, arrange the oysters, rounded side down, on the grill over the coal bed. Those who like them rare will want to pull them from the heat as soon as the shell yawns one iota. This is when they are juiciest, so apply caution and kitchen towels.

5. As the oysters remain over the coals, they cook and shrink and eventually dry out entirely. But as I previously said, tastes in shellfish-eating vary infinitely. This is a good opportunity for experimentation.

6. Use the knife to pop off the top shell, then slide the knife under the meat to free it, trying not to mangle it. Eat immediately, with the sherry butter if so inclined.

The Grill

JERKED PORK LOIN

This treatment works when I am faced with a boneless pork loin. Given the choice, I prefer to cook a bone-in roast, seasoned more subtly, on a spit or a low grill like the schwenker. But I find that the often over-trimmed boneless roast profits from more aggressive flavors and a little added fat.

You can certainly grill it whole, but in this recipe I quarter it lengthwise. Not only does that trick expose more surface area to the smoke and heat, it also magically multiplies the number of people you can serve with a few pounds of meat. Once grilled and thinly sliced, this pork can be paired with large and tasty sides, like a gigantic noodle and vegetable salad, or beans and rice and fried plantains, to expand it to feed a small multitude. Or serve with a pile of rolls and grilled vegetables for sandwiches.

1 tablespoon espresso-roast coffee beans (optional)
1¼ teaspoon whole allspice
¾ teaspoon brown mustard seeds
1 teaspoon peppercorns
1 teaspoon coriander seeds
1 ½-inch piece of cinnamon stick or ¾ teaspoon ground cinnamon
¼ of a nutmeg
3 cloves garlic
1 teaspoon kosher or sea salt
1 bunch scallions, roughly chopped
1 cup parsley, chopped
1 tablespoon fresh oregano, chopped
2 teaspoons fresh thyme, chopped
1 habanero chile, seeded and minced
1 teaspoon lime zest
3 tablespoons olive oil
1 (2–3 pound) boneless pork loin roast
Juice of 1 lime

8 to 15 servings, depending on sides

I. In a dry frying pan over a medium flame, toast the espresso beans and whole spices for a few minutes. Shake the pan to keep things moving and as soon as it gives off a toasty aroma, pour the contents into a large mortar (or spice grinder). Pulverize.

2. If you are using the mortar, add the garlic and salt, and work it over to a chunky powder. Add the scallions, parsley, oregano, thyme, habanero, and lime zest, in batches if necessary, pounding it all to a mash. Scrape it up from the bottom and work in the olive oil. If you don't have a mortar big enough for this job, use either a food processor or a cutting board and chef's knife.

3. Bisect the pork loin lengthwise, then bisect each half again. Slather each quarter with the rub and place in an airtight container for an hour on the counter or up to a day in the fridge (but bring to room temperature before grilling).

4. Grill over hot coals, flipping on all sides, until crisp and brown on the exterior and registering 145°F within. Remove from the grill, tent with foil, and allow to rest 10 minutes. Slice thinly across the grain, drizzle with lime juice, and serve with accompaniments.

TESTING WITH TOAST

There's no better or quicker way to find out about the evenness of the heat from your coal bed than to make toast. If you load up a hot grill with slices of bread, smoke plumes will quickly call your attention to the location of hot spots among the coals. First, flip and shift the bread around with tongs to even out the cooking and to avoid any fatal burning. Rub the finished toast with the cut face of a garlic clove and drizzle with olive oil, or just serve with cheese or spreads as an appetizer instead of crackers.

Once you have removed the finished toast from the grill, you have a chance to attend to the coals if you feel it's necessary before you move on to cook more substantial foods.

I also very frequently serve grilled or roasted foods on toast. In that case I usually grill the toast more slowly in the last heat left after cooking the rest of the meal so that it's nice and fresh.

Really good toast can be a wonderful supper if you put it in a soup plate and top it with a ladleful of excellent stock and maybe even a poached egg. It's also requisite with toasted cheese.

THE SCHWENKER

What about suspending the grill from on high? Cooks in the Saarland region of southern Germany use a grill called a *schwenker* — a heavy-gauge grill with three lug handles welded to the rim that allow it to hang from a tripod or gallows. Its traditional use centers on one particular dish, *schwenkbraten*, marinated pork sirloin steaks, but we have found it to be very adaptable and a wonderful all-around grill with remarkable low-and-slow capabilities.

Typically the *schwenkermeister* keeps the thing moving — swinging and rotating from its chains — which, along with the ease of adjusting the grill's height from the coals, makes it simple to cook items which are usually a bit of a challenge because of size and shape. Cooking such foods, like large whole chickens and small roasts, on the schwenker is a long, but leisurely process, feeling rather like making real barbeque. And the results carry some of the weight of real barbeque in smoke and juiciness.

A swinging schwenker keeps meat moving over the coals.

The Schwenker

SAARLÄNDISCHER SCHWENKBRATEN

In the schwenker's homeland, this preparation reigns. This recipe is courtesy of my friend Astrid Weins, whose father hails from the Saarland. If neck meat is unavailable, ask your butcher to cut boneless country style ribs in large (3- by-4-inch) pieces.

4 pounds pork neck meat, cut into 8-ounce pieces
¼ cup canola oil
3–4 onions, cut in large strips
4 cloves of garlic, pressed
7 juniper berries, crushed
1 tablespoon prepared mustard
½ teaspoon dried thyme
1 teaspoon dried oregano
1 teaspoon good curry powder
2 teaspoons paprika
½–1 teaspoon cayenne pepper
1 teaspoon freshly ground black pepper
2 teaspoons kosher or sea salt

8 servings

I. Place the meat in a sealable container. Mix the remaining ingredients together and work into the meat. Seal and chill for at least 24 hours, up to 3 days.

2. Allow meat to come to room temperature while you make a fire under the schwenker. Beech wood is traditional in the Saarland, but your schwenkbraten will be delicious cooked over any hardwood coals. Once you have a decent coal bed, and more wood burning alongside to generate additional coals, place the meat on the preheated grill grate, and start it swinging gently yet continually. Adjust the height of the grill or the coal arrangement to get a moderate steady heat.

3. At this point, there's nothing to do but keep the schwenker swinging and drink beer. When the first side looks crispy and luscious, flip the schwenkbraten with tongs. Keep the schwenker moving, and cook until meat registers 145°F internally.

"Planking" food by a fire is a perfectly viable method to add to your technical arsenal, but like most techniques that use few tools, it benefits from some forethought and practice. Trickiest of all to master is the vernacular method for plank-baking unyeasted breads, like jonnycake and shortcake, regionally popular in eighteenth-century America. These treats, described elegiacally by nostalgic memoirists long after their extinction, are utterly compelling to me in that they are completely vernacular, sparsely documented, archaeologically invisible foods. It was worth having a few slide into the fire to have the fun and satisfaction of re-creating their singular flavor.

The planking of fish, another homespun practice, has never entirely gone out of style. The method has been particularly associated with shad, as they arrived on their spawning ground in spring. Like so many special seasonal foods, planked shad always seems to have had a festive edge. Late in the nineteenth-century, tony resorts on the Delaware and Chesapeake watersheds specialized in a rather gentrified version, while good-ol'-boy political rallies grew up around annual shad-planking events from Connecticut to North Carolina.

PLANKED FISH

Shad populations plummeted in the last century, as rampant pollution and dams blocking access to spawning habitat took their toll. Another hint to its demise lies in the fish's scientific name, *Alosa sapidissima*, which loosely translates to "most luscious." Although conservation efforts are bringing shad back from the brink, it behooves most of us who wish to plank a fish to broaden our horizons. So if you haven't a hope of catching a shad, experiment with other mid-sized to large, firm-textured, flavorful fish.

You'll need a nice smooth hardwood plank — oak, hickory, and birch are variously suggested by nineteenth-century writers — about two inches thick, and roughly one foot by two foot in size. You'll also need a hardwood fire, and something — bricks, firewood, a stick — handy for propping up your plank; plus a palmful of stainless steel or wrought iron nails (never galvanized) and a claw hammer.

---

2 skin-on sturdy fish fillets (about 2 to 3 pounds)
2 tablespoons olive oil
½ teaspoon kosher or sea salt
1 fat pinch of cayenne or other powdered hot red pepper
2 tablespoons butter

4 to 6 servings

I. Make a good hardwood fire on level ground or in a slight depression. Develop a nice bed of coals before you start and have plenty of small hardwood chunks standing by.

2. Inspect the fish fillets for bones, especially if you did manage to get shad, which are as notorious for boniness as they are delicious. Use tweezers to extract any you find.

3. Put the olive oil in a large plate and run the fillets through it on both sides. Sprinkle with salt and cayenne, and stack on the plate for ten minutes while you preheat the plank.

4. Prop the empty plank before the fire. This is a good opportunity to test both the heat of the fire and the security of your propping system. Meanwhile, gather up the fish, fastenings, and hammer. When the plank is heated "to the point of ignition" as one period description has it, pick it up with hot pads and convey it to a solid heatproof surface.

5. Working quickly, arrange the fillets, skin-side down, on the plank and nail them in place. Remembering that you will be turning the board top for bottom at least

once, test your fastening arrangement against the rigors of gravity. Then return it to the fire.

6. Melt the butter before the fire in a small earthen or other pan. Brush the fillet with butter every now and again. After about 10 minutes, overturn the plank so that the fillets get a good even roasting. Test for doneness by prodding with a small knife.

7. Pick up the plank with pot holders and serve immediately, as soon as you have discreetly drawn out the very hot nails.

8. Serving suggestions: An April 1894 issue of *Boston Cooking School* magazine accompanies planked shad with *maitre d'hotel* butter (mash 4 ounces soft butter, ¼ cup minced parsley, juice of half a lemon, salt, and pepper) and, today, the now rather recherché pickled walnuts or butternuts. A slightly earlier South Jersey description lays out a full shad-centered spring celebration, featuring new potatoes, fresh green peas, asparagus, and waffles.

SEARING WITH HOT IRON

Early modern cooks made creative use of the heat-retaining qualities of their fireplace tools for an array of culinary quick fixes. All sorts of foods and beverages were assailed with super-heated shovels and pokers for a quick volcanic blast just before serving.

The poker, heated red hot in the coals of a cooking fire, can be a very efficient, and dramatic, immersion heater. A school of early American beer-and-rum beverages called "flip" employed this party trick. Why get a pot dirty when you can quickly heat a beverage right in the tankard with a handy hearth tool? Most fun of all, each drinker gets to perform the alchemy for himself. The flip hisses and seethes like an espresso machine, growing warmer, smokier, richer, and bitterer the longer the poker remains. The result — a hot velvety-textured ancestor of the boiler-maker — is unlike anything I've ever had. A compelling fireside activity and a warming beverage all in one!

When first used, the term "salamander" cumulatively encompassed all super-heated iron tools (even those used for lighting pipes), but by the eighteenth-century, a well-appointed kitchen might boast a specific implement by that name. That salamander, a robust lollipop-shaped unit forged of iron, was used red hot for crisping up toppings of breadcrumbs or cheese and for melting sugar on creamy desserts long before broilers and hand-held blowtorches came along.

An omelet recipe published in 1823 closes with: "A Salamander is necessary to those who will have the top brown; but a kitchen Shovel may be substituted for it." In these latter days, we are not so lucky. Our stamped steel shovels are poor stand-ins for wrought iron tools when it comes to both retaining and withstanding heat. Fortunately for those interested in experiencing this kind of fun, iron fire shovels, salamanders, and pokers are not rocket science to reproduce for those who know how to work metal.

Red-hot iron transfers searing heat to food and drink. The salamander, pictured here, caramelizes and crisps surfaces, while a super-heated poker can be used as an immersion burner.

BURNT CREAM

Both the technique and the scenting with lemon peel and cinnamon make this 18th-century English member of the *crème brûlée* family a dead ringer for the *crema cremada* still served in Catalonia.

2 cups milk

1 cup cream

1 lemon peel (white pith excluded)

1 3-inch cinnamon stick

2 tablespoons cornstarch (white flour in original recipe, but cornstarch makes a nicer texture)

⅓ cup and ¾ cup organic sugar, separately

5 egg yolks

6 to 8 servings

I. Slowly heat the milk, cream, lemon peel, and cinnamon in a heavy saucepan over low heat; do not boil. In a medium bowl, whisk together the cornstarch and the ⅓ cup sugar. Whisk in the yolks until smooth.

2. When the milk mixture is steaming, whisk about ¼ of it into the yolk mixture, then scrape the yolk mixture back into the saucepan, whisking continually. Continue to cook, whisking and occasionally scraping the bottom of the pan with a spatula, until mixture thickens and just simmers. Pour through a sieve into a flat heatproof dish (like a pie plate). Cover very tightly with plastic wrap and chill at least 3 hours.

3. Heat your salamander or iron fire-shovel until red hot in the coals of a fire. Set the unwrapped dish of cream on a stable surface and sprinkle evenly with a good layer of sugar. Carefully touch the flat of the hot salamander to the sugar all over until molten. Let cool a minute to harden, but eat very soon.

Searing with Hot Iron

FLIP

A favorite sea beverage, tavern treat, and mid-morning refreshment in Federal America. It can also be used to make Flip Pancakes. (See Resources, page 306.)

1 ounce light rum

1 tablespoon old-fashioned molasses, or less, if your beer has some sweetness

1 bottle or can not-very-bitter ale or beer, room temperature best

---

1 serving

---

1. Set the business end of an iron fire-poker directly over hot coals to heat.

2. Stir together the rum and molasses in a large heatproof mug. Stir in beer to fill no more than three-quarters full.

3. Immerse the red-hot poker. Try not to touch the sides of the mug, and generally be careful. Enjoy hot.

BURNT WINE

A probable ancestor of flip, burnt wine is just a cup of wine, spiced or not, heated with a hot poker. Also, like flip, it is associated with sea voyages, where it was an easy fix. Apparently, it was understood that some alcohol is lost in the searing process; Samuel Pepys drank burnt wine for a while when he was trying to not be such a sot.

Searing with Hot Iron

HOT POKER MUSTARD

Another creative misuse of a fireplace tool is found in this 19th-century recipe for mustard, where once the condiment is packed in storage pots, a hot poker is "thrust into each" for a quick jolt of searing heat.

Honestly, this would be a very nice preparation even if you didn't have the fun of sticking a hot poker in it; it's great with roast lamb or beef, or in a smoked-turkey sandwich. Use Coleman's dry mustard for an intense sinus-clearing experience.

1 clove garlic

Fat pinch of salt

A few sprigs each parsley, celery leaves, chervil, and tarragon (or any combination)

4 anchovies (optional for vegetarians)

1 teaspoon sugar

4 ounces dry mustard

¾ to 1 cup cool water

2 teaspoons cider or white wine vinegar

Makes about 1 cup

1. Mash the garlic in a mortar with the salt. Mince the herbs, add to the mortar, and continue mashing. Work in the anchovies and sugar, and then the mustard and the water little by little until it forms "a thinnish paste."

2. Heat a poker until it is red-hot in the fire.

3. Scrape the mustard into a jar. Carefully stick the red-hot poker into the middle of the mustard, without grazing the jar. Be prepared for a pretty alarming odor. Pour a fine skim of vinegar on the surface and pop on the lid. Let stand an hour or so before using, or keep as long as you want. It grows mellower in time.

PEBBLE-SEARED PARSLEY SAUCE

Barcelona, 1529: Aromatic herbs are compounded with vinegar and honey. The cook must then take "two smooth pebbles from the sea or river, and cast them in the fire; and when they shall be quite ruddy and red, cast them with some tongs in the mortar in such a manner that they are quenched there."

What results from this exciting alchemy project is an *agrodolce*-type condiment, wonderful with grilled meat, poultry, or fish. The 16th-century Catalan cookbook from which this recipe is adapted suggests grated horseradish or minced clary sage as variants from the parsley. In any event, the effect of the stones on the texture and aroma of the sauce is remarkable.

Do try to get pebbles from the sea or a river, as smooth as possible. Always be wary when heating stones; eye protection is not a bad idea.

1 fat slice rustic white bread, toasted dry, no crusts
3 tablespoons (about) white wine vinegar
1 packed cup finely minced parsley
Fat pinch of kosher or sea salt
Freshly ground black pepper
1 tablespoon honey
1 tablespoon water

Makes about ⅔ cup

1. Place your "two smooth pebbles" on the coal bed of your fire.

2. Break the toast up roughly and steep it in the vinegar while you prepare the parsley.

3. Grind the parsley and salt in a mortar very thoroughly. Mash in pepper and the soaked bread, holding back any unabsorbed vinegar for the moment. When it's amalgamated, work in the honey, then the water and leftover vinegar. The texture should be loose.

4. If your pebbles seem "ruddy and red" enough, carefully pick them up with tongs and place into the sauce. Mind the spatters. Remove pebbles when things have cooled down a bit. Stir the sauce and check the seasoning. Correct it so that it "tastes a little of pepper, and a little sweet-sour, and of parsley."

3.

POTS AND PANS

The global pantry — stocked with durable cooking containers made of clay and metal — is a recent innovation. For most of our existence, we humans have used naturally occurring objects and substances as utensils. Cooks have manipulated wood and other plant fiber; stone, including raw clay; and animal parts, like bone, shell, sinew, and hide, to mediate between fire and food. For hundreds of thousands of years, that's what our kitchen equipment looked like. The world of pots and pans didn't begin to exist for most of us until an explosion of technologies in the Neolithic period ushered it in, among many sweeping changes.

In this cook's opinion, the game-changing technologies of ceramics and metallurgy were the children of one mother skill — cooking. Sure, it could be a coincidence that the pottery kiln and the smelting furnace developed in the same region as had the cylindrical masonry oven known as the *tannur*. But it requires less imagination to picture the tannur's salient characteristic — furious heat, produced by containing fire while controlling its draft — as the underlying concept that set humans on the path toward pottery and metalworking. Whether the raw material was sheets of dough, vessels of clay, or lumps of ore, understanding the tannur principle allowed the artisan to wreak unprecedentedly dramatic effects on the product.

We'll get to tannur baking in chapter 4. For the moment we're more interested in the cooking tools produced in the pottery kiln and the smelting furnace, and how you can use them in your hearth.

We'll start with the griddle, since it can be made of good old stone, fired earthenware, or hammered or cast metal; then move on to cooking pots, first clay, then metal.

THE GRIDDLE IN ALL ITS GUISES

A griddle is a flattish surface of clay, stone, or metal that is supported or suspended directly over a fire or coals. Anyone who has ever tried to bake bread on a hot rock near a fire will have an innate understanding of the griddle's convenience. If you could add only one item to your wood-fired *batterie de cuisine*, the griddle is the A-number-1 artifact to beg, borrow, or steal. It supports the addition of more techniques to your repertoire and foods to your menu than any other one piece of equipment, save a wood-fired oven, but without any of the work or money entailed in acquiring one of those. Plus it takes up very little room.

Selecting a Griddle

To cook all the recipes in this section, you will need two different shape griddles — flat and convex. Aside from that basic requirement, though, there is a great deal of latitude in what constitutes a griddle. Along the way to discovering your ideal utensils, you may find yourself trying out all kinds of found objects. What ultimately works for you will depend as much on your willingness to experiment as on your fire setup and your desired menu.

Flat cast-iron griddles are widely available; unless you plan to carry it around a lot, select the largest one for greatest flexibility. A sheet of steel or a piece of cast iron salvaged from a scrap pile can work just as well, or better, since most purpose-made griddles are designed for indoor use and needlessly small for an outdoor fire.

All the recipes in this section may be cooked on a flat griddle, with the exception of the large wheat-based flatbreads. These prefer a convex baking surface, a more specialized griddle type known as a *saj* among Arabic and Turkish speakers and a *tava* among South Asians (including those in the Caribbean). Online shopping or a visit to an ethnic grocery may reward you with such a pan, but be careful to avoid aluminum and nonstick tavas.

A steel wok inverted over the fire worked very well as a saj for me for years, although try as I might to protect the wooden handles from the heat, they got pretty scorched from this perversion of the wok's design. Recently we came across a very heavy piece of a defunct industrial artifact — a perfectly smooth dome-shaped iron boiler cap 16 inches in diameter. Its weightiness calls for a bit of care in the setup, but allows it to heat very evenly; its size has pushed me to pursue the challenge of making huge, delicious flatbreads.

The only recipes in this section that cannot be easily cooked on a convex griddle are those for foods that would tend to slide off (asparagus, shrimp . . .) or that require a level surface (English muffins).

Griddle Setup and Fuel Prep

The classic way of supporting a saj, or convex griddle, is to arrange three similar-size stones as a tripod. I prefer to set the stones up stably and try for symmetry, height, and levelness before even starting the fire. Then, so that I have a nice coal bed, I'll remove the saj and make a fire of hardwood sticks and split kindling between the rocks. Once you're an old hand with your griddle setup, you may be able to roll any three rocks into a fire and be good to go, but it's wise to be methodical at least the first few times out.

Observe the height the saj stands from the ground when it's supported on the tripod; your fuel will need to fit easily under it, along with some air and maneuvering room. Prepare a nice pile of fuel accordingly. I use finely split pine or dry twigs from the forest floor, fuels which I have in abundance; depending upon their location and lifestyle, other cooks favor agricultural by-products like straw or dried dung. I take an 8-inch wrought-iron tava with me camping, and have always found something suitable locally, from loblolly pine needles to desiccated cowpats. Having read about gorse (a thorny evergreen bush) as a cooking and baking fuel in early modern England, I decided to try snipping up some of the briers that grow around my neighborhood. Except for the lacerations to my hands and arms, this experiment was very successful; even green, that stuff really goes up! Half an hour's work using heavy leather gloves and long-handled pruning snips yields enough potential flame for stacks of flatbreads.

Whatever fuel you choose, have enough, properly sized and on hand, so that you can easily keep a brisk small fire going throughout your cooking process without the distraction of juggling a rolling pin and a Gurkha knife. Learning to make flatbreads is challenge enough for one day.

Having a nice bed of small coals before you start makes it easier to maintain a moderate fire to heat the metal plate evenly; with practice you may learn to keep light quick-burning fuels, like straw, burning steadily. But, once again, there's already plenty to tend to in forming and cooking the breads. Have fun with the multitasking inherent in this kind of cooking by learning in partnership with a friend.

The nature of your griddle will have an effect on how much fire you need. Something thin that transfers heat quickly will need a very even low fire under it; you may need to increase the distance between the griddle and the heat. A heavy cast-iron griddle will distribute the heat and take longer to heat and cool.

The food on the griddle also determines the type of fire you want. Seared vegetables, for example, can take all the heat you throw at them, as long as you move them around and don't leave them too long. Some very thin breads are extra delicious if the fire licks around the edges of the griddle and chars them directly just a little. Thicker griddle-breads like English muffins, on the other hand, need to bake through to the middle without immolating the exterior; a low flame is key.

If you're not much for crouching on the ground or in your hearth, consider setting up your griddle along the lines of a British bakestone or Mexican comal. Experiment with stacking bricks to build a sturdy support for a piece of sheet metal, cast iron, or heck, even a real comal. This arrangement is comfortable to use, especially if you are engaged in a time-consuming cooking project like baking a huge pile of tortillas or crackers.

Pull up a chair, or at least a stump. Seventeenth-century Dutch genre paintings are full of pancake makers, both housewives at home and professionals on the street, working their griddles while sitting on little milking stools. You've got to be comfortable, or this is no fun.

SETTING UP YOUR WORK AREA

Arrange a work surface with all the ingredients and equipment you need at hand. It's nice to have enough surface area to have a bread or two "on deck" waiting for the griddle. It's a wonder to watch Middle Eastern bakers working with trays and cloths around them on the ground, tending fires, baking, rolling, and stretching dough, and telling stories all at once. Take their cue and have everything organized and at arm's reach before you start.

CAKES ON THE GRIDDLE

Part of the fun of griddles is that they are global. Many, many cultures feature characteristic foods cooked on them. It's tempting to say that the griddle's utter simplicity has dictated its dispersal all over the planet, but a brief consideration of the complex processes undergirding so many griddle-cooked foods (contemplate corn tortillas, for example) suggests we think again. This deceptively simple baking technique is in many places simply the last link in a chain of ancient and intricate cultural evolution.

The fact is that baking technologies develop to suit the grains available. With its smooth horizontal surface allowing even and controlled baking, the griddle has been used by cooks the world over to convert gluten-free grains and even tubers into tremendous breads.

By contrast, the tannur, and later, the wood-fired oven, developed in tandem with gluten-bearing wheat. For many centuries, these ovens remained localized to the complex societies situated in the swath of the planet where domestication of that grain family had first occurred. To bake in these specialized ovens is to appreciate wheat's particular handling and baking characteristics. Wheat's gluten allows it to stretch and cling to a blazing hot tannur wall in the form of naan; it traps fermentation gasses and lets loaves rise when enclosed in a dome-shaped oven.

Before so much of the world was ruled by wheat, the griddle was all you'd need to convert the dough or batter that was the end result of your agricultural efforts into the tasty staple of your region, whether you were making an oatcake on the far reaches of the Shetland archipelago or a corn pupusa in ancient El Salvador or a lentil dosa in South India.

Unlike the tannur or wood-fired oven, the usually portable griddle can be used quickly and almost anywhere, to bake breads made out of a great array of ingredients, from millet to cassava. This is not to say that the griddle is inappropriate for wheat-based breads. On the contrary, some of the very tastiest combinations of flour-water-yeast-salt I've ever tried were baked in seconds on a fire-heated slab of scrap iron propped up on three rocks.

Some griddled breads have survived as the dominant staples in their home regions into the twenty-first century. In most cases, these breads — chapati, tortilla, pita — successfully made the leap to industrial production and global diffusion. At the same time, though, many home bakers still provide them for their families.

In other parts of the world, even those whose populations once relied entirely on griddles to bake their daily bread, the tradition has all but vanished. Especially in Europe, many regional griddle breads remained inseparable from small-scale home cooking and resisted large-scale production and marketing. The lefse of Norway, the oatcakes of Yorkshire, the many bakestone cakes of Wales and Brittany — those are still celebrated today as a part of regional heritage, but they are rarely made and eaten among populations who now share the same commercial white bread habit dominant in much of the world.

Consider, though, that those European griddled breads, when they were first described as distinctive regionalisms a couple of centuries ago, were really just the last holdovers for a continent fed on a huge variety of local non-wheaten flatbreads since the inception of agriculture. The further north and west one travelled into Europe away from the wheat center of, say, Anatolia, the longer these regional breads held sway.

Even centuries after the introduction of wheat into Western Europe, it remained the luxury of the well heeled and well connected. In the early modern period, people of moderate fortunes might rejoice to eat wheaten bread during a flush year or season, conscious that they may soon lower their sights to barley, oats, millet, or rye when weather ruined the harvest, or when war, chicanery, or politics propelled the wheat elsewhere. (By extension, the real dearth experienced once in a generation or so kept cooks up on how to make bread out of lupine seeds, acorns, or bark.)

PITA

For home cooks, pita is a great entry into the world of flatbreads, even into baking in general. Its formula is simple and the dough is easy to handle. The loaves' thickness and relatively small diameter doesn't demand any daredevil dough-stretching skills. You don't need anything fancy in terms of equipment; because pita may be small, you can get away with using a 10-inch cast-iron frying pan. The dough can be held over in the fridge for a day before baking, helping it fit conveniently into a busy schedule. A bagful of pita in the freezer is like gold at lunch-making time. I find the griddle method irresistibly fun. but if you'd rather, you may bake the prepared pita in a hot wood-fired oven.

EQUIPMENT

Flat heavy griddle, any size
Rolling pin
2 or 3 clean cotton kitchen towels
Non-serrated tongs or a metal spatula or asbestos fingers

INGREDIENTS

16 ounces bread flour
8 ounces whole-wheat flour
2 cups plus 2 tablespoons warm water
1 teaspoon dry yeast
1 tablespoon kosher salt (only 2½ teaspoons if you omit the leaven)
5 ounces white or whole wheat leaven (optional)

Makes 14 or 16 small pita

1. Mix the flours and water in a large mixing bowl, or in the bowl of a stand mixer if you'd like to use one. Stir the mixture with a fork just until well combined with no dry patches; add a touch more water if necessary. Let stand at room temperature, covered airtight, for 30 minutes.

2. Add the remaining ingredients and mix well for a few minutes, by hand or with a dough hook. Scrape into a nice ball and cover airtight.

3. Ferment at warm room temperature 90 minutes, scraping the dough out onto a floured surface every 30 minutes to stretch and fold it — pull it into a rough oblong, then fold it in thirds like a letter, once on one axis, and once on the other. Incorporate as little new flour as possible. (If you would like to retard the dough overnight, place it in an airtight container into the fridge directly after the second stretch-and-fold exercise.)

4. When you are ready to bake, prepare your fire setup, griddle, and fuel as described on page 95. Divide the dough into sixteen 2½-ounce balls, and preshape them evenly round. (Dough will make only 14 portions of that size if you omit leaven.) Keep covered to keep them from drying out while they rest 15 to 30 minutes.

5. Preheat your griddle over a moderate flame. Use a short rolling pin to roll one of the balls out to an even circle about 6 inches in diameter. Place it gingerly on the griddle. Start rolling out the next one, while another part of your brain slowly counts to 15. Flip the bread. If the heat is right, the side that was down should be just beginning to set up but not brown. Return to your rolling pin and finish rolling out the second pita.

6. Peek under the pita on the griddle. If it looks baked and is flecked with brown, flip it over again. (Take a second to check your fire; does it seem steady? Should you add more twigs or whatever?) By now your pita may be puffing up. If it just bubbles a bit and then stops, take action to help it: holding a towel bunched up to protect your fingertips, press down gently on one of the bubbles. This almost always has the effect of spreading the steam out between the upper and lower "crusts" of the pita and forcing the pocket to open. If nothing happens, flip it over and try the other side; on rare occasions you'll have a dud, in which case you'll have to eat it.

7. Remove the pita from the griddle soon after it has puffed. If it bakes too long it will be undesirably crisp; pita should remain soft. Place the pita on a cloth and cover lightly; it's fine to stack them as you go along.

8. Once you figure out your rhythm, you may find you can add another griddle (or cook two pitas side-by-side on an oblong cast-iron griddle).

NOTE: You may use a saj or other convex griddle to bake this dough into larger, flatter breads that are decent for wrapping falafel or other fillings. Divide the dough into twelve 4-ounce portions, preshape, and roll out into 9-inch circles. Bake on the preheated saj, turning once.

FLATBREAD VARIATIONS, ANCIENT AND MODERN

In its most authentic form, shrak (see facing page) is baked on a hearth of river pebbles in a tabun (see page 291). A similar Persian bread, *sangak*, is baked on a bed of blazing hot pebbles in a very large wood-fired oven, even when commercially produced. Very good versions of this wonderful bread, however, are also made on the saj, the large convex griddle.

Archaeologists have turned up shards of large perforated clay griddles on Iron Age sites in the Levant. These griddles seem to have been installed in hearths and were certainly the predecessor of the saj. It's impossible to say, based on the current research, what sorts of breads were baked on these clay griddles, and why they would be used in one place and tabuns in another not so far away.

Diffused during the Ottoman Empire, the brass, and then steel, saj has played a part in Middle Eastern baking for centuries. It is relatively portable and very efficient on fuel if well used.

SHRAK

A close relative of the more familiar Armenian or Persian *lavash*, shrak is a spectacularly large thin sheet of flatbread made by Levantine bakers. I first encountered it integrated into one of the most delectable meals I've ever eaten, the Palestinian roast chicken dish, *mussakhan* (see page 290 for recipe).

To make your shrak, you'll need a large saj, at least 16 inches in diameter. So scrounge up some convex sheet metal, or flip over your wok for this one. Have plenty of nice, dry light fuel. Shrak is best baked very hot, with flames reaching around the lip of the griddle to lightly scorch and flavor the bread.

Making shrak is a great opportunity to try out a virtuosic Middle Eastern dough stretching technique, an ancestor, surely, of the Neapolitan pizza toss. While it's admittedly unlikely that most of us will master this skill at its spectacular best, it is nonetheless possible to imperfectly use the technique to bring about some pretty awesome results. I would recommend starting privately until you build a little confidence. A hole or two in your shrak makes no never mind.

16 ounces bread flour, about
½ teaspoon dry yeast
1½ teaspoons kosher or sea salt
1½ cups water

Makes 8 large flatbreads

1. Mix all the ingredients in a work bowl and turn it out onto a lightly floured surface to knead until very smooth. Place in a bowl and cover airtight.

2. Ferment for 2 hours, turning it out onto the surface for a brief stretching and folding, as in the pita recipe (see page 99), halfway through.

3. Divide the dough into eight equal bits, and round each one up nicely to rest, covered lightly, for 30 minutes.

4. Meanwhile, set up your baking arrangement, and get a smart fire going.

5. Give yourself plenty of elbow room. On a floured surface, pat one of the balls into a flat disk. Using a long straight rolling pin, roll the disk as large as it will go. Remove any jewelry from your hands and wrists and push up long sleeves. Take a deep breath and pick up the dough lightly but decisively by an edge. Quickly flap the circle from one open palm to the other, exerting kinetic stretching pressure on the perimeter as you work your way methodically around it. Back away from your work surface to give the growing circle of dough plenty of room.

6. When it's as large as you think you can get it without disaster, flip the shrak onto the hot saj. Centering the dough takes some practice, too; you have about 2 seconds to pull the edges out if they wrinkle up at all. Flip the dough with your fingers when it's done on one side, and give a brief scorching on the other side. Whip it off the saj onto a waiting cloth as soon as it gets enough black flecks for your liking. Less cooking, of course, will leave it tender and pliable, while more will give a more cracker-like result. (If you are planning to make mussakhan, leave it pliable.)

7. Continue forming and baking the remaining shrak.

FLATBREAD FOR WRAPS

Have you ever ordered a "wrap" that didn't prove to be constructed with damp light-gauge cardboard? No matter how they flavor or tint the dough, the "bread" usually has very little to offer beyond holding the filling together. These naturally leavened whole grain breads are pliable, strong, and *tasty*. They are best made on a convex griddle, but it needn't be large; ten inches will do.

16 ounces whole-wheat flour
1 cup buttermilk
⅔ cup warm water, about
4 ounces white or whole-wheat leaven
1½ teaspoons kosher salt

Makes 14 or 15 flatbreads

1. Mix the flour, buttermilk, and warm water into a rough dough, adding a few more drops water if dry spots remain. Cover airtight and let rest 30 minutes.

2. Chop the leaven in 8 bits and add to dough along with the salt, mixing with a wooden spoon or your hand until the dough is well combined and begins to develop some strength, about 2 minutes. Scrape up the edges into a ball, cover, and ferment at cool room temperature for 4 hours. Stretch and fold the dough two or three times, every hour or so.

3. Prepare your fire setup, griddle, and fuel as described above. Divide the dough into 2½-ounce balls (making 14 or 15), and preshape them evenly round. Keep covered to keep them from drying out as they rest 20 to 30 minutes.

4. Preheat the saj. Use a rolling pin to thin one of the balls out as far as it will go, and then pick up the dough and gently stretch it to 10 inches in diameter. Place it on the hot saj and cook, turning once, until flecked

on both sides with deep brown, and even a few black, spots. The fire should be considerably hotter than that for pita.

5. Place the baked bread in a towel and keep covered to conserve its moisture and wrapability.

THREE BOREKS

These boreks are adapted from types still found in central Turkey. The first is a quick-to-put-together turnover using a straight yeast dough. When I bake pita, I'll often squirrel away eight ounces of dough in order to make a couple of these for breakfast or lunch the next day. The second borek, a crispy packet of goodness, uses a very simple unyeasted dough and affords a great opportunity to develop your rolling and stretching skills. You may use a flat or convex griddle for both versions. You may also mix and match doughs and fillings.

VERSION I: HALF-MOON BOREK

Improvise the filling with what you have on hand — I like to use part feta, or other salty cheese, and part mozzarella for the stretchy, melty quality.

DOUGH

10 ounces (2¼ cups) bread flour
½ teaspoon dry yeast
1 teaspoon salt
⅞ cup lukewarm water

FILLING

1 tablespoon butter
1 cup minced leek, scallion, chives, or scapes
5 ounces mixed cheeses, minced or grated
¼ cup parsley, chopped
1 tablespoon chopped fresh mint or ½ teaspoon dried
   Pinch of Aleppo red pepper
   Kosher or sea salt

GARNISH

1 teaspoon butter (optional)

---

4 servings, as an appetizer or accompaniment

1. Stir all the dough ingredients together with a fork in a work bowl. Turn the dough out onto a floured work surface and knead well. Overturn the bowl onto the dough and let it rest for about 45 minutes.

2. Meanwhile, make the filling. Melt the butter in a medium pan and cook the leeks until tender. If you use chives, this is just a brief wilting. Mix with the rest of the filling ingredients in a small bowl. Check for salt; some cheeses are much saltier than others.

3. Divide the dough into four 4-ounce pieces. Preshape each quarter into a nice round ball, and allow to rest 30 minutes, covered.

4. Start preheating your griddle over a medium fire.

5. Roll and stretch a ball of dough fairly thinly — about 10 to 11 inches in diameter. Scatter one-quarter of the filling on half of the circle, moisten the perimeter with water, then fold over the unfilled half to make a half-moon shape. Press the edges together. Very lightly run the rolling pin over it to flatten.

6. Bake a few minutes per side over a low flame, until golden brown with dark flecks. Transfer to a plate and rub with butter, if you like, before serving hot.

VERSION 2: CRISPY MUSHROOM BOREK

This filling is not authentic to Central Asia, or any-where, exactly, but it is really delicious in these little griddled pies. Substitute the previous cheese filling (on page 103), or experiment for yourself with any filling you like, as long as it's not too wet.

DOUGH

7	ounces unbleached all-purpose flour
½	teaspoon kosher or sea salt
⅔ to ¾	cup lukewarm water, approximately

FILLING

1 ounce dried porcini mushrooms, or a mix of porcini and oyster mushrooms
2 tablespoons butter or bacon fat
1 medium yellow onion, finely chopped
1 tablespoon port or sherry
2 tablespoons fine bread crumbs (dark Russian rye adds depth)
Kosher salt
Freshly ground pepper

TO ASSEMBLE

4 tablespoons butter, melted

2 servings

Make the Dough

1. More than an hour ahead, make the dough. Mix the flour, salt, and ⅔ cup water together in a small mixing bowl with a fork, adding a bit more water as necessary to make the dough come together. Knead the dough until it is very smooth and uniform.

2. Divide the dough into four equal pieces (about 4 ounces each) and knead each one into a nice smooth ball. Cover airtight and let rest about an hour.

Make the Filling

1. Put the mushrooms in a small heatproof bowl and just cover with very hot water. Place a plate over the bowl and steep mushrooms until soft, at least 20 minutes.

2. Strain mushrooms from soaking water, reserving the liquid. Either very carefully decant the liquid to leave any grit behind, or pour through a coffee filter. Chop the mushrooms finely.

3. Melt the butter in a frying pan over moderate heat. Sauté the onion until translucent. Add mushrooms and cook a couple minutes. Add the port and the reserved mushroom liquid, and move the pan closer to the fire. Reduce, stirring, until only a little syrupy liquid remains. Remove from the fire. Stir in the bread-crumbs and season with salt and pepper. Set aside to cool a bit.

Assemble the Boreks

1. Depending on how much you like to multitask, either start preheating your griddle now, or assemble all four pastries first, and then turn your full attention to cooking them.

2. Flour your work surface and remove any jewelry from your fingers and wrists. Take one ball of dough and press it into a disk. Using a straight rolling pin, roll it into as large a circle as possible. Pick up the dough and place your hands, knuckles upward, under the center of the dough circle. Gently stretch your fingers and hands apart, rotating the dough to stretch it evenly.

3. You will soon find that the center has stretched pretty thin, but the edges are holding you back. (Hold the dough up toward a window or a light source and the awkward thick places become immediately apparent.) Now, working quickly and gently, take the dough by an edge and work your way around the perimeter, stretching little sections as you go. If you make a little tear by the edge, no matter; it'll be buried in the pastry. Be careful, though, not to rip the center.

4. When you get to the point where you're sure you're about to wreck it, place the pastry back on a very lightly floured surface. Brush the surface of the dough with butter and deposit one-quarter of the filling in a 3-inch squarish blob in the center. Fold the upper and lower dough edges in partway, covering the filling. Brush a touch more butter on any unbuttered surfaces, then follow suit with the left and right flaps. You should have a nice compact square packet. Continue with the remaining pastry and filling.

Bake the Boreks

If you haven't already done so, start preheating your griddle over a medium-low fire as previously described. Place one or more packets on the hot surface, brushing any exposed unbuttered surfaces with butter. Bake for about 4 to 6 minutes per side,

until golden brown and puffed up. (If you have a large griddle, you may be able to cook all four at once.) Enjoy soon.

THE SPRAWLING BOREK FAMILY

Borek is the very ancient root name for a constellation of foods made by layering, wrapping, or stuffing filling in a wheat-based dough before cooking. The first Anatolian borek was probably the common ancestor of almost any treat we can think of today that fits that ridiculously broad description — from tortellini to pierogi to strudel to scallion pancakes. Today, the borek family encompasses a great variety of dough types and fillings, and derivatives of the word are found across two continents, from Italy to Tunisia to Armenia to India. Some versions are baked, boiled, or fried; the doughs used are appropriate to the technique (that is, boiled variants use a pasta dough, while baked borek might use filo or, more recently, puff pastry). Probably the oldest is the griddled type.

VERSION 3: SWEET CRISPY BOREK, OR CAMPFIRE BAKLAVA

I am resigned to the fact that I will never have the hand-skills to roll or stretch *yufka* or *filo* like a pro, but I still enjoy trying to improve. Putting together a down-home version of this palace sweet in minutes and cooking it on a campfire elevates that fun to an almost perverse level.

Make the dough from the Crispy Mushroom Borek recipe on page 104, and treat it in exactly the same way.

¾ cup walnuts, finely chopped

1½ tablespoons sugar

½ teaspoon cinnamon

¼ cup honey

¼ cup water

4 servings

1. Make the filling by stirring together the walnuts, sugar, and cinnamon.

2. Fill and bake as for the Crispy Mushroom Borek. Meanwhile, in a small skillet or clay pot, stir together the honey and water. Place down in the coals of the fire and remove from the heat as soon as it arrives at a bare simmer.

3. When the baklava packets are crispy and golden brown, remove them to a cutting board. With a large knife, cut each into four quarters, and transfer them neatly to a small bowl. Pour a quarter of the syrup over each pastry and enjoy right away.

CHIVE PANCAKES

Central Asian wheat techniques — stretching or rolling and layering or stuffing — migrated west, as we have seen, to the lands of *lasagne* and *strudel* and *brik* and *pastizzi*, but they also strove eastward. Ever wilder dough-stretching techniques were invented by cooks of many cultures — from the Uygur to the Indonesians. Many of the more virtuosic are the province of professionals, whether in the palace kitchen or at a brazier on a street corner. But a few of these techniques may be easily mastered by mere mortals and are very handy to know and adapt to your own purposes. These chive pancakes employ what has got to be the simplest way of creating flakiness in a griddled bread.

FOR THE SAUCE

- 1 tablespoon light soy sauce
- 1 tablespoon dark soy sauce (or another of light soy sauce)
- 1 tablespoon rice vinegar
- 1 teaspoon *sambal oelek* or other Asian hot chile paste
- ¼ cup chicken broth (or water, plus another dash or two of soy)

FOR THE PANCAKES

- 1¾ cups (8 ounces) all-purpose flour
- 1¾ cups (6 ounces) unbleached cake flour
- 1 teaspoon salt
- 2 tablespoons peanut, canola, or corn oil, plus more for frying pancakes
- 1¼ cups boiling water
  Asian (toasted) sesame oil for brushing
- 1½ cups chives or scallions, finely chopped

---

4 to 6 servings

I. Make sauce first to let flavors marry. Mix all ingredients and let rest while you make the dough.

2. With a food processor or by hand, mix together flours and salt. Stir in 2 tablespoons oil, then, gradually, the boiling water. (You may need a few more drops water, but wait and see.) Once it comes together in a ball, knead by hand a few minutes, then let rest airtight for 30 minutes.

3. Roll the dough into a cylinder, and cut into 12 even-sized pieces. Roll each into a smooth ball. Cover with a moist towel or plastic wrap so they don't dry out.

4. Roll one ball out thinly, brush with sesame oil, sprinkle liberally with chives, and roll up snugly in a cylinder. Coil the tube of filled dough in a spiral, keeping the seam to the inside. Press together a bit, and set aside, covered, while you fashion the rest.

5. Gently roll each pancake flat. They should be 4 or 5 inches in diameter and about ¼-inch thick. (Light-handed rolling preserves all-important layering for the best texture.) Set up a couple large skillets or a griddle; heat ⅛ inch of oil over medium heat. (You can continue rolling as you fry.)

6. When the oil is hot, fry the pancakes (as many as you can at a time without crowding) until golden brown and crispy and cooked through — they should take about 3 minutes on the A side, and 2 minutes on the B side. Drain briefly on a rack or paper, cut in quarters, and serve hot with dipping sauce.

TORTILLAS

The griddled breads we've discussed so far originated in antiquity in the wheat belt from Mesopotamia to Central Asia. But, meanwhile, on the other side of the globe, people in south-central Mexico were also busy inventing both a grain and the techniques necessary to transform it into bread. These folks had to start from whole cloth, though, since — unlike wheat — corn's natural parent plants barely even provided gatherable food. And, if that weren't troublesome enough, they then had to somehow figure out that corn treated with calcium hydroxide would not only make a delicious tortilla but be far more nutritious than corn in its natural state. This "nixtamalized" corn was and is the basis for many elaborate breads and other dishes. To this day, despite the deep cultural disruptions of colonialism, the corn tortilla has not only persevered as the staple of a large region but has diffused, in commercial form, over much of the world.

For the reasons discussed in the introduction to this chapter, the griddle is the ideal cooking surface for breads made of glutenless grains like corn. For most of the tortilla's lifespan, that griddle, the comal, was a smooth disk of burnished earthenware. The clay comal is still made and used today, but the sheet-metal comal has eclipsed it in availability and popularity.

Traditionally, beautiful clay comals have long served as tortilla griddles in Central America. As pictured, a not-so-lovely piece of broken refractory clay chimney flue works, too.

CORN TORTILLAS

I'm not lucky enough to live in an area where freshly made tortilla *masa* is commonly sold, so I use the dry *masa harina* sold in grocery stores. (See Resources, page 306.) My tortillas, as a result, cannot compare in exquisiteness with those made by someone who nixtamalizes his or her own corn and grinds it with a *mano* and *metate*. On the other hand, the simple tortillas I make at home, even with my cheating on ingredients and methods, are tremendously superior to any premade tortillas available in stores and even most restaurants.

Because tortillas are small and cook quickly, it's no problem just cooking them in a cast-iron pan, if that's what you have. A large griddle or true *comal*, of course, will let you crank out a lot more if you're a great multitasker or have a cooking-partner. You may multiply the formula as needed.

6½ ounces (1½ cups) *masa harina*

1 cup water

Makes 14 tortillas

1. Set up your griddle arrangement and get a nice fire going. Since the dough takes no time to make and doesn't need to ferment, it's a good idea to have the fire first.

2. Mix the ingredients together in a medium bowl with a fork. Stir well until a soft dough forms, adding a touch more water as necessary. If you experience any cracking while rolling out the dough, you can still add more water. Cover the dough airtight while you heat your griddle.

3. Set up to form the tortillas right near the griddle. I use a rolling pin, but by all means use a tortilla press if you have one. Keeping the remaining dough covered, pinch off a golf-ball sized piece of dough and roll it into a sphere. Place it on a piece of plastic wrap, and place a second piece of wrap on top. Press the dough into a flat disk with the flat of your hand. Use a small straight rolling pin to roll it out very thinly and evenly. Carefully peel up the upper sheet of plastic, and use a small pot lid (approximately 5 to 6 inches in diameter) like a cookie cutter to excise a perfectly round tortilla. Quickly scrape up the overage from around the tortilla; the "waste" dough will be none the worse for wear and can be easily used in another tortilla as long as you don't let it hang around uncovered.

4. Pick up the sheet of plastic wrap with the tortilla adhering to it and invert it onto your free hand, pulling back the wrap carefully. Gently place (do not fling) the tortilla onto the hot griddle. Bake about 30 seconds, until well set and flecked with pale brown, then flip to bake another 30 seconds. Flip again and bake on the first side to steam through, and deepen the flavor, and hopefully puff up. Do not overcook, though, or the tortillas will be hard. Stack the cooked tortillas in a cloth, and keep in a warm spot. Serve immediately.

FLOUR TORTILLAS

The post-Hispanic flour tortilla is unlike its predecessor, the corn model, in most every way except that, no matter how imperfect looking, fresh homemade is invariably better than store-bought.

10 ounces unbleached all-purpose flour
½ teaspoon baking powder
½ teaspoon salt
2 ounces (¼ cup) bacon fat, lard, or other solid fat
⅔ cup water, approximately

Makes 16 tortillas

I. Combine the dry ingredients in a medium bowl or in a food processor. Cut in the fat, blending until the texture is like cornmeal. Add the water and mix well by hand or briefly by machine, moistening further if dry.

2. Set the dough on a lightly floured counter and knead a few minutes. Place into an airtight container and allow to rest at room temperature for 30 to 60 minutes.

3. Meanwhile, make a fire in your griddle arrangement. You can use a flat or convex griddle, or even a cast-iron frying pan, of at least 10 inches in diameter for 7- to 8-inch flour tortillas. (Naturally, if you want to make very large tortillas for burritos, you'll need something larger; and you'll want to divide the dough into 8 to 12 pieces instead of 16.)

4. Divide the dough in half and return one half to the airtight container. Divide the other half into 8 equal bits (each a touch over an ounce), and roll them up into neat round balls. Cover with plastic wrap. Heat your griddle over a smart fire.

5. Roll out one lump of dough on a very lightly floured surface to about an 8-inch diameter. Place it on the hot griddle. Flip it after it has bubbled up and has nice brown flecks on the first side, about one minute; then cook the other side. Slide the finished tortilla into a cloth to keep warm and pliable. Repeat with the remaining dough. Serve hot, reheating briefly on the hot griddle if necessary.

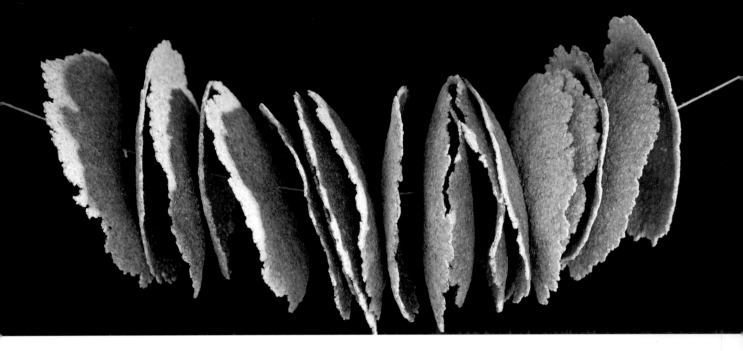

GRIDDLED BREADS OF NORTHWESTERN EUROPE

Ancient Scandinavians solved their grain storage problems by baking loads of flatbreads and stringing them up in their warm, dry rafters. They not only keep well, they are crunchily delicious.

Cold and damp areas that favored the culture of rye, oats, buckwheat, and barley also favored the bakestone, since those glutenless grains respond so well to unleavened baking. For most of the bakestone's preindustrial heyday, it literally consisted of a slab of appropriate rock installed in a hearth. Particular, geologically appropriate quarries were dedicated to sourcing bakestones, which must be "capable of withstanding high degrees of Heat, without melting or falling to pieces," according to an early English geologist. Bakestone mining left behind both place-names (in Britain) and a dense archaeological record (in Norway). The reputedly superior bakestones from Hardanger, Norway, accompanied the Norse folk on their famous sea adventures of the early medieval period; tell-tale shards have turned up in quantity in the British Isles, especially the Shetland archipelago, and in Iceland.

Evidence seems to show that the people of ancient Britain, whose cultural toolbox held much in common with that of the Scandinavian cultures, possessed their own preexisting bakestone tradition dating back to at least the Iron Age, if not much earlier. (Once again, consider Stonehenge, a much larger-scale quarrying project.)

The breads baked on these bakestones varied over time, and with cultural tradition, microclimate, and harvest. Two or more varieties of grain were frequently milled and baked in combination, because until the modern period, Northern European farmers often sowed a couple of cereals together in one field, a hedge against total crop failure. Marginal conditions also encouraged the use of short-season cultivars such as *bere*, a barley relative that could be baked into flatbreads and malted for ale, and which is still grown and milled in Orkney. Thus the characteristics of the breads reflected the agricultural reality of life on the chilly, wet edge of Europe's arable zone, at least until well into the nineteenth century.

PROTOHISTORIC MULTIGRAIN FLATBREAD

There's nothing like thinking about charred remains in cremation burials to make you want to get cooking! Nonetheless, that's the best source of physical evidence for the actual breads people lived on over a millennium ago in Scandinavia. Charring is an excellent preservative, and archaeologists have found hundreds of fascinating ancient bread specimens in Swedish cremation interments from the Viking period and much, much earlier. These excavated flatbreads were shaped as disks, rings, or half-circles, from tiny to large, and composed of mixed cereals, legumes, flax seeds, and animal fats or even blood.

This recipe is based on that data, uses ingredients easy to lay hands on today, and surprisingly results in a completely addictive treat. The ancient Scandinavians are said to have accompanied their many sorts of crisp flatbreads with a range of dairy products — butter, curds, whey, buttermilk, or *skyr*, a strained yogurt. And, indeed, this bread's crunchy nuttiness proves to be a delicious complement to any kind of cheese. Also, broken up in a bowl of whole-milk yogurt, it makes a soul-satisfying supper or breakfast, better only with a handful of blueberries or lingonberries.

3 ounces (½ cup) steel cut oats
2 ounces (½ cup) dark rye flour
⅛ teaspoon kosher or sea salt
½ ounce (1 tablespoon) rendered animal fat or butter — lamb or mutton tallow is appropriate and extraordinary
¼ cup water

Makes 4 medium flatbreads; multiplies easily

---

1. Set up a griddle arrangement and get a fire going. A large flat griddle is handy for this project, since these breads cook rather slowly. Also set out cooling racks for the finished breads.

2. If you happen to have a grain mill and want to start with whole grains, by all means grind both grains coarsely together. Then it's easy to mix the rest in by hand, cutting in the fat first, then stirring in the water and salt.

3. Otherwise, place the oats, flour, and salt in the bowl of a food processor. Pulse the grains several times. This makes the texture pleasantly less uniform. Add the fat and pulse until evenly cut in. Add the water, mixing just till a soft dough forms.

4. Preheat the griddle over a moderate fire.

5. Divide the dough in four, and round each quarter into a ball. Lightly flour your work surface with rye flour. Pat out one dough ball into a disk, keeping the edges nice and round. Flip it over, flouring a bit beneath. Use a rolling pin (or just keep patting) to make a circle as thin as the oat groats will comfortably allow, 6 to 7 inches in diameter. Poke a hole less than an inch in diameter in the center.

6. Use a bench knife or metal spatula to help transfer the bread to the hot griddle. Keep half an eye on it while you roll out the next bread. The baking bread should begin to look crier and perhaps curl a bit after a few minutes. You don't really want it to take too much color at this point. Flip it over and cook the other side. After a couple of minutes, when that side seems done, use your cooling rack to prop up the bread (which should now be totally rigid) on one edge before the fire. The idea is to let it continue to dry and toast a bit while you bake the rest. I like them to get some brown flecks at this point, but, unlike some wheat flatbreads, they're not tasty if they burn at all.

7. Use the hole in the center to string the bread up in your kitchen for storage.

BRITISH GRIDDLE BREADS

In the bakestone lands of Northern and Western Britain, industrialization brought access to sheet- or cast-iron and wheat, changing the nature of the griddles as well as the composition of the breads on them. Bannock, made of whole-grain, roughly milled local flours (mixed simply with a little dripping from the roast and some water) gave way to those made with patent wheat flour, chemical leavenings, and currants or sultanas. And in turn those soon upgraded from grease to butter, and acquired sugar and a genteel attitude to go with it. But from the perspective of the modern baker, every one of those bakestone breads, from havercake to bannock to scone to muffin, is fun to make and splendid served with a cup of tea or something stronger.

Cream Scones (see page 118) bake on a griddle over hot coals.

OATCAKE, OR HAVERCAKE

Even today, oatcakes from the traditional oat-growing regions of the British Isles vary from crunchy biscuits (Scotland) to flexible pancakes (Staffordshire). This traditional Welsh version has every earmark of being quite an ancient type of bakestone bread.

Those who don't care about authenticity may add the optional sugar for extra crispness and a fugitive sweetness.

If you have a grain mill, you can grind 7¾ ounces of whole oat groats coarsely; if not, the proportions below allow you to use a food processor to work up commonly available forms of oats into a nicely textured result.

5¾ ounces (1 cup) steel cut oats
2 ounces (½ cup) rolled oats (not instant)
Pinch kosher salt
2 teaspoons sugar (optional)
¼ ounce (½ tablespoon) bacon fat (or other fat or butter)
Around ½ cup warm water

Makes 4 very filling oatcakes

---

1. Set up a griddle arrangement and get a fire going. A large flat griddle is handy for this project, since these breads cook rather slowly. Prepare a cooling rack or some other rig near the fire to finish drying and hardening the breads after baking.

2. Place the steel cut and rolled oats, the salt, and the sugar into the bowl of a food processor fitted with the steel blade. Whiz it around for 20–30 seconds or so to break up the rolled oats into coarse powder. Add the fat and pulse to cut in. (If you milled your own oats, you may cut in the fat with two knives, or just rub it in with your fingers.)

3. Add ¼ cup of water and process or stir thoroughly. Add more water a tablespoon at a time until a stiff, but not dry, dough forms. Make a ball and knead it a bit. If it cracks easily, add more water. (Oats are very variable in their thirstiness, I find, so you may have to add more water than the ½ cup in total.)

4. Preheat the griddle over a moderate fire.

5. Divide the dough in four, and round each quarter into a ball, each about 2½ ounces. Keep three of them covered with plastic or an upside-down bowl. Take the fourth and press it very firmly together into a blunt cone shape on the counter to consolidate it. Flatten into a disk, trying to keep it perfectly round and smooth-edged. Use a small straight rolling pin to roll as thinly as the oat groats will allow, to a diameter of about 7 inches. I find that I don't need to flour the counter at all unless I have included the optional sugar in the dough.

6. Use a bench knife or metal spatula to help transfer the oatcake to the hot griddle. Be ready to slacken the heat if it cooks too quickly. The oatcake should begin to look drier and perhaps curl a bit after a few minutes. Do not allow it to get darker than a pale tan. Flip it over and cook the other side, again, without browning. When that seems done, which should take at least two minutes, use your cooling rack to finish hardening the oatcake (which should now be totally rigid) on one edge before the fire while you bake the rest.

BANNOCK

Originating in the northern tier of ancient Britain as a homely griddle cake of barley, oats, or peas, "bannock" transitioned to life in 17th-century America by assuming a composition of corn, and adopting the regional nickname "johnnycake."

Through a wide swath of 19th-century Anglo-America, the word endured to describe any griddle-baked bread you threw together when you didn't have a "proper" oven, or when you ran out of bread between bakings. Still pretty good for a stopgap, this bannock is like a missing link between the ancient bakestone cakes, Irish soda bread, and the scone.

6 ounces unbleached all-purpose flour

4 ounces whole-wheat flour

½ teaspoon baking soda

½ teaspoon kosher salt

1 teaspoon sugar

½ ounce (1 tablespoon) solid fat — beef tallow, lard, bacon fat, butter, or coconut oil

¾ cup buttermilk, approximately

3 tablespoons currants or raisins (optional)

3 or 4 servings

I. Set up a griddle arrangement. You may use something approximating a bakestone as described on page 97, but a 10-inch cast-iron griddle or even a frying pan works also. The important thing is a moderate-to-low heat under the pan; it works to nestle a heavy pan into a bed of coals, their heat dampened with plenty of ash.

2. Combine the flours, soda, salt, and sugar, and cut or rub in the fat. Use a fork to stir in the buttermilk and currants. Add a few more drops of buttermilk as needed to make it adhere in a lump; do not overwork.

3. Preheat your griddle.

4. Flour a work surface lightly, and scrape the dough out onto it. Pat it lightly into a flattish cake about 8 to 9 inches in diameter. Transfer the disk of dough to the hot griddle. (If you hear much sizzling, slacken the heat a bit.) Cook a minute, then moisten the blade of a bench knife or straight-edged metal-bladed spatula and cut down through the bannock to make 6 or 8 even-sized wedge-shaped pieces. In about 12–15 minutes, when you suspect it to be browning, peek under one of the pieces, and turn them all if it is time.

5. Bake on the second side, paying heed to the intensity of the heat under the griddle. Make adjustments so as to bake your bannock through without scorching the outside.

HANNAH GLASSE'S MUFFINS

Even though current-day Brits generally repudiate them, American "English muffins" are our only contemporary specimen that even vaguely resembles the 18th-century English small bread called a "muffin." The concept certainly sprang from one of the bakestone backwaters of the British hinterland. But once introduced into London, the original muffins were a big hit in tea and coffee houses — a tasty, crisp receptacle for lots of butter. Soon they were propelled into posterity by best-selling cookbook author Hannah Glasse, who gave them a very full run-down in her 1774 *Art of Cookery*. Besides the simple and wonderful formula, another highlight of her recipe is her description of how an iron-topped brick and mortar muffin griddle could be built into a cooking range: "Build a place just as if you was going to set a copper, a piece of iron all over the top fixed in form just the same as the bottom of an iron pot, and make your fire underneath with coal as in a copper."

Mrs. Glasse wrote her recipe on an industrial scale, and she uses fresh yeast from a brewery (from which she carefully washes the bitterness). I've divided the recipe by 32 (yes, 32) and adapted it for instant yeast.

10 ounces unbleached all-purpose or bread flour
1 teaspoon dry yeast
¾ teaspoon kosher or sea salt
1 cup warm water (90°F)

Makes 8 muffins

1. In a medium bowl, stir together the flour, yeast, and salt. Stir in the water, and work it together to a nice soft dough, either with your hand or a wooden spoon, which takes 2 or 3 minutes. Scrape down the sides of the bowl, cover airtight, and let rise in a warm place for 1 hour.

2. On a lightly floured surface, divide the dough into 8 equal pieces. Form each gently into a taut ball, incorporating as little flour as possible. Give them a little pat to flatten a bit and place them on a well-floured board or cloth. Cover lightly with a cloth or plastic wrap and let rest 30 minutes.

3. Meanwhile, set up your griddle arrangement and burn enough hardwood to get some glowing coals. Preheat the griddle, but with moderation. Muffins want a gentle and even heat, so that they can fully cook within before they get too dark.

4. I'll let Mrs. Glasse take it from here: ". . . by that time [the rising muffins] will be spread out in the right form; lay them on your iron; as one side begins to change colour turn [to] the other, and take great care they don't burn, or be too much discoloured, but that you will be a judge of in two or three makings. Take care that the middle of the iron is not too hot, as it will [tend to] be, but then you may put a brick-bat or two in the middle of the fire to slacken the heat." (Yesss! Great idea!)

5. Set the baked muffins on a rack to cool for at least ten minutes. Split by gently pulling apart with the fingertips, "but don't touch them with a knife, either to spread or cut them open, if you do they will be as heavy as lead, or when they are quite buttered and done, you may cut them across with a knife."

CREAM SCONES

You may, of course, bake these scones in a wood-fired oven, well after the fiercest heat has abated. But the griddle is the original, and to my mind, still the best, way to cook them. I am indebted to my friends Liz Lodge and Tom Gerhardt for this recipe. These are just great with butter and marmalade.

10 ounces unbleached all-purpose flour
 2 tablespoons sugar
 1 tablespoon baking powder
 ½ teaspoon kosher salt
2½ ounces (5 tablespoons) lightly salted butter, cold
 1 egg, plus 1 egg yolk
 ½ cup cream
 ½ cup currants, or other dried fruit chopped to the size of currants

Makes 8 scones

1. Set up a griddle arrangement and get a fire going. You may use something approximating a bakestone, but a 10-inch cast-iron griddle or even a frying pan works fine, with low heat under it. You can nestle a heavy pan into a bed of coals, provided the heat is dampened with plenty of ash.

2. Combine the flour, sugar, baking powder, and salt in a bowl or food processor. Cut or rub in the butter until the flour looks like meal. In a separate bowl beat the egg and yolk together, then beat in the cream. Use a fork to lightly stir the egg mix into the flour mixture, tossing in the currants as you go. Scrape it up into a ball, but do not overwork.

3. Preheat your griddle.

4. Flour a work surface lightly, and scrape the dough out onto it. Pat it lightly into an even cake about 8 to 9 inches in diameter. Use a bench knife or scraper to cut the scone into 8 wedge-shaped pieces, and transfer them to the hot griddle. (If you hear any sizzling, situate the griddle in a cooler location or spread out the coals or diminish the blaze under it.) Bake for 10 to 15 minutes per side, peeking underneath to monitor and turn when lovely and brown. Let cool several minutes before serving.

JUST-FOR-FUN CRACKERS

Using a hand-cranked pasta machine makes it easy to form the thinnest and crispiest all-purpose crackers. They can also be baked in a hot wood-fired oven.

  6 ounces (1 cup) semolina flour
6⅔ ounces (1⅓ cups) unbleached all-purpose flour
  ½ teaspoon salt
  ½ teaspoon dry yeast
  1 tablespoon butter, cold
  ¾ cup cool water

Makes about 80 crackers

I. Place flours, salt, and yeast in the bowl of a food processor. Whiz briefly to combine. Drop in the butter and process until invisible. Add the water while the motor is running, and process for at least a minute. Place the dough in an airtight container.

2. Ferment at room temperature for one hour. Turn the dough out on the counter and press it gently to degas it. Return it to the container and refrigerate at least an hour, but up to a day.

3. Set up a griddle arrangement and get a fire going. You'll want a long-lasting moderate heat. A large cooking surface is preferable, but I have made these on a 10-inch griddle; it just takes a lot of batches.

4. Start heating the griddle.

5. Slice about one-quarter of the dough off the blob and return the rest to the fridge. Do not knead it; but if it seems to have reinflated significantly, just press the gas out of it gently on the counter. Run it through the pasta roller repeatedly, starting at the widest setting and working down gradually to the second narrowest. Use a pastry wheel or sharp knife to cut the dough strips into whatever size or shape of crackers you desire.

6. Place them on the hot griddle, close together but not touching. Turn them and move them around so as to cook them evenly for 5 minutes or longer, adjusting the fire as necessary to achieve a very pale tan cracker with a few darker brown spots. Make sure they feel entirely dry — no pliability in the center. Heap on a rack on a cookie sheet when they are done. Repeat with the rest of the dough.

7. When completely dry, the crackers may be piled in an airtight tin.

OTHER THINGS TO COOK ON THE GRIDDLE

Once you get comfortable cooking things on a slab of metal perched over a fire, your culinary gears may start turning: what else can I slap on this thing?

Well, what about meat and vegetables? For sturdy meats, I'll generally prefer a grill over a griddle, if one is available; the flavor impact of the extra smoke and sizzle from the direct exposure to the coals cannot be lightly dismissed. However, if no grill is at hand, most any grillable food can be cooked on cast iron or sheet metal, as long as you give some thought to a couple of issues.

The critical aspects to consider are mainly two: release and temperature. And generally speaking, they are intertwined: if the surface is hot enough, and you are patient enough, the food will release. But you can help yourself out by applying the finest coat of neutral oil to the food just before dropping it on the blazing-hot griddle. Then stand back and just wait for it to begin to carbonize just a bit before molesting it in the slightest. Turn it once, returning to the griddle in a new spot, which will be hotter, and cleaner, than the one just vacated by the food.

Conversely, some foods that are notoriously tricky to cook on a grill, like fish fillets, or that are just plain silly, like green beans, do extremely well seared on iron or steel.

And then there's the issue of cooking things together for a delicious melding of flavors. I think of the full Sunday breakfasts made in the home of my friends Cairbre and Eithne McCann — where the fat rendered from rashers of the most incredible Irish bacon provided the foundation for a griddle full of sizzling mushrooms and tomatoes and eggs, to be accompanied by platters of the world's best toast, amply buttered. All those components cooked separately simply wouldn't have the same impact.

BLISTERED VEGETABLES

This technique works best with tender vegetables of small diameter. The long structured ones can be cooked on any large slab of metal; the unruly spherical ones — cherry tomatoes, especially — need a railing to keep them from abandoning ship. A skillet or steel wok works fine. You want a hot fire.

1 bunch asparagus or 1 pint cherry tomatoes or
   1 pound green beans or 2 bunches scallions or
   1 pound tiny baby eggplant or a dozen jalapenos
1–2 teaspoons olive oil or peanut oil
   Kosher or sea salt

2 to 4 servings

1. Trim any tough or inedible parts off the vegetable, but otherwise leave as whole as possible. (You can leave the stems on baby eggplant.) Place in a large bowl. Drizzle with oil and sprinkle with salt. Toss to coat.

2. Get your griddle good and hot.

3. Dump the vegetables on the hot surface and use tongs to spread them into a single layer. When they begin to show some black flecks, move them all around, exposing all sides to the direct heat and collateral steam. Sample, and remove from the griddle when crisp-tender. (No reason not to put them back in the bowl they started in — these aren't pork chops.)

SALT-ROASTED SHRIMP

A bed of salt diffuses the heat of the iron without overseasoning the shrimp. Use head-on shrimp by all means if you can get them.

Solar salt (see Salt-Roasted New Potatoes,
   page 128)
Shrimp in shell
A pepper grinder

1. Spread out a solid ½-inch bed of solar salt on a sheet of iron or an actual griddle, and start heating it over a hot fire.

2. Meanwhile, toss the shrimp with copious freshly ground black pepper.

3. When the salt is very hot, quickly lay the shrimp down on it. Turn each shrimp as soon as translucency appears to have crept through more than half of it, using the tail as a handle (or tongs if you prefer). The second the flipped shrimp attains curliness, remove to a serving platter.

4. Allow 4–6 shrimp per person for an appetizer, depending on size of shrimp and appetites.

123

SEA SCALLOP LOLLIPOPS WITH SPICED OLIVES

One of the culinary joys of life in my southeastern Massachusetts home is the Atlantic sea scallop. Our major port, New Bedford, rules the waves when it comes to fishing these delectable bivalves.

A shopping trip to one of New Bedford's many Portuguese groceries inspired these simple appetizers, which are, of course, no more than a reworking of the old scallops-wrapped-in-bacon standby. The difference with these is that, because both *presunto* (Portuguese air-cured ham) and super-fresh scallops are delicious raw, there's no need to overcook the poor shellfish — just a blazing hot quick sear to crisp up the edges and take the chill off. You'll need a pile of bamboo skewers, and you may substitute prosciutto for presunto.

2 pounds very large, super-fresh sea scallops

1 pound presunto or prosciutto, sliced extremely thinly

Optional spiced olive accompaniment:

8 ounces mixed tasty olives

1 small dry hot chile

½ teaspoon cumin seeds

½ teaspoon black peppercorns

3 cloves garlic, lightly crushed

3 tablespoons extra-virgin olive oil

A few sprigs parsley, minced

Few slices lemon

Serves a gathering of 10 or 12, but not for long

1. Up to three hours ahead, prep the lollipops. Lay out a slice of presunto flat. Set a single scallop at one end on edge, and roll it up like a wheel in the presunto. Fasten through with a skewer, lollipop-wise. Continue with the rest, and stack them all carefully in an airtight tub. Keep chilled until cooking time.

2. You may make the optional accompaniment 4 hours to 2 days ahead. Drain the olives of their brine and put in a jar. Heat a small griddle or cast-iron pan over a medium flame. Toss in the dry chile, cumin seeds, and peppercorns. Toast for about 30 seconds or until aromatic — do not scorch. Add to olives, along with garlic and olive oil. Close the jar and shake it to coat the olives with the flavorings. Chill until needed.

3. When you're ready to serve, put the olives in a serving bowl, and toss in the parsley. Wring in the lemon slices, and then toss the rinds in, too. Give it a stir.

4. Set up a griddle over a wood fire and get it pretty hot.

5. Line up the lollipops, one flat side down, on the griddle. Cook until some surfaces are golden brown and crispy, then flip. When the second side is done, serve on a heated platter. Your admonishments about mouth-burning will go unheeded by your guests.

THE GRIDDLE ON STEROIDS: THE ARGENTINE *INFIERNILLO*

So far we've seen how small and thin foods are natural candidates for cooking on a blazing hot sheet of metal — by the time the heat has penetrated to the center, the outside has developed a perfect deep sear. Quite reasonably, bulkier and thicker foods don't immediately suggest themselves for griddling. But an Argentine tradition brings in a second sheet of metal, and yes, a second fire, to sandwich the food in a "little hell" of great heat. An encasement of salt around the food diffuses the heat, prevents burning, and seals in the moisture. The whole thing is basically a clever way to create an oven-like atmosphere just by using two pieces of sheet metal and some bits and bobs to hold it up.

While I suppose you could hire a fabricator to build you an infiernillo, I suggest looking around your garden shed and basement for parts that can serve. We've had good luck with stacking a bunch of mismatched castoff items into an unsightly, but effective, pyre. We started with a stable base of steel angle-iron driven into the soil beneath the fire pit. Crosspieces athwart those held the piece of sheet iron, basically the griddle to support the food. Upon that we sat a fabricated steel tripod that was all that remained from a friend's cracked chiminea. It just so happened that a saucer-shaped patio "firepit" someone gave us fit right in there, to perfectly suspend the fire from above.

Preheat the infiernillo with a nice big hardwood fire above and below, while setting up the food. For the greatest ease in sliding the food in and out of "hell," use a sturdy half-sheet-pan.

SALT-ROASTED NEW POTATOES

Although these potatoes are a great first project for your infiernillo, we love them for themselves and do not think of them as a mere training exercise. They are the apotheosis of potatoes, as more than one true spud-lover has told me.

Once you have mastered this technique on tubers, though, apply the same principles to cook other foods that you might otherwise roast or bake with medium-high heat, like a chicken, a whole fish, or a tender joint of meat or small whole animal. (Conversely, you may also, if you like, make salt-roast potatoes in a wood-fired oven.)

Incidentally, the first few times we made this we included thyme sprigs and garlic, thinking that the potatoes would be perfumed by them. Nope; the garlic was good (if surprising) to eat, but, perhaps because of the desiccating effect of the salt, neither it nor the thyme imparted anything discernible to the potatoes.

10 pounds new potatoes, scrubbed
 1 bag solar salt*
 2 boxes kosher salt

* Solar salt is sold in 40-pound bags (as a water softener) at home-improvement retail stores. It's by far the cheapest way to go with this technique, and works fine as long as you improve the mix with a portion of kosher salt. If you've ever mixed concrete, it may help you to think of the solar salt as the aggregate, and the kosher salt as the cement.

Serves 12 to 15

1. Use your largest mixing bowl or other clean vat for making the salt mortar. Dump about 10 or 15 pounds of the solar salt (depending on the size of your mixing vessel) and half a box of the kosher salt in the bowl. Add a couple cups of water and work together with your hands. The kosher salt will begin to melt and surround the larger crystals. Add more water as needed until the mixture feels damp throughout. If you begin to have a deep puddle on the bottom, dump in more kosher salt and continue mixing.

2. Transfer the salt mortar to a half-sheet pan with your hands and press into an inch-deep layer with no gaps. Dump on the potatoes, and pile them into a compact form (making sure that the height will be accommodated by your infiernillo). Leave a border of a bit more than an inch potato-free.

3. Cover with more damp salt to a thickness of about an inch (I usually have to mix another batch at this point). Pat the whole monolith into stability, closing gaps. If you are nervous about any particular place, mix up some straight kosher salt with a dash of water to fill in.

4. Slide the pan with its salt dome into the hot infiernillo and keep everything moderately stoked for about an hour or so. We like to slide the potato dome out and let it rest for 10–15 minutes; you can also let them stand longer if you have other unfinished cooking going on, as they stay hot a long time. If you want to be sure about doneness, whack one edge of the dome with a heavy sturdy object, and poke a potato with a fork. When it comes to serving time, let your guests do their own excavating.

5. We usually serve these unaccompanied, but you can set out whatever you like, if you want to make it seem more like you're working to entertain your guests. Let your conscience be your guide.

The Griddle on Steroids: The Argentine Infiernillo

POTS OVER FIRE

Clay and metal pots really opened up a world of cooking in liquid. While much fun may be had using hot rocks to boil food in an animal hide or stomach, sometimes it's a relief to just use a purpose-made container. The metal pot seems like the lowest common denominator of ordinary cooking equipment, and so it has become, virtually worldwide, since the Industrial Revolution. But the real revolutionary moment came thousands of years before, when the fired clay pot came onto the scene. Perhaps I'm revealing a presentist attitude, but I can't help but imagine how exciting it was to move up to a clay pot after preparing food in a bitumen-and-plaster–lined basket.

Beef Shanks with Chile and Cranberry Beans (see page 140) simmer near a roaring fire.

THE CLAY POT

Even during the Neolithic Period, when widespread ceramic technology was new and developing, potters were already working out how to compose and fashion clay vessels in the service of cooking in some very sophisticated ways. Neolithic potters at Tell Sabi Abyad in Northern Syria, for example, used several strategies to increase the usefulness and lifespan of their wares. They selected clay types that were especially suited to the rigors of the hearth; isotope analysis shows that the clay for their best cooking pots was imported from a region over a hundred miles away. They tempered the clay with minerals or crushed pottery, now a time-honored method for conferring resistance to heat-shock on cooking pots; then, cutting-edge technology. In building the pots, they strove for even wall thickness and smoothly arced forms, both helpful in creating resistance to thermal shock; they added lug handles to give the cook something to grab. The artisans enhanced the naturally low porosity of their special clay by burnishing, intentionally smoothing the surfaces of the cooking pots before firing them, improving their cooking and storage qualities. In short, to a startling degree, some of the earliest known cooking pots were highly functional, and often beautiful, implements.

This is a small sampling from the global clay pot tradition, including examples from Turkey, Italy, Vietnam, England, and Thailand.

Today, potters are still making great cooking pots all over the globe, even though cooks now have many other choices. I have acquired pots of all sorts on my travels and, although I'm fiercely protective of those from the remotest locations, I do use every one of them, whether in a hearth or in a wood-fired oven. And even here in the States, I never enter an ethnic market without inspecting the housewares aisle for a hidden pottery gem. Southeast Asian grocery stores are especially fruitful in this regard.

Clay Pots and Safety

Most of the pots I have collected over the years have proved extraordinarily durable. I used to expect them to break at any moment, but have found that with a few ordinary precautions, they can provide many years, even decades, of tasty and beautiful service.

When you get a new pot, wash it in hot soapy water, rinse it well, and fill it with hot water. Put it on a very low flame and bring it to a simmer slowly. Then let it cool down slowly.

Leery of thermal shock, I tend to use certain clay pots only for simmering and baking. I'm very careful not to add cold liquid to a hot pot, and I always set a hot pot down on a forgiving surface like a folded up towel. But some pots are more bulletproof than others. Asian "sand pots," particularly those cased in wire, have considerable antishock qualities. Since they are inexpensive and easily available to me, I have been a bit cavalier, and have subjected them to some pretty rigorous treatment. I reach for a sand pot when a recipe starts out with sautéing, which is a particularly challenging technique for the vessel since one section of the pot, the base, is subjected to much higher temperatures than the rest.

So far I've talked about the safety of the cookpot — what about the safety of those eating from it? Most of the pots I have accumulated over the years come with no guarantee as to their composition, so one wonders a bit about the dangers of lead contamination in the food. First, many of my more interesting pots are unglazed, so are unlikely to be a problem. I do have a few with particularly beautiful lustrous glazes, some from Mexico, and some made by a friend down the road. While I'm pretty sure that the Mexican pots have lead in the glaze, I'm utterly certain that my friend's do, since he told me so. He feels that lead, skillfully handled, shouldn't be accessible to contaminate the food. I take no position on the matter except to say that I do not serve salads or any other acidic foods in those nice shiny pots.

Using a Clay Pot in the Hearth

This is one of the simple joys of hearth cooking. Have a moderate hardwood fire underway; you'll need the supply of coals and ashes it provides. Use a fire shovel to rob a nice mix of the two and deposit it a few feet from the main fire. Select a spot that is easy to tend, yet is unlikely to get in the way. (I know more than one person who broke an earthen pot by upsetting an andiron onto it.) Nestle the pot, full of the food to be cooked, down into the coal bed.

If you are nervous about your clay pot's durability, or if you are heating it for the very first time, make a thermal cushion by laying a second shovelful of ash over the first little pile of mixed ashes and coals. When the heating capacity of that coal bed begins to slacken, merely pick up the pot with a potholder or rag and set it aside — in a warm place! — while you steal more coals from the fire to fortify your little cooking hearth.

What's So Special about a Clay Pot?

If the food I intend to cook is small enough to fit in a clay pot, I will most always choose clay, which transfers heat slowly and can be maintained on a coal bed at a very gentle heat, poaching more than boiling the food. The difference may be appreciated by thinking about cooking a chicken covered with a gallon of seasoned water in an iron pot hung over a fire, versus tucking that same chicken in a snugly fitting clay pot with a glass of wine and some salt, pasting the pot lid on with a flour and water slurry, and setting it down in the coals and ashes. Each result is excellent in its own way; it all depends on whether you are looking to make chicken in an excellent broth or an elixir of chicken.

Some seventeenth-century cooks intensified this effect with a technique called "smoring": sealing the seasoned chicken or rabbit or duck into a small clay

Buttered Gooseberries (page 134) are underway, in a clay pot nestled in a custom coal bed.

pot and immersing that in a kettle of simmering water. (A bit reminiscent of the recent *sous vide* craze . . .)

In a rather extreme case of pot-abuse, an Anatolian lamb dish is made by seasoning small kebab-sized bits of meat with onions, herbs, spices, and tomatoes; forcing the mixture into a tall vaselike pot with a narrow neck; stopping up the top; and burying it in coals and ashes to cook slowly for several hours. Serving is accomplished by means of a skillful sharp rap with a hammer, bisecting the pot neatly with a single blow. This is single-service disposable cookware, convenient as long as you have a production potter at hand.

One of the real advantages of clay is obvious to those of us who do not smash our pots after one cooking, but use them over and over. Earthenware vessels absorb some mojo from each delicious food that has gone before, as fat carries each dish's essence deep into the clay. You would think that there would be a limit to the benefits from this tendency, that the cookware would develop sour, off, or rancid aromas. But I clean the pots promptly after use and do not store foods in them; perhaps these practices account for my lack of trouble on this score. Somehow, the effect of the *je ne sais quoi* imparted by the pots seems altogether positive, merely adding depth and nuance to dishes. (This characteristic of clay vessels also helps archaeologists learn what people cooked in those pots. The residual lipid profile in a cookpot shard reveals all.)

Another culinary advantage of clay over most metals is its nonreactive nature. For our simple boiled chicken example that may not matter, but if you want to make an intense little sauce for your chicken using, say, tart fruit like grapes, or maybe the juice of a lemon, or even a glass of wine, and then you thicken that sauce with an egg yolk, a small clay pot is far and away the superior choice. Acids and compounds, when exposed to reactive metals, can unleash some powerful funky aromas and flavors (wet golden retriever, anyone?) and unusual colors (George Carlin was wrong — there *are* blue foods).

That same theoretical sauce also illustrates another wonderful benefit of cooking in clay. Whereas a metal pot transfers heat quickly to the foods within it, clay diffuses it. Thickening a sauce with egg yolks or making a *crème anglaise* in even a nonreactive metal pot will always be more fraught with the risk of curdling than cooking the same food in a friendly, gentle clay pot.

Any of the clay pot cooking done in the wood-fired oven in chapter 5 may be done in a gentle coal bed in your hearth.

BUTTERED GOOSEBERRIES

This recipe is straight from the manuscript recipe book of a 17th-century English noblewoman. Both the ingredients (acid fruit and egg) and the technique (thickening with yolks) cry out for a clay pot to cook it in.

When a bumper crop of gooseberries first persuaded me to try this recipe, I was astounded: this is what English ladies ate before they invented lemon curd! Since gooseberries are very seasonal, I have on occasion substituted other tart fruits like cranberries and diced rhubarb. You can use it as a filling between cake layers or in tart shells, or just straight-up lashed with *crème anglaise* or whipped cream.

2 ounces (4 tablespoons) butter

9 ounces slightly underripe (green) gooseberries

1 cup sugar

6 egg yolks

¼ teaspoon rosewater (optional)

1. Prepare a little nest of coals and ashes that just holds your clay pot. Add the butter, and, when it starts to melt, the gooseberries and about ¾ of the sugar. Heat slowly, cooking until the berries explode. Remove the pot from the heat and place on a warm, forgiving surface.

2. Beat the yolks with the remaining sugar and optional rosewater in a medium, heatproof bowl. Look at the fruit in the clay pot: is it still simmering even though it's off the fire? If so, wait until it stops, and then be patient another minute or two while the mixture cools a bit more. Then, whisking the yolks with one hand, add a dollop of the hot fruit to them and combine quickly and thoroughly. Use a silicone spatula to scrape the tempered yolk mixture into the clay pot of fruit, instantly stirring the whole mess thoroughly together, scraping up from the bottom. The residual heat in the berries and the clay pot should be enough to cause the yolks to thicken the mixture subtly. (If somehow it has cooled too much, return the pot to the coals for a moment, never leaving off stirring from the bottom, until the mixture coalesces and coats a spoon without running.)

The Clay Pot

IRON POTS AND PANS

When it comes to rapidly heating large volumes, metal vessels are impossible to beat. Copper alloy and cast-iron pots and pans have long been valued for their quick heat transfer and relative durability and portability, but their ubiquity is rather recent. The culinary presence of these useful pots and pans has waxed and waned over thousands of years with the availability of raw materials and the vagaries of metallurgical technology — with hot spots from the ancient Indus Valley to fifth-century BCE China to Classical Rome to medieval Tanzania to early modern Europe. Only with the Industrial Revolution did metal pots begin to rule kitchens worldwide.

The largest pots, whether cast in one piece or assembled out of sheet metal, were usually built into a masonry surround, which both supported the pot and created a very efficient, safe containment for the fire. This arrangement was called a furnace, and was used by early modern Europeans in many industrial applications (salt making, sugar boiling, brewing) and in feeding crowds (crews at sea, orphans). Households with many mouths (human and otherwise) to feed, heaps of laundry to boil, and barrels of beer to brew also made use of a "copper" built in along the hearth. Along with an oven, it supplied the full range of kitchen needs.

Less capacious brass and iron pots were furnished with bails so they might be suspended from the lug pole up in the chimney by means of pot hangers, chains, or trammels. In eighteenth-century Europe and America, the crane became a common hearth furnishing. A convenient wrought-iron arm, the crane didn't just hold the pots up, it allowed the cook to swing them right out into the room at working level.

Three long or short legs built into the base of a pot made them efficient cookers without hanging, as they could be set upon a great heap of coals to just simmer away on the hearth.

Learning to use metal pots with a wood fire is pretty intuitive, although pots vary a great deal as to their strengths and weaknesses. The best way to learn is to do — just make your favorite soup or stew in a cast-iron kettle to find out how the process is the same yet different from how you always do it. Remember that cast iron, although strong, is brittle. Don't drop it on a hard surface. And, as with virtually any cooking vessel, try not to add very cold liquid to a very hot pot.

Restoring a Rusty Iron Pot

It's wonderful that a few companies are still turning out good quality, inexpensive cast-iron pots and frying pans. That small investment should provide you with a lifetime of great cooking, indoors and out. (See Resources, page 307.)

However, the range of sizes and shapes available today pales in comparison with the panoply of terrific pots churned out in the last few centuries. Keep your eyes open for sound but disused and inevitably rusty old pots shoved aside by people eager for the dubious conveniences of aluminum and Teflon. Unless your salvaged pot has been at the bottom of the Gulf of Mexico for a few centuries, it is likely that it can be brought back into good working order with just a little care. And as you use it, it will grow more and more beautiful and functional.

First, make sure the pot *is* sound — that it has no fatal cracks hidden by the rust. A chip, or even a small crack by the rim, probably will not spell doom, so I'd commit a little time and work to a full investigation.

Aside from big bumpy accretions, which might merit the application of a heavy paint-scraper, most of the cleanup work is best tackled with a wire wheel attachment of a handheld electric grinder or electric drill. Don't forget the safety goggles, gloves, and ear protection. And for goodness' sake, don't do this job in a bikini top, no matter how hot it is out; when those hot little wires dart into your flesh, they don't want to come out!

Once you've run the grinder over both the inside and outside of the pot to your satisfaction, rub it clean with an old chunk of towel. Fine steel wool can be helpful for touchups in out of the way spots. Wash it all over very well with hot soapy water.

Rub it all over with neutral vegetable oil, and pop it in a cooling oven (wood-fired or otherwise). Remove when cool, wipe with paper towels, and enjoy.

THE MESS O' GREENS

All the proof you'll ever need that al dente is not the only path to essential vegetal goodness.

Bones and fatty bits from smoked pork or turkey
1 head garlic, cloves chopped
1 or 2 small hot dried red chile peppers
5 pounds or much more collards, turnip, mustard greens (add some chard, dandelion, scallions, what-have-you from the garden if you like), washed and chopped
Salt

1 Put 4 or 5 inches of water in a big iron pot over the fire. Add the rest of the ingredients, cover, and simmer until incredible, at least an hour or two. Correct salt.

(If all the greens don't fit in the pot at once, add them by degrees as they cook down.)

2 Serves a crowd with cornbread and hot sauce. Barbeque ribs a plus here.

THE ORIGINS OF CHOWDER

True fish chowder is unthinkable without a cast-iron kettle.

Admittedly, in chowder's scrappy multinational seaborne infancy on the fishing grounds of the North Atlantic, a brass pot or even a clay marmite was more liable to be the cooking vessel available. The shadowy but fascinating first generations of chowder eaters — a mix of sailors and fishermen from France, Brittany, the Basque country, Cornwall, Wales, and England — were simply using the materials at hand, flavored and filled out with the provisions (and traditions) in their boat's cookroom, to make a filling and tasty quotidian dish. In its first appearance in documents in the eighteenth century, it's clear that chowder was defined as the technique of layering freshly caught fish with common shipboard ingredients like salt pork, onion (if there were still some left), and ship's biscuit, and perhaps some wine and other oddments, depending on the voyage; the whole thing then covered with water and simmered a bit.

In New England, chowder survived the transition from innovative working people's food to charter fishing party standby. By the mid-nineteenth century, it reached its apogee as de rigueur celebratory summer fare, the kettle banging along out to the beach in a catboat, on a wagon, or simply suspended on a stick between two chowder-loving pedestrians. The technique of layering the food in the kettle, "building the chowder," was so intrinsic to the dish that its abandonment in the early twentieth century spelled doom for real chowder everywhere. The ultimate result has been a sad proliferation of flour-thickened nasty messes winning awards in every once-proud chowder town ever since.

This situation need not be. With a little trouble sourcing equipment and ingredients, anyone can experience the real deal. Once you have your kettle, the trickiest part of chowder is getting the essential pilot or water crackers. One bakery in the world still makes them (see Resources, page 307) or you can make your own (see chapter 5). The next-trickiest part is the salt pork. Commercial salt pork can be used, but if you can find a butcher or local farmer selling some, stock up the freezer; or, again, make your own. The difference is astounding.

PLYMOUTH FISH CHOWDER

This recipe captures a very common style of chowder for Plymouth, Massachusetts, in the second half of the 19th century. It's way more delicious than the sum of its parts.

4 ounces (about a 1- by 2- by 3-inch chunk) salt
    pork, thinly sliced
2 medium onions, thinly sliced
6 medium potatoes, peeled and thinly sliced
2 to 3 pounds fresh cod or haddock, each skinned
    fillet cut crosswise in thirds
  Salt
  Freshly ground pepper
  Boiling water or fish stock, if available*
8 or 10 (real) common crackers or pilot crackers,
    plus more for serving
3 cups whole milk

---

8 servings

I. In a large heavy soup pot, fry the salt pork over medium-low coals until the fat renders and the pork becomes golden brown. (Commercial salt pork may require the addition of a tablespoon of butter or bacon fat to get it going.) Remove the pork (at this point irresistibly called "scrunchions" by Newfoundlanders) and reserve, retaining the fat in the pot.

2. Remove the pot from the heat. Layer up the onion, potato, and fish slices alternately, ending with potatoes. Season each stage with salt and pepper (even though the pork is really salty, you need to be surprisingly liberal here).

3. Pour on boiling water, just covering the uppermost potatoes. Cover snugly and return to the heat to bring to a bare simmer. Cook thus for about 25 to 30 minutes; test a potato slice for doneness.

4. As soon as you get the chowder on, split and/or break up the crackers a bit in a medium bowl; pour over the milk and let soak. Add this mess to the chowder as soon as the potatoes are tender. Mix very gently, keeping the fish in as large pieces as possible, and heat through. Adjust seasonings and serve with additional crackers and scrunchions on the side. It's even better the next day, strangely enough.

*If you have fish heads and frames, make simple fish stock first in a separate pot. Just cover with water, bring to a simmer, and cook, uncovered for 20 minutes. Remove from the heat. Proceed with the recipe, straining in this broth instead of the boiling water.

BEEF SHANKS WITH CHILE AND CRANBERRY BEANS

You may substitute other firm, tasty dried beans and other tough flavorful cuts of beef, but there's no getting around the New Mexico red chile, the cast-iron pot, and the campfire to get this right.

½ pound dry cranberry beans

2–3 tablespoons lard or vegetable oil

1–2 pounds beef shank or other tough flavorful beef*

1 medium yellow onion, roughly chopped

2–3 large cloves garlic, chopped

3 tablespoons medium or medium-hot New Mexico ground red chile

1 tablespoon cornmeal

2 teaspoons salt

4 cups boiling water

½ teaspoon oregano, preferably Mexican

---

4 servings

I. Rinse the beans and put into a medium pot. Cover with cold water by about 2 inches. Let soak while you proceed with the recipe.

2. Select a deep cast-iron pot with a lid. Melt the lard in it over pretty good heat, and brown the meat on all sides, whether it is in pieces or one chunk. Add the onion and stir until browning.

3. Add the garlic and stir well for a few seconds. Quickly stir in the chile, cornmeal, and salt. Fry that around for a minute without scorching, then pour on the boiling water, stirring. As soon as it comes to a boil, adjust the pot or the fire so that you achieve a very gentle simmer. Add the oregano, cover the pot, and cook slowly the rest of the afternoon.

4. Two or three hours later, have a look at your beans to make sure that there's still a good inch of water covering them. Set the pot over a low fire to simmer for another hour or so, or until the skins wrinkle when you blow on them.

5. Haul the beef carefully out of the pot, and put it in a big bowl. Using a knife and tongs or a fork to hold the meat, cut between the bones of the shank. Pull and cut the meat apart a bit, then return it to the chile pot. Add the beans and their liquid.

6. Simmer, covered, at least another hour, but preferably longer. Serve with a stack of fresh flour tortillas. Make sure you excavate the marrow from the shank bone and share it among the guests — it's incredibly good napped with the chile sauce on a crisped tortilla.

*You can cook a small top round or piece of chuck this way, browning it whole, braising until tender, and then slicing or shredding. Return it to the broth to finish flavoring the beans.

Pots and Pans

SHALLOW FRYING

If you've already learned to use the griddle and cast-iron pots, you really already know how to shallow fry over a live fire. The skills are simple and the essential tools — cast-iron skillets — are available widely, both new and old.

When it comes to shallow frying, you have a lot of latitude in your cooking arrangement. Three support stones stably cradling your pan (a favorite since Neolithic times at least) can work fine, with nice hot coals shoveled in between the stones. Or, a strong trivet of about a foot of height can be a good support, as long as everyone moves with deliberation around it. Have a pile of light pine, split small, to jump the heat up. As ususal, you'll need a decent coal bed before you start cooking.

Fried food is irresistible when the fat is kept good and hot. A good bed of coals under a frying pan keeps the heat steady and makes for snappy ignition of softwood bits when the temperature starts to drop.

Pots and Pans

GAETANO'S FRIED PIZZA

Fried pizza was big news to me when my Roman friend, the archaeologist and bon vivant Gaetano Palumbo, showed this off. We were working in a very remote section of the Jordan Valley and amusing ourselves during our non-digging hours by beating the bushes for promising ingredients and cooking improbable foods for each other and drinking Ramos Gin Fizzes on the roof of the dig house. Gaetano was shocked by my ignorance concerning the real foods of Rome, and I in turn was amazed by how great these simple pizzas are.

The basil we used on these Jordan Valley pizzas was a sort that grew in pruned woody hedges, like privets, around the dig house. At least it tasted and smelled like basil, and made pretty decent pesto, and no one ever told us not to eat it. Whatever sort is growing in your garden will be great.

You'll only need about an inch of oil for frying these, so you can get away with a deep cast iron frying pan if you don't have a wide-mouthed open pot. (Also, if you've ever wondered what might be a good use for less-than-virgin olive oil, this is it.)

You'll note that this pizza is made without cheese. The richness and flavor created by frying in olive oil take its place subtly and deliciously. You may, however, find that you need to salt your sauce a bit more than usual. And it may not be authentic, but I sometimes melt a couple of anchovies in the olive oil before adding the garlic and tomatoes to the sauce.

24 ounces bread flour

2 cups warm water, plus 1–2 tablespoons

½ teaspoon yeast

1½ teaspoons kosher or sea salt

2 tablespoons extra-virgin olive oil

2–4 cloves garlic, crushed and chopped

1 28-ounce tin crushed tomatoes

1 teaspoon dried oregano or ¼ cup fresh basil leaves, torn in bits

2–3 cups olive oil, depending on the size of your pan

Makes 12 to 16 small appetizer pizzas

1. Mix the flour and the 2 cups water together into a rough dough, adding a bit more water as necessary if dry spots remain. Cover airtight and set in a warm spot for 20 to 30 minutes. Stir in the yeast and 1 teaspoon of the salt, and work the dough with your hand for a couple of minutes until it is uniform and elastic. Cover airtight and allow to ferment for 90 minutes, scraping the dough out onto a lightly floured counter halfway through that period to stretch and fold it.

2. Meanwhile, make the sauce. In a medium saucepan, heat the 2 tablespoons olive oil over a medium flame. Add the garlic and stir and cook gently for 10 to 15 seconds, then stir in the tomatoes and ½ teaspoon salt. Cook gently 10 minutes or so. If you're using oregano, add it and remove the sauce from the heat. If you're using basil, save that for later. Adjust seasoning and set sauce as de.

3. Have a nice hardwood fire burning, and ascertain exactly how you will support your pan of oil securely.

4. Divide the dough into 12 to 16 even-sized blobs, and round up neatly. Let them rest covered lightly. Put the sauce near the fire to reheat, then just keep warm. Start heating up about an inch depth of oil as you roll out a few pizzas to about 4 to 5 inches in diameter.

5. When the oil begins to look a bit wavy and hot, put in a little pinch of dough and observe it. If it fries actively right away, you may begin. If it just sits there with slow bubbles around it, keep heating. You may use an instant-read thermometer to check your oil temperature if you don't like the seat-of-the-pants method. Slide in the first pizza when the oil's at 375°F.

6. Turn the pizza gently with tongs when the bottom looks brown, probably less than a minute. When the other side is done, in half a minute to a minute, remove, hold over the pot a second to drain, and place on a cookie rack to drain further. Meanwhile slip in another pizza, and check on your fire to keep the same heat coming if you like it.

7. Keep it up until the first pizzas have been out of the oil long enough to no longer be a burning hazard to eat. (If necessary, blot them with paper towels, but usually the rack alone allows very good drainage.) Anoint with a light skim of sauce and sprinkle with fresh basil, if using. Serve hot.

A NOTE ABOUT ADVANCE PREPARATION: You may prepare both sauce and dough the day prior and chill airtight. Take the dough out, preshape the balls, and cover about an hour before you want to roll out the pizzas and cook.

CAJUN RICE AND EGGS

My Georgia friends Pat and Shirley Puckett taught me this most foolproof of all breakfasts, a legacy from their mother's Louisiana childhood. This "recipe" has saved my bacon many a morning when a guest or two has shown up and the cupboard was bare. But there's almost always a tub of leftover rice in the fridge! The proportions are extremely elastic; it seems that no matter how I make it, everyone is always surprised by how good something so simple can be.

1 tablespoon butter, at least
3 cups cold cooked rice, give or take
2 or 3 eggs
  Salt and pepper to taste
  A bottle of Louisiana hot sauce, to accompany

Serves 2 or 3 hungry folks

I. Melt the butter in a 10-inch skillet over a medium fire. Add the rice, breaking up the lumps. Stir it around with a wooden spoon, warming it through, not frying it crisp.

2. When the rice is all buttered up and hot through, make divots in it, one for each egg. (If the pan seems very dry, drop a bit of butter into each hole.) Crack the eggs and drop them in the prepared divots. Let cook unmolested until the eggs have begun to set up, around a minute. Then stir the whole thing around once, breaking the eggs all over the rice, yet trying to leave some of the eggs in discernible chunks. Cook another minute until set through but not dried out. Add salt and pepper to taste. Give it another gentle stir, then serve on hot plates, passing the hot sauce.

MAGYAR MIGAS

A half loaf of stale bread and a few eggs could result in French toast, but our tastes generally run a little earthier. *Migas* is the brilliant Spanish dish of soaked and fried bread, a concept we enjoy taking in, whichever direction the contents of our larder point us.

This imaginary Hungarian version is merely an example of the versatility of the idea. Made with week-old caraway sour rye, duck eggs, and duck fat, it results in a remarkably meaty and serious breakfast, although it contains very little actual meat. Change it around as you like — bacon fat, hen's eggs, an old focaccia, garlic?

3–4 cups of stale rugged bread, cut/torn to ½-inch
    pieces
2½ tablespoons olive oil
2½ tablespoons duck fat
1 medium onion, sliced in fine (¼-inch) wedges
¼ teaspoon hot paprika or smoked red pepper, or
    more to taste
Kosher or sea salt
4 serrano chiles, stemmed and sliced in half length-
    wise (I leave the seeds)
4 fresh duck eggs
Freshly ground black pepper

2 servings

1. Put the bread chunks in a mixing bowl and cover with water. Let soak from 30 seconds to 5 minutes, depending on degree of staleness. Drain water and squeeze the bread to remove the excess.

2. Meanwhile, put a 10-inch skillet over a medium fire. Add 2 tablespoons of the olive oil and 2 tablespoons of the duck fat. As soon as the fat melts, add the onion and sauté until translucent. Give the bread a final squeeze and add it to the skillet. Push it around with a spatula, frying it very thoroughly for 5 to 10 minutes — each crumb should be crunchy on the outside and chewy on the inside. Sprinkle paprika and salt to taste.

3. When the migas are about ready, heat the remaining oil and fat in another skillet until quite hot, almost smoking. Toss in the pepper halves and allow to blister a little bit. Move the skillet to a cooler part of the fire, and crack in the eggs. Season with salt and pepper, and cook sunny-side up or over easy. Serve the migas and eggs and peppers on hot plates.

SPAGHETTI ALLA CARBONARA

Since at least the Bronze Age, Mediterranean peoples have been converting their forests into charcoal to fuel metalworking and other proto-industrial pursuits. The process involves a lot of chopping and stacking of hardwood, the burying of that wood in a mound of earth, and the controlled burning of the wood in the resulting oxygen-starved environment. Thus, although the name doesn't show up in printed cookbooks until the 20th century, "charcoal-makers' spaghetti" is by definition a vestigial campfire dish, quick-cooking food for folks working and living in the woods away from home. Its ingredients, dry pasta, salt pork, salt, butter, onion, and hard cured cheese, are long-keeping and easy to transport. Having cooked it myself on several occasions while actually engaged in making charcoal, I can indeed vouch for it as the ideal dish — hearty, sustaining, basic, yet delicious — for hard-working people whose weary bodies are inundated with smoke and dirt.

1 ounce (2 tablespoons) butter

4 ounces streaky bacon or jowl meat, cut in small cubes (classically, unsmoked, but I personally prefer it salt-cured and smoked)

1 medium yellow onion, chopped
Freshly ground black pepper

2 eggs
Salt

16 ounces spaghetti

½ cup freshly grated *parmigiano reggiano*

½ cup freshly grated *romano*

4 servings

1. Put a large pot of salted water, covered, over a brisk fire to boil the spaghetti.

2. Place half the butter and the bacon in a 10-inch iron skillet and set over coals or a small fire. When the butter has melted and the bacon is starting to sizzle, add the onion. Cook, stirring occasionally with a wooden spoon, until the bacon and onion are golden brown and crispy and irresistible. Remove from the heat and grind over plenty of black pepper.

3. Meanwhile, uncover the pot, cook the spaghetti al dente and drain in a colander. Return it to the pot, away from the fire. Add the remaining tablespoon of butter, crack in the eggs, and stir to coat the spaghetti. Scrape in the bacon mixture, along with the cheese, and stir it all well together. Serve instantly with a robust red wine.

DEEP-FRYING

This is where I throw aside my usually cavalier attitude to safety, and begin with an admonishment: always use utmost care when deep-frying over an open fire. Double-check your cooking gear ahead of time for stability, have all the tools you need present, including a fire-shovel, and select your fuel carefully so that you can anticipate the size of your blaze. Have plenty of headroom in your pot so that there is never the slightest fear of overflow. Keep careful tabs on the pace at which your oil heats; if it seems like it is gaining heat faster than you like, make an adjustment to the fire, rather than trying to adjust the heavy kettle full of hot oil. Brief your guests sternly on safety, especially if there are children involved.

(Reading these sensible words will amuse people who have seen me fry doughnuts for a hundred on an open fire in a thatched underground hovel, walled away from the only exit by planks of rising crullers, while wearing a devil costume, all because I thought that "Dungeon Donuts" was a great concept for Halloween entertainment. Or what about the time we made Scotch eggs in a fire pit dug into a glare sheet of ice on a hillside while drinking Bloody Marys? My friend Stephen had to keep pushing me in my tractionless boots back up to the high side of the fire pit; I'd slide back down, tending the frying as I went, and he'd slide me back up. Who knew that crampons were essential deep-frying tools?)

Think through the process before committing to heating the oil, so that you can anticipate all of your equipment needs. I like to have the eventual serving platter standing by in a warm spot, a roll of paper towels handy just in case, a pair of tongs, a wire skimmer or slotted spoon, and for draining, wire cookie racks (which I feel leave fried food much crisper and less greasy than the spell they're commonly given on absorbent paper). Definitely use an instant-read thermometer if you're new to this; but once you gain experience and build confidence, you'll probably find that you can leave it in the drawer.

Ideally, the temperature in your pot should remain steady throughout the process, but achieving this goal requires some focus. Each time you add a lump of cold dough, you're bringing down the temperature of the whole shebang, so calibrate your additions both to the oil and to the fire accordingly. Try to anticipate by keeping a steady flame under the pot. The bed of coals helps tremendously here. And if the heat should suddenly climb more quickly than you like, push the fire aside for a moment and take advantage of the fact that the most efficient way to cool down a pot of hot fat is to introduce some cold food to it.

Although they'll never be confused with healthy choices, well-fried foods should not seem greasy or heavy. They should taste like the apotheosis of their ingredients, not like the frying medium — whether it's lard, clarified butter, seed oil, or whale blubber. (Yes, blubber. American whalers joyously celebrated rendering a voyage's thousandth barrel of whale oil with doughnuts for all hands — fried

right on deck in the seething try-pots. One 1858 verdict: "right good were they too, not the least taste of oil — they came out the pots perfectly dry.")

Once I started deep-frying outdoors, I realized I would never voluntarily do so in my house again. Much as I love the occasional deep-fried food, I hate the mess, and worse, the lingering smell. Outdoors, none of that is an issue (but do remember that a greasy paper towel thrown in the fire will flare up). When the fun is over, there will still be used oil to deal with; I advise cultivating friendships with folks who power their vehicles with biodiesel.

FRIED SMELTS WITH RHODE ISLAND RELISH

You'll need a medium hardwood fire to start, and some small dry softwood to spike the heat. Select an open-mouthed cast-iron pot that can safely hold 2 to 4 inches of oil and still have an equivalent amount of freeboard.

RHODE ISLAND RELISH

- 1 cup kalamata or other firm, flavorful black olives, pitted and coarsely chopped
- 1 cup pickled hot pepper rings (preferably banana peppers)
- 1 cup pickled hot cherry peppers, coarsely sliced or chopped
- 4 cloves garlic
- ¼ cup extra-virgin olive oil

SMELTS

- 1 cup semolina flour
  Kosher or sea salt
  Freshly ground black pepper
  Cayenne pepper
- 4–6 cups olive oil (not extra-virgin)
- 2 pounds smelts, cleaned

GARNISH

- ½ cup parsley, chopped
  Lemon quarters

4 to 6 servings

1. Mix relish ingredients and set aside while you prepare the smelts.

2. Mix the semolina with fat pinches of salt, pepper, and cayenne in a clean paper bag.

3. Set up a deep-frying arrangement over a bed of coals and feed the fire with small dry wood, gradually heating the oil. Have all the ingredients and equipment ready to go.

4. Shake about a quarter of the smelts at a time with the flour mixture, then fry them quickly in the hot (375°F) oil. Drain on racks for a few minutes, then serve hot, sprinkled with parsley. Accompany with lemon wedges, relish, and crusty bread or boiled new potatoes.

OLIE-KOECKEN

A delicious and fun cool weather treat. Twenty-first-century Dutch children still enjoy these fritters under a different name, but the formula has endured substantially unaltered. Why mess with success?

The original recipe calls for turnip-seed oil, the ancestor of the modern canola, as the frying medium, a striking regional practice in a mostly lard-frying post-medieval Europe.

I've halved the proportions of the 1668 recipe and adapted it from ale yeast to commercial yeast.

2 cups raisins
2 cups boiling water
¾ cup milk
4 ounces (8 tablespoons) lightly salted butter
1 pound unbleached all-purpose flour
2 teaspoons dry yeast
2½ teaspoons cinnamon
1¼ teaspoons ginger
¼ teaspoon cloves
2 ounces (½ cup) blanched almonds, coarsely chopped
1 large apple, pared, cored, and chopped
Canola oil, for frying
Powdered sugar, for serving

Treats for 10 to 12

1. Place the raisins in a heatproof bowl and pour over the boiling water. Stir, cover, and let steep 30 to 60 minutes.

2. Warm the milk to 90 to 100°F. Remove from the heat. Add the butter and let it melt.

3. Mix the flour, yeast, cinnamon, ginger, and cloves. Add the raisins and their water, and the milk mixture, and stir it all well with a wooden spoon. You should have a stiffly stirrable dough; correct with additional milk or flour if necessary. Cover airtight and allow to ferment 90 minutes at room temperature, stirring once after 45 minutes. Stir in the almonds and apple at the end of the fermentation.

4. Prepare a deep-frying setup with a cast-iron pot deep enough to hold 2–3 inches of oil and still have at least 2 inches of freeboard. Make a hardwood fire, and have scraps of dry pine on hand to spike the heat.

5. Get your tools ready — cooling racks, skimmer or tongs, serving basket, paper towels, sugar, dough, and two spoons.

6. When the oil begins to look a bit wavy and hot, use two spoons to ease in a little sample of dough. If it just sits there with slow bubbles around it, keep heating. If it fries smartly as soon as it enters the oil, start adding lumps of dough the size of a walnut. If you're using a thermometer, that'll be at 375°F.

7. Fry, turning as necessary, until golden brown. Transfer to cooling racks to drain thoroughly, then make an impressive pyramid, sprinkling with sugar as you go. Serve hot or warm.

Pots and Pans

BAKING BREAD IN A CAST-IRON POT

The masonry oven is not the end-all and be-all of wood-fired baking. As we've seen, people have baked bread on earthen and iron griddles, on planks, and right under the coals and ashes, all over the world and for centuries. For a small investment and with a little enjoyable practice and experimentation, you can also bake a very tasty loaf of bread in cast iron.

The earliest full description of the baking technique that I've come across demonstrates the ingenuity of the desperate. A British military officer posted to deepest Scotland in 1746 simply couldn't deal with the flat local oat and barley breads; he began keeping his own leaven and churning butter and used the buttermilk as the liquid for his bread. And as for baking:

"[H]aving not the conveniency of an oven, I made use of a large iron pot that would bake two large bricks or loaves at a time. I prepared it by covering it with

what they call an Irish gridle [*sic*] for baking oaten bread over the fire, and putting fresh coals under the pot of turf or wood, until the air within the pot became sufficiently warm, I then caused my bread to be fixed in the pot and covered again, and fresh coals to be put under the pot, and the griddle covered all over with them, and thus constantly supplied, till your bread be sufficiently baked, which will be in a very little time; and when you take it out, put it before a good fire, constantly turning it to harden the crust; and after this manner I have as good French bricks, and wheaten and household bread baked as ever you saw come out of a baker's shop."

By sometime in the late eighteenth century, enthusiasts like this anonymous officer would no longer need to improvise to bake in the hearth. The Industrial Revolution and the migration of Europeans all over the globe brought on an explosion in the production of cast iron for domestic and industrial purposes. Iron foundries extended their repertoires of holloware to include the "bake pot" or "bake-kettle," the ideal utensil for the purpose: a straight-sided round pot with a bail, three short chunky legs, and a tight fitting lid cast with a peripheral ridge. The legs allowed it plenty of room to nest on coals and embers without smothering them. The shape of the cover made it easy to heap coals on top, as well as to look inside without sullying the food.

Because a portable mini-oven was so helpful when cooks were on the move, the innovation really took off in restless North America. Iron foundries throughout the Northeast and the Midwest of the United States turned them out in quantity. The bake-kettle became a standard feature of the kit of any cook on the cattle drive, at the logging camp, in the wagon train. But though they are associated with American frontier life, their use was by no means limited to that context. During the nineteenth and early twentieth centuries, they also pop up in accounts of travelers and settlers and even recreational campers throughout the rest of the British sphere of influence: Canada, Kenya, South Africa, Australia, and the West Indies.

Baking in a kettle was not just for travelers; many cooks in America and the British Isles who had no masonry oven relied on the technique for all their home baking. Others who had ovens turned to their bake-kettles when unexpected company turned up for tea, or when they had only one or two things to bake and couldn't justify firing a big oven. Biscuits, shortcake, and other quick breads using the newly developed chemical leavenings like bicarbonate of soda, were often cooked in bake-kettles because they could be thrown together easily in no more time than it took to prepare the fire and kettle for baking.

Tips for Kettle Baking

ACQUIRING YOUR EQUIPMENT. If you are lucky, you may find a bake-kettle at a junk shop or yard sale. Snap it up and marvel at your good fortune if it still has its original, snug-fitting cover.

Thanks to a small, but persistent, market of enthusiasts, new bake-kettles are still available, squat legs, straight sides, ember-holding lid, and all. A quick web search ("dutch oven"), a few mouse-clicks, and a valid credit card number will have one at your door in a jiffy.

A fire-shovel, a pothook, and a whisk broom are handy to have around, but their absence is not a deal breaker. Much can be accomplished with an old shingle, a stick, and a rag or two.

PREPARING YOUR FIRE. It only takes a few minutes to heat the kettle enough for baking, but naturally you need to have an ample supply of coals all ready to go before you start.

If I am making a dedicated fire for this purpose, I like to burn small-diameter round hardwood stock (i.e., sticks), for a few reasons. A big pile of oak or maple sticks or brush combusts aggressively and quickly, even if it's not 100 percent dry, leaving a nice bed of coals. And small-diameter wood, even as half-burned embers, will fit conveniently underneath your bake-kettle without putting it off-kilter.

Err on the side of abundance, and, later, when you are baking in the kettle, keep a little fire going to the side so that you will have a source of coals should you need them to refresh the heat under or over your kettle.

If, however, you already have a hearty cooking fire going, just use a shovel to steal some coals from beneath the fire and set them in a little heap, making a new hearth about the diameter of your kettle a couple feet away. Do not overdo it. Remember that the rule of thumb is to use about half as many coals below the bake-kettle as above. Cast iron is an excellent diffuser of heat, but restraint is key — the trick here is setting up just the right amount of heat to bake your food through without scorching it.

PREHEATING THE KETTLE. Place the empty covered bake-kettle upon this small nest of coals and allow to preheat about 5 to 10 minutes. This is a convenient time to accomplish the final mixing and any necessary shaping for quick breads. This is also the time to check and make sure you'll have everything you need close by.

When the preheating time has elapsed, pick up the kettle by the bail with a pothook or potholder, and have a look beneath. (Check with a quick touch first, but it is unlikely you will need to use a pothook or potholder yet.) Add another small shovel of coals to the bed unless it's screaming hot. When you put the pot back into its nest, turn it 180 degrees from how it was sitting before, and try to get it pretty level, especially if you're baking something with a liquidy batter like cornbread.

BAKING THE BREAD. Bread at hand, remove the kettle's cover. (Again, you will probably be able to bare-hand it still.) Nestle the bread in the kettle, close it back up, and place the lid on top. Check to see that it's really seated down. Sometimes they catch where the end of the bail curls back from the pot. As you're baking, any visible steam, or even more than a subtle aroma, may mean that your lid is ajar.

Retrieve a good shovelful of small coals from your source fire and rain them evenly on your pot lid. If you are baking out-of-doors and it's cold or windy, make a little skirt of coals and ashes around the perimeter of the pot, too. Look at the clock or set a timer, since you won't get many physical cues from this food when it's ready.

Throw an armload of very small-diameter hardwood — twigs, really — on the main fire. Quick-burning small stuff will replenish the coals should you, in a pinch, require more.

A little before halfway through the cooking time, pick up your pot by the bail and rotate it 180 degrees. This time, you'll probably need your pothook or potholder. Turning the kettle compensates for hot spots in your coal bed, and for one-sided exposure to the main fire.

When you think it's about time, use whatever comes to hand to brush the coals back into the fire from the lid. Use a whisk broom if you like to clean off the ashes, too. Lids can be tippy when lifted, and grittiness is unwelcome seasoning.

Finding the center balance point, lift the lid straight up and out of the way. If things look very underdone, instantly close it back up, and refresh the coal supply over and under. Some foods — biscuits, in particular — are very steamy-seeming when first opened. If they've browned on top, keep the lid off, and put some new coals beneath. They should crisp up in just a minute or two and be wonderful.

For large yeast- or naturally leavened loaves, you'll want to turn the loaf out of the pot to test the bottom by tapping, same as you would with any kind of baking. Usually, the bread draws away from the sides of the pot and releases without a fight, but a long, thin spatula (like for cake frosting) is helpful in the case of recalcitrance. If you're baking in the rough without a frosting spatula at hand, any bowie knife will do.

The anonymous British officer quoted earlier mentioned placing his loaves near the fire to crisp up the exterior after their time in the bake-kettle. I have never had to do this, but be aware that it is an option.

KETTLE BAKING, STEP-BY-STEP

1. Preheat the bake-kettle on a bed of coals.

2. Nestle the proofed dough in the kettle.

3. Cover the pot securely.

4. Shovel more coals onto the lid than are under the kettle.

5. Bake the bread, rotating the pot a half-turn halfway through the baking time.

6. Brush most of the coals and ashes from the lid.

7. Lift the lid carefully with a pothook.

8. The result can be as delicious and crusty as bread baked in a wood-fired oven.

CLASSIC WHITE BREAD FOR CAST-IRON BAKING

This 2¼-pound loaf of bread bakes perfectly in my ten-inch bake-kettle. The recipe was inspired by looking at mid-20th-century photos of Welsh home bakers and their beautiful loaves of kettle-baked bread.

18	ounces bread flour
¾	ounce (⅓ cup) dry milk powder
2	teaspoons sugar
1½	teaspoons kosher salt
1½	teaspoons dry yeast
¾	ounce (1½ tablespoons) butter, soft
3	ounces leaven (whole wheat or white), optional
1½	cups lukewarm water

Makes 1 big loaf

I. Mix all the ingredients in a stand mixer with the dough hook, or by hand. (If you mix by hand, work the butter into the dry ingredients first, then stir in the leaven, in bits, and water.) Add a few drops more water as necessary. Once everything is combined, mix for 3 minutes. Scrape down the bowl and stir up from the bottom. Cover airtight.

2. Allow to ferment 2 hours, interrupting it halfway through to stretch and fold it on a lightly floured counter. If you don't already have a cooking fire going for another purpose, start a lazy fire now. Small dry hardwood sticks (about 1- to 2-inch diameter) are great for this.

3. When the bulk fermentation time is up, line a round medium basket with a floured cloth. Turn the dough out onto a lightly floured counter and knead it gently for a few seconds, gathering it up into a nice smooth ball with good surface tension. Flour the good side, and put it, good-side down, in the basket to rise. Cover well with plastic or put the whole thing inside a plastic bag.

4. Allow the loaf to rise about 40 minutes. Place the covered pot upon some moderate coals, away from the main body of the fire to preheat. When the loaf is proofed, move the pot off those coals and augment the coal bed a bit. Remember to save plenty of coals to place on the lid of the pot, where the greater proportion of them should ultimately be. Ease the risen loaf into the pot, nice-side up. Return the lid, and place the pot on the prepared coal bed. Shovel some nice embers all over the lid of the pot.

5. Turn the pot 180 degrees after 20 minutes for even baking. Taking precautions against spilling ashes in the pot, very carefully lift the lid and peek at the loaf after about 50 minutes. If it appears golden brown, tap the bottom of the loaf to check for doneness.

BUTTERMILK BISCUITS

If these are all you ever make with your bake-kettle, your investment has paid off. I like to use about one-quarter whole-wheat flour, and we mash together butter and molasses or sorghum molasses on our plates as the accompaniment.

10 ounces flour — whole wheat, unbleached all-purpose white, or a mixture
½ teaspoon salt
1 teaspoon baking powder
½ teaspoon baking soda
1 ounce (2 tablespoons) butter or other solid fat
¾ cup buttermilk, about

Makes 8 biscuits

1. Mix the flour, salt, baking powder, and baking soda in a medium bowl, and cut in the butter with two knives or a pastry blender. (Or use a food processor.) This part can be done ahead while you mess around with the fire.

2. While you preheat your bake-kettle, add ¾ cup buttermilk to the flour mixture. Use a fork to stir lightly and try not to overwork as you mix. Add another tablespoon or two of buttermilk if some of the dough remains dry.

3. Turn the dough out on a lightly floured counter and press it together lightly. Use a rolling pin to roll it out ½-inch thick. Cut it in half with a dough scraper, and set one half evenly on the other, without incorporating any additional flour. Roll it gently out to ½-inch again. Cut biscuits with a 3-inch cutter, and transfer them to a board so you can easily carry them to the fire.

4. Bake in your preheated bake-kettle for about 20 minutes, remembering to turn the kettle about halfway through. The biscuits should be brown, but steamy, not crisp, when you remove the lid. To crisp them, put them over some new coals, uncovered for a few minutes.

MORE GEAR

In this chapter, we'll look at some of the diverse ways in which people have altered the environment of a cooking fire in order to modify its effects. For their own culinary reasons, cooks in various places and times have contrived to create situations for food that were hotter, cooler, smokier, clearer, steamier, or drier than that which is endemic to an ordinary cookfire. In many of these cases, the cook has also had an interest in efficiency, since fuel crises of one sort or another have been part of the human experience for millennia. Most any kind of built installation improves fuel efficiency over that of an open fire; not hard to do since so much of the heat released in your average hearth fire — in fact, in all the fires described in this book up to this point — just flies out the chimney or diffuses into the air.

Encircle a fire in a narrow heatproof enclosure, and induce a draft through it, and you will create a lot of intense heat, enough to fire pottery and smelt metal if you really push it. But if you pull back and apply the principle with moderation, you can control the effect to foster a very hot, efficient cooking fire. This technology seems to have been independently understood and developed thousands of years ago by disparate civilizations in Mesopotamia, China, the Andes, Mexico, the Indus Valley, and sub-Saharan Africa. After a recent period of fossil-fuel-addled neglect, the idea is currently making a comeback, reengineered and very thoroughly tested, in the guise of the super-efficient rocket stove (see Resources, page 308).

Those of us whose tastes run more Bronze Age than high-tech may be surprised when our sweet little cooking installations, built of friendly stone and clay, turn out to be pretty efficient. And a little planning and experimentation can help make them more so.

THE TANNUR, THE FURNACE, AND THE POTAGER

I group these devices together here because, even though they are generally thought of as different technologies, they have a lot in common from the perspectives of both the builder and the cook.

The tannur is composed of a chamber, traditionally masonry and usually more or less cylindrical, fed with fuel and air from below. It has been in use since at least the Neolithic period, according to the archaeological record in the Middle East. As the early writers in the region, ancient Sumerians did us the favor of recording the word *tannur* for the first time. But like us, they were only the inheritors of both the word and the invention it denotes; the time, place, and circumstances of tannur's origin will surely never be known.

Over the course of millennia, the tannur has spread far and wide, with cooks and bakers from the Arabian Peninsula to Uzbekistan to India to North Africa putting their own regional spins on the equipment and its products. Tannur traditions range from the simplest unleavened flour/water/salt flatbreads to spiced stuffed naan to tandoori chicken and beyond. In some areas (interestingly, closest to the tannur's origin-point), the baking is actually done in retained heat after the fire lapses. But globally, most tannur bakers take advantage of the snappy heat of an active fire for a delicious sear as well as continual production capability.

The business part of a tannur is the core, which is made of clay tempered with grog, gravel, salt, hair, chaff, or dung, depending on local tradition. It is shaped, usually by the coiling method, into a large barrel, truncated cone, or cylinder form, with a small door cut into the base for fuel and draft; then it is air-dried or low-fired. Since the core is thin — about an inch thick when made by a skilled person — it wants to be set into something for thermal mass, traditionally a mud-brick bench or patio, or, if it's left freestanding, just several inches of clay mortar. (The baker works standing in the latter case, but seated in the former, reaching down through the mouth of the tannur, for all intents and purposes, a hole in the floor, to bake the bread.)

Sometimes installed indoors, tannurs are more often incorporated into a courtyard. A recent innovation — available today in at least Yemen and Pakistan — imbeds the core in mortar in a lightweight metal barrel, and makes a tannur that is more self-contained and shippable. I fear that many of these are destined to be fired with gas, but that's up to the installer and the client.

Like the tannur, the furnace is a masonry cylinder that encloses a fire fueled from below, but its cooking surface is usually a metal pot on top. For millennia, the furnace was deployed in many industries to boil huge volumes of liquid efficiently — from reducing brine to salt in ancient China, to simmering pease pottage for throngs of sailors and soldiers on early modern English naval vessels, to boiling down sugar at plantations in Brazil and the Caribbean, to rendering oil from blubber on whaleships. A smaller version, the copper or set kettle, was an ordinary feature in the back kitchens of households of any size and complexity in Europe and America, allowing laundry, brewing, and other large-scale tasks to be tackled in house.

These furnaces could be built to churn out a lot of aggressive heat. The masonry found in their archaeological remains appears every bit as scorched and superheated as that of bread ovens. But a mini-relative of the furnace, essentially an early stove, allowed for gentler cooking of small quantities of more refined foods and became very popular in the better establishments of early modern Europe and her colonies. Called *potager* in French, and the far less felicitous *stew-hole* in English, they were set in ranges (usually two to eight) in a high masonry counter, often under a window. This arrangement allowed cooks to stand upright and really see the nice things they were preparing, a boon for turning out multi-course meals with complex and fragile sauces for discerning diners.

Potagers were generally fired with charcoal, affording steady, moderate heat. Since charcoal makes no visible smoke, ventilation doesn't seem to have been a priority; potagers were rarely effectively flued into a chimney. By at least locating potagers beneath windows, employers graciously kept their woozy cooks from succumbing altogether to carbon monoxide poisoning.

A tannur may be free standing, but it is often set into a patio or floor, as in this Afghan bakery.

The Tannur

If you live in a hot, and more importantly, dry, place, you may enjoy experimenting with building tannurs along the traditional lines described above. Well, you can experiment in cold, wet climes, too, but only if you are ready to watch your handiwork suffer fatally in the first freeze/thaw cycle of the winter (leaving an interesting archaeological feature as consolation).

Those of us in the temperate zones may prefer to take a different approach. Here's one idea: find a potter willing to build a cylinder (say 16 inches high and wide) of highly tempered earthenware, and kiln-fire it at a low temperature (around 1,650°F or 900°C). Build a base for this prefab tannur, including an air channel, out of dry-laid brick, and set the fired top, the interior walls of which serve as the baking surface, on it. Surround with more bricks for some thermal mass and then backfill all around with earth and rubble. If you are serious about using it a lot, consider creating a thermal break with insulating firebrick all around the core about six to eight inches out.

If you don't know a potter, try playing with some found or salvaged items; castoff clay flue liners, for example, work very well if they're big enough. Our very first "tannur" was just a section of steel pipe, 12 inches in diameter and about 2½ feet high, stuck into a retaining wall with a little stokehole-air channel. So much fun! It heated quickly and baked perfectly as long as we used it every day

A tannur can be approximated in the backyard, using a clay flue liner.

The Tannur, the Furnace, and the Potager

(which we did for weeks). The catch came when we left it idle for a few days, and a crust of unstable rust built up on the inside and proceeded to spall off and literally weld itself to the bottom of our naan. So, unless you fancy a go-round with a grinding wheel every baking day, clay is really the ideal medium for the tannur.

The Furnace and the Potager

That steel pipe scrap, once it was forcibly retired from naan-baking, was repurposed as a furnace, when I happened to notice that my wok happens to fit it just right. I arranged a few strips of iron across the top of the pipe, more to allow draft around it than to support the wok. The power of the furnace was instantly clear. As someone who is often frustrated by the lame output of the domestic gas stove, I was truly awed by the instant, extraordinary blast of heat shot from the combustion of a handful of sticks in my little furnace. True wok-seared stir-frying at last!

You can replicate these results using all sorts of flameproof materials. Compared to a tannur, a furnace or potager is much less persnickety to build, since its inner walls, not being a baking surface, need not be smooth, clean, or even cylindrical. It's just a sort of silo to hold the fire, draw air, and support the cooking vessel. Also, since you're not slapping bread against the walls, you may size your furnace at any scale and ultimately burn your fire at any intensity, depending on the job at hand. Using the basic concept, you could fry doughnuts in a wok-on-a-pipe unit or heat ash lye in a cauldron for boiling proofed bagels before baking. Or scale back the intensity and build a more potager-like model, suitable for gentle cooking — simmering mulled wine, for example.

Depending on your inclinations, you may design and build a furnace to be long-lasting and highly efficient, or you can throw one together out of dry-laid bricks just for tonight's party. Even the latter will take less tending and burn less fuel than an open fire with a kettle suspended over it.

Tannur trials with a steel pipe encountered rust issues, but were successful enough to goad me into further experimentation with clay versions. Though unsuitable for bread, this thing is still unbeatable as a furnace for jet-powering a wok or generally blasting insane heat at anything.

More Gear

Firing a Tannur

Building a decent functioning tannur from scratch presupposes an understanding of the baking process; so read this first to get the mechanics.

Build a fire inside the tannur using pretty much any fuel — as usual, the dry, light, and small variety makes starting easy. Given the mix of wood I have around the yard, I usually start a blaze with shavings and sticks, and add a few pieces of hardwood that will burn down to coals over time. This is not traditional in the tannur lands generally, if only because chunks of hardwood are not available on the steppes, and straw is. (The last hardwood there was made into charcoal five millennia ago to support all the vanguard metallurgical industries that allowed those famous Bronze and Iron Age empires to rule the world. Since then, not so much.) Straw, dung, twigs, olive pits, pomace, and dried-up cotton plants have been documented as used by contemporary bakers in the Middle East. (A Czech archaeologist mentioned in her 2012 dissertation observing the unfortunate use of plastic bottles as oven fuel in northern Syria. Not recommended.)

Surrounding a clay flue liner with earth or masonry, like the brickbats pictured, affords it some thermal mass, so that a steady heat for baking bread is maintained in the clay after preheating.

Air should draw in from the small door built into the bottom of the tannur and whoosh a lot of life into the fire. Keep a bit of brick or tile on hand to play with closing off the mouth of that door, until you find what works best given your tannur's geometry, your fuel, and the day's breeze. As much fun as it is to burn your tannur like a rocket, remember that the greatest heat of fire is at the tips of the flames, so keeping the fire in the masonry is helpful

Aim to saturate the walls of the tannur with plenty of heat and to build up a sustaining coal bed in the bottom of it. Observe the char buildup on the wall. Once that starts to burn away, you're getting to the end of the preheating phase. Charge it with one more load of fuel while you move your dough toward readiness.

Once I'm getting ready to start baking, I cease tossing wood in the top, and slide it solely into the lower stokehole. Obviously, sticks, twigs, straw, and other long thin fuel work best after that point. Add fuel gradually, remembering that air must also enter by the same door; stuffing it full of even highly burnable fuel will tend to stifle and cool the fire. The coal bed should instantly ignite any newly added fuel.

Remember that each bread removes heat from the walls, so having deep heat, plus a continual small but smart fire, will help you get through your whole batch.

If there's a lot of cold or moisture in the surrounding masonry, you may find that the walls of the tannur quickly grow black with char again, signaling a temperature drop. If the heat does grow sluggish, quit loading bread, and recharge the fire.

Naturally, bakers in those places where it is traditional to allow the fire to die before loading bread must be sure that the walls of their tannurs have absorbed heat to capacity. Because that kind of retained heat baking is so suitable for the wood-fired oven (see chapter 5), I prefer to keep the tannur for the exciting live-fire application that only it can achieve.

The Tannur, the Furnace, and the Potager

Baking in the Tannur

It's really helpful, and fun, to enlist the help of some intrepid partners. Remind anyone nearby how very hot it is directly over the mouth of the tannur. Tie back long hair, and no loose flammable clothing.

Have everything you need on hand before you start: your dough, a rolling pin and floury surface, some long oven mitts, a set of long spring-loaded tongs or two long metal skewers or perhaps one of those otherwise useless long barbeque forks, a small dish of cool water, a heavy kitchen towel or clean board to put the finished bread on, maybe some melted ghee and a brush. Real tannur bakers use a wooden-backed firm cloth pillow the size of their breads to support the dough into the oven as it is slapped against the searing hot wall. If you start to make large naan, you'll want to build yourself one of these; for smaller breads you can fake it with a large oven mitt and a wadded-up kitchen towel.

Roll out a lump of dough and stretch it to the desired thinness and shape (lavash as thin and large as you can handle; naan a bit thicker and egg-shaped). Start small, and suit the size to your tannur, in any case. Now move quickly and purposefully. Spread the dough on your transfer pillow, dip your fingers in the water and lightly moisten a couple inches of the part of the dough that will be uppermost in the tannur (the pointy part of the egg-shape). Now, remembering your personal safety, pick up the dough-pillow in your dominant hand and slap it against the inside of the tannur, striving for positive contact with that damp upper section.

Repeat with more dough, eyeballing carefully exactly where you intend to slap it. Meanwhile keep watch on naan number one. It should bake visibly, its bottom half browning rapidly and pulling away from the wall of the tannur. Left too long, it may pull itself right off the wall as the moistened section bakes, dries, and separates; you must be standing by with your tongs or skewers before that moment comes. Snatch the naan up and toss it on a towel or board; brush with ghee, if desired.

Back to rolling, stretching, and baking; don't neglect to tend the fire to keep a nice sharp heat leaping up the walls. We enjoy the naan that is ever-so-slightly burned best; you will find your own taste, and setup will dictate your work rhythm.

NAAN

These are so delicious baked in a tannur that people tend to wolf them down beyond all limits of decorum. For this reason, and because you will probably have a conflagration or two, make more dough than you think you need; the recipe scales up easily.

1 cup milk
⅔ cup boiling water
1 pound bread flour
2 teaspoons kosher or sea salt
1 teaspoon dry yeast
4 ounces white or wheat leaven (optional — see page 268)
2 or 3 tablespoons melted ghee

Makes 8 naan

1. Mix the milk and boiling water in a mixing bowl, then stir in the flour and mix well. Cover, and let rest at room temperature about 30 minutes.

2. Add the salt, yeast, and optional leaven, and stir well with a fork. Turn onto a lightly floured surface and knead for 1 or 2 minutes.

3. Cover airtight and allow to ferment at room temperature for 90 minutes. Halfway through that period, turn the dough out onto a lightly floured counter and stretch and fold it. (I usually start my fire around the time of the stretching and folding, depending on the weather, the size, and the state of the tannur, etc.)

4. Divide the dough into 8 equivalent sections (about 4 ounces). Round them up and cover lightly with plastic wrap to rest for 10 to 20 minutes.

5. Follow the general directions in the previous section, "Baking in the Tannur," page 168.

VARIATION: POTATO-STUFFED NAAN

1. Set aside half the dough to make 4 filled naan. Peel and mash 1 large baked or boiled potato. Work in a teaspoon grated fresh ginger, 1 clove minced garlic, 1 minced scalion, 1 minced serrano chile, a sprig of cilantro chopped, and a fat pinch each cumin seeds, garam masala, and salt. Divide mixture in 4.

2. Roll out one of the pieces of naan dough to about 4 inches. Seal up one of the filling lumps inside, pinching dough together. Pat the ball flat and roll out thinly. Bake as regular naan.

MAKING GHEE

Heat butter in a heavy-bottomed saucepan over a low flame. Cook gently until it stops spluttering and the milk solids at the bottom have turned golden brown. To separate the milk solids from the ghee, pour it through strainer lined with a bit of cheesecloth or a scrap of an old kitchen towel into a heatproof bowl or jar. I do a pound at a time, because, refrigerated, it keeps forever.

BAKING NAAN, STEP-BY-STEP

1. Preheating the tannur is lots of fun and may be easily accomplished by burning most any kind of twigs, deadfall, or prunings.

2. A resting period makes the dough more extensible. Be sure to set the dough on a board so that you can easily carry it, along with the rest of the supplies, tannur-side.

3. Roll out the dough, situate it on your mitt top-down, moisten the bottom with a bit of cool water . . .

4. . . . and pick a spot on the wall of the tannur, take a deep breath, and gently but decisively slap it into place.

5. The naan bakes quickly, filling with steam and lightly scorching on the edge closest to the fire.

6. Be on your toes to catch the baked naan; sometimes it just lets go when it's done.

7. Brush the hot naan with melted ghee.

8. They're just not as good if you don't get a little char on the n, but it's up to you.

GLÖGG

Mulled wine completes an outdoor winter party. A wee little brick enclosure protects the fire from the wind, keeps the process fuel-efficient, and warms the wine without boiling. All the components can fit on a toboggan — set up your glögg station in the middle of a frozen lake!

Select a pot — a stainless steel soup pot will do — and build the brick furnace to fit around it. It's just a firebox beneath, bricks all around; you can adjust the draft by sliding bricks here and there. For fuel, it's not cheating to base the fire in a small pile of hardwood charcoal, and feed with twigs or other light stuff as necessary. Then your glögg will scarcely take any attention at all, allowing you to skate, fish, tell jokes, and do all the other important winter tasks.

By the way, if you're the pyromaniac I think you are, you'll appreciate the traditional method of compounding glögg: Drench an old-fashioned sugarloaf (the cone-shaped type — how the best sugar once came to market) with hot aquavit. Set on fire. Quench with hot spiced wine. Enjoy.

1 orange
1 tablespoon whole cloves
1 bottle (750 ml) dry red wine
2 tablespoons green cardamom pods
½ cup sugar, and possibly more
1 cup raisins
1 cup blanched almonds
2 cups brandy or aquavit

8 to 10 servings

1. Slice the orange across at about ⅜-inch intervals. Use a skewer to poke a few holes in the outer rind of each slice and insert cloves. Add to the wine, along with the cardamom, sugar, raisins, and almonds. You can do this well ahead of time.

2. Begin warming the wine slowly over a low flame. Stir and taste for sweetness; it shouldn't hit you as sour, so add sugar to get the right balance. When the wine is good and hot, stir in the brandy. Try to keep it well below the boiling point, if possible. Serve in mugs.

THE CAST-IRON COOKSTOVE

In hindsight, the nineteenth-century rise of the cast-iron cookstove seems inevitable. Scarcity of fuel and resulting high prices were pinching city dwellers all over Europe and North America. Iron-casting technologies were developing rapidly as the Industrial Revolution kicked into overdrive. Forward-thinking tinkerers like Benjamin Franklin and Count Rumford had already laid the technical groundwork decades before, although their paths were a bit too radical for immediate acceptance. But even though widespread change did not come in their lifetimes, these fireplace visionaries were ultimately very influential.

In the early nineteenth century, most Americans probably first encountered heating fires that were enclosed in stoves in workshops and in public places like schools and houses of worship. At sea, using a woodstove for cooking displayed immediately appreciable advantages; and thus ship owners seem to be in the vanguard of early adopters. Acceptance may have thus been strongest in locales with a strong maritime strain (admittedly that would be at least a section of most U.S. cities in 1830) populated as they were with many men and women for whom stove culture was already the norm at their places of employment.

Between 1840 and 1860, the revolution came. In one generation, cooks set aside their inheritance of accumulated knowledge and all their personal experience with open-fire technology in order to take up a new, very different, way. For every cook who touted the benefits of the cookstove — no more crouching in the hearth, and all those savings on fuel — there was another who bemoaned the loss of real cooking. Sure, a stove can boil and steam many foods at once, but what about a crisp-coated savory roast and springy deep-crusted real bread? Putting aside spit-roasting and brick-oven-baking was not an easy sacrifice for many cooks and eaters; their palates told them that open fire and masonry were (and still are) the best media for certain types of cooking.

Nineteenth-century cooking trends reflect the strengths of the cookstove, where a variety of stovetop cookery may be done all at once using one enclosed fire. It's no problem to simultaneously cook chicken and dumplings, Boston brown bread, a variety of vegetables, a pot of applesauce, and a steamed pudding, all on the surface of a good-sized cookstove. A glance at any woodstove-era cookbook shows a real proliferation of these recipes.

The oven of the cookstove was a perennial weak link. The butt of much criticism, it was the feature most frequently characterized as "improved" in the promotional literature. Cooks made do as best they could, and were helped in that regard by the new chemical leavenings. Soda-leavened breads and cakes were not much worse baked in a cookstove oven than in a brick oven. And since cornbread or biscuits are best hot and fresh, it made sense to cooks to whip up a pan once or twice daily, in lieu of baking yeasted bread once or twice weekly in the much more capacious old brick oven. Also a great variety of griddlecakes served to fill in the gap, taking advantage of the stove's prodigious cooking surface as well as the new leavenings.

And some big changes in kitchen technology and home economy were entirely predicated on the existence of the cookstove. For example, after the middle of the century, home canning and other kinds of large-scale domestic preserving took off, a development unthinkable without a heavy-duty level cooking surface fed with constant heat.

As time passed, cookstove manufacturers marketed refinements and attachments meant to compensate for the stove's deficits when compared to hearth-cooking. Easily my favorite is a large oblong grill, designed to take the place of the two lids that sit directly over the firebox. Spectacular hardwood coals and even a little flame provide an unparalleled indoor grilling experience. No matter how infernally hot and sizzly you get it, all the smoke just draws down into the body of the stove and out the chimney, no overhead ventilation needed!

Acquiring a Cookstove

If you happen to have a spare flue in your house (or are planning a new house), a wood-burning cookstove is a very worthwhile investment. It has tremendous cooking capacity with its large surface area and serious thermal output. It can bring so much more possibility to your cooking life than an ordinary gas or, heaven forbid, electric range. And how else can one have the satisfaction of simultaneously steaming a pudding, warming the kitchen, reducing maple sap to syrup, heating wash water in a reservoir, grilling pork chops, and making an omelet all with one little fire?

I must admit that I had always thought that firing up a woodstove in the middle of the house in summer would necessarily be dreadful. Indeed, many nineteenth-century cookstoves migrated to porches and cellar kitchens for several months each year in an attempt to keep houses cool. But careful use of dampers by the cook can go a long way to dumping all the heat that is not used directly on the stove's cooktop up the chimney. On one of the hottest days of last August, I walked into a kitchen where tomatoes were being reduced to sauce on the back of a beautiful 1880s cookstove and was surprised to find that the kitchen's ambient temperature was still somehow cooler than outdoors. The cook, Skip Mull, who also happens to be a crackerjack restorer of cast-iron cookstoves, showed me with a flick of his wrist exactly which damper to slide where to effect that magic.

Which brings me to the bottom line: When you get your woodstove, you will be many months in becoming its expert and companion. If you buy it from a restorer like Skip, you should be able to benefit by that person's experience at the

outset. In time, though, it will be you who understands your cast-iron friend's moods and capitalizes on its strengths.

In selecting an antique stove, consider that buying a popular model built by one of the big manufacturers will make it easier to find replacement parts and essential "optional" add-ons, like a grill. If budget is a concern, be aware that the cost of re-nickeling all those bright-shiny gewgaws can really add up; don't neglect more understated models that may cook as well as their glamour-puss cousins. Above all, pay attention to the state of the oven's guts. It's crucial that cracked castings be replaced. Restorer Skip Mull told me that he likes to start out working with at least three versions of any stove that he intends to sell. If he's lucky he ends up with one Grade A beauty, one perfectly functional but less resplendent model, and one picked-over carcass. The mint edition goes for big money, someone like me buys the Grade B unit, and he hangs onto the cannibalized remains for parts for the next batch.

What about a new one? For many years, very few manufacturers worldwide were still making and marketing wood-fired cookstoves. As of the first decade of the twenty-first century, however, the customer once again faces a wide selection of radically different types of wood-fired cookstoves and ovens. From traditional "solid-fuel cookers" like the English Aga to ultra-modern versions of the Northern European masonry stove to boxy and businesslike, welder-fabricated North American brands, a broad range of aesthetic and price-point choices are available today with a quick web search. In most cases, these stoves have been utterly redesigned for greater efficiency, safety, and bakeability, and will operate quite differently from their nineteenth-century forebears.

One last option: the barrel oven and stove are clever do-it-yourself riffs on the wood-fired stove and are especially popular in South America. A metal barrel serves as the cooking chamber; it is built into a clay mortar base and casing. This unit's advantages are efficiency and quick preheating. Since the food is isolated from the fire, it is not baking in retained heat as in most masonry wood-fired ovens. The clay enclosure does retain some heat, and helps keep the temperature of the chamber steady, but firing is done from a firebox below. (See Resources, page 309.)

Recipes for the Cookstove

Since the functioning of our modern gas and electric kitchen stovetops flowed from their wood-burning ancestor, it should be no surprise to find that you can transfer your favorite recipes pretty literally. Just for kicks I'll pass on a few tasty dishes from the woodstove's mid-nineteenth-century American heyday.

CORN OYSTERS

This treasured recipe is a late-summer rite of passage. My dear friend and neighbor Marion Crocker learned it during her childhood in Pennsylvania German country. Nineteenth-century cookbooks sometimes dubbed these Artificial Oysters, which today sounds just a little bit alarming.

2 eggs, separated
2 cups corn pulp (grated from tender fresh ears)
2 tablespoons flour
½ teaspoon salt
¼ teaspoon pepper
Butter for frying

4 servings

1. Lightly beat the egg yolks in a medium mixing bowl. Add the corn pulp, flour, salt, and pepper, and mix well.

2. In another bowl, whip the egg whites until they form firm peaks. Fold into batter without deflating.

3. Heat a griddle or frying pan over medium flame. Rub with butter and fry oyster-sized lumps of the batter until brown. Drain on a cooling rack in a warm place.

More Gear

BROILED FILET OR PORTERHOUSE WITH MAITRE D'HOTEL BUTTER

Maitre d'hotel butter was one of the few compositions from the professional French chef's repertoire simple enough to cross the line into American home cooking. A century and a half ago, it was the go-to accompaniment for tender grilled beefsteak, and it's still fabulous today.

Period recommendations were to cut steaks a minimum of ¾ of an inch thick, or up to twice as thick if preferred. Nineteenth-century cooks did not share the modern love for (some might say obsession with) grill marks on food, and did their best to avoid them. They might encase lamb chops in paper, or turn a filet mignon every ten seconds in an effort to keep the meat from getting those telltale lines. Although I don't particularly care about grill marks, I am otherwise a product of my own times, and I do like a good sear on meat. My drill is to set it on a clean, super-hot grill and not touch it until turning in 4 or 5 minutes, and then, after a similar interval on the B-side, to remove it to a hot platter for a brief rest before serving.

Naturally, you needn't have a cookstove to make this; any sort of grill or gridiron over hardwood coals will do.

4 thick (1½ inch) tenderloin steaks or 1 massive porterhouse
2 ounces (4 tablespoons) butter, soft
1 tablespoon lemon juice
1 tablespoon finely minced shallot (optional)
1 tablespoon very finely minced parsley leaves
Kosher or sea salt
Freshly ground black pepper

4 servings

1. Let the beef come to room temperature while you cultivate a bed of very hot coals, and then preheat a clean grill over it.

2. Mash the butter in a small bowl with the lemon juice, shallot, parsley, and plenty of salt and pepper to taste.

3. Salt and pepper the steaks all over. Place on the very hot grill of your woodstove (or any very hot grill), and cook to desired doneness, turning once with tongs. (Feel free to experiment with the every-ten-seconds technique if you have filets.) Let rest on a hot platter for 3 to 5 minutes. Spread with the compound butter, and serve. If you have a porterhouse, carve so that each diner receives some each of the loin and tenderloin.

BOSTON BROWN BREAD

This bread was a by-product of the woodstove. New England's staple brick-oven-baked brown bread disappeared when homeowners far and wide stopped up their cooking flues with woodstoves. Folks took advantage of the stove's steam-producing strengths and adapted the mixture to cook like a steamed pudding. Even though steamed brown bread uses chemical leavening, it still wants long cooking to develop its full deliciousness, just as the earlier brown bread took many hours of baking (see chapter 5).

Use coffee, juice, or large tomato cans as molds. (Smaller ones are cute and cook in less time, but it just takes a lot of them.) Whatever size they are, fill them just ⅔ full.

---

2 cups (9 ounces) whole rye flour
2 cups (11 ounces) medium or coarse corn meal
1 cup (4½ ounces) whole-wheat flour
2 teaspoons salt
1 teaspoon baking soda
3 cups milk or combination of milk, water, and plain yogurt
⅓ cup molasses

Depending on your molds, makes 2 or more loaves

---

1. Get out a large pot, and fit it with a rack. (Make sure that the molds will fit in, with a little room around and over.) Add water, just covering the rack, and set the pot on to boil. While you're at it, fill a teakettle and put it on to boil as well (you'll need more hot water to replenish the steamer from time to time later).

2. Lightly butter your molds. Cut little squares of foil to serve as lids.

3. In one large bowl, whisk together the dry ingredients; in a separate bowl, whisk together the liquids. Stir the liquid into the dry with a fork or spatula, just until no dry spots remain, and scrape the mixture into the molds, filling about ⅔ full. Put the foil on top and crimp down smooth along the outside of the cans. Place in the steamer, and keep at a simmer for at least 3 hours; 4 hours makes a better bread. (Less time for teeny molds — say an hour or so for tomato paste cans.) Do not neglect to add boiling water every 30 minutes or so, because it *will* boil away.

4. Take the tins out of the steamer carefully with mitts, and place on a rack to cool 10 minutes, without the foil lid. After the rest period, pick up each can and shake it back and forth a bit; the bread will loosen up from the edges. Then shake it out of the can gently onto the rack to cool completely. (If the bread absolutely refuses to come out, use a can opener to remove the bottom, and give it a shove.) Brown bread slices most cleanly when cool.

SMOKE

Smokiness — treasured by today's grill and barbeque cooks — has been a general and mostly inevitable flavorant in foods from cooking's birth until its relatively recent divorce from wood-burning. The desirability of that smoke flavor has not exactly been a constant in human taste, probably because of that very ubiquity.

Most refined cooking of early modern Europe, for example, eschewed smoke-scented foods, associated as they were with the diets of coarse country people. Dainty foods poached or sautéed over a discreet charcoal fire in a *potager* denoted wealth and refinement in a way that smoked ham-based pea soup cooked in an iron kettle on a hearth fire did not. Rustics had to eat their smoky food and like it; a striving bourgeois housewife took care that her roast did not spatter into the fire and impart that low-life telltale odor.

But aside from flavor considerations, smoke has long been understood to act as a preservative. How long is hard to say since the act of smoking food leaves a scant and easily obliterated archaeological record. A rare exception is a Paleolithic site along the Nile where archaeologists found abundant remains of processed (headless) small fish in the vicinity of several shallow charcoal-filled pits These hearths were even flanked by post molds showing where industrious fish smokers had installed their wooden racks some 13,000 years ago.

Prehistorically, the smoking of foods — first fish, then meat, and then dairy products is a likely global sequence — was very widespread, and was an extrapolation from the prerequisite understanding that desiccation retards spoilage. These techniques permitted the preservation of protein when it was available in abundance, a boon to the diets of hunter-gatherers and settled farmers alike. Temperate, clammy regions fostered an especial dependence on smoking as a preservation technique: places with wood to burn, fish to catch, and not much hope of sun or air alone being effective drying agents. Whereas desert dwellers might just set out on their roofs a rack of meat strips, a string of fish, or a basket of yogurt, the cooks in a humid clime could not count on the elements alone to dry their food. Sheltering the food from the weather and applying smoke did not just compensate for the ambient moisture; these additional steps, of course, produced a distinctive result. Thousands of years later, some of these damp locales — Scandinavia, the Pacific Northwest, and Japan, for example — still identify with smoke as their local flavor.

The earliest accounts of Europeans visiting the Americas suggest that one common thread running through the extraordinarily varied culinary habits of the native peoples of two continents was an expertise in smoking fish and meat, both with and without salt. When fish and shellfish were abundant in summer on the Massachusetts coast, for example, Wampanoag people would remove to the shore to fish and set up a preservation operation. Unsalted seafood, from herring to bass to lobster, had to be smoked until it was very, very dry and packed away carefully in order to last as a winter provision. A couple thousand miles south, Spaniards described Maya cooks roasting and reroasting haunches of meat on racks high above fires (the famous *barbacoas*). The resulting foodstuff was rock hard, but lasted, even in a hot, humid climate; it was reconstituted by boiling. In case we're feeling smug about the vast variety of foods available to us today, it's humbling to read about the tremendous spectrum of preserved fish that was available in the average Maya market five hundred years ago, not to mention the smoked tapir and manatee on offer.

Getting Started

Smoking, like most culinary processes, can be made as easy or as complex as you have a mind to make it. I've come to prefer the former, having in the past engaged in the protracted brining and smoking process required for curing large bone-in hams. Today, most of the smoking I do is much lighter-duty, requiring only the briefest of brinings, and an hour or two in the smoker. It is almost always a surprise activity, brought on by a windfall of wonderful fresh fish. Unlike the smokers of old, I'm into it just for the special flavor and texture, and the fun of doing it; my results could scarcely be called preserved at all. Although they do hold up perfectly in the fridge for a good week, most often they disappear too quickly to be sure!

COLD SMOKING

Preservation through cold smoking requires that foods first be thoroughly salt-cured, and then subjected to a long stretch of 70 to 90°F smoke carried out during cool weather. A firebox remote from the smoking chamber helps to keep the temperature down.

Hot smoking can be done any time of year using a smoker with an attached firebox. The foods are treated to a flow of smoky air between 130 and 180°F. Although delicious, these smoked foods are not "preserved," and must be kept refrigerated and used soon.

Efficient smoking demands a covered chamber in which the food to be smoked is laid out or hung up, and a separate firebox. The firebox must have a vent through which it draws in air and a connecting tube through which the smoke exits the firebox and enters the food chamber, which itself must be furnished with a vent for the smoke to finally exit the whole shebang. All of these vents should be adjustable, to control the flow of oxygen to the fire, and the draft, throughout.

The chamber and firebox may be contiguous if you plan to hot smoke just to create flavor and texture. This simple technique is a great entry into the world of smoking, producing some tremendous results with very little fuss. Different times and temperatures create different results; experiment with the ingredients that come to hand to find the smoking style you enjoy. Adhere to basic food-safety principles (use fresh ingredients, keep them clean, and don't let them linger needlessly in the temperature danger zone of 40 to 140°F). How smoky and how dry you like the product is up to you. Remember, these foods are not preserved, just cooked in a smoky atmosphere at low temperature. Enjoy right away or wrap and refrigerate and use within a week.

Choosing Wood for Smoking

Around the world, different smoking traditions hold certain woods absolutely indispensible for an authentic product. Naturally, these subjective tastes are based on the reality of terroir: I suggest that you establish your own products based on your own local reality. For us, that's oak, apple, maple, and sassafras. (I know, sassafras is supposed to be toxic to ingest. But really, isn't *all* smoke toxic? Everyone will have to decide for themselves about the risks inherent in eating a sassafras-smoked scallop . . .)

Classic are fruitwoods, vine cuttings, oak, hickory, chestnut, maple, beech, ash, or alder. Cut and split the wood into smallish chunks and store in a "special" place so it doesn't accidentally land in a campfire.

Hot-Smoking Tips

I generally use a wood-burning roaster/smoker with an offset firebox. The modest rack area allows me to smoke two huge bluefish fillets or about two pounds of scallops or enough pork belly to kill us. When I have more, I just count myself lucky and smoke it in batches.

I brine most foods before smoking to improve flavor, texture, and appearance. With sturdy, bulky foods like turkey or pork, an overnight brining is helpful. The brining time of fin fish can be measured in minutes, but it has a distinct effect, slightly tightening the texture and helping create that lovely mahogany-tinged semigloss finish. I skip this treatment altogether with shellfish, since it seems to come out of the shell already briny and firms up perfectly in the smoke without any help from me.

To make brine: dissolve 1 cup kosher salt in every 2 quarts cold water. Optionally, you may add ¼ cup sugar (which will deepen the color) and some flavoring if you are inclined, like a jot of soy sauce, some juniper berries, or a bay leaf. (Personal confession: unless I'm making a brine that is intended as a real cure, like for cold-smoked bacon, I just wing it by stirring salt in cold water until it tastes as briny as the mouthful of freezing-cold ocean I inevitably swallow each time I go body surfing.)

After brining, fish, especially, will need time to air-dry before greeting the smoke. Leave an hour to be on the safe side.

About 30 minutes before smoking time, make a fire in the firebox of the smoker. Make sure all the vents and dampers are open. Use the usual sort of tinder and light wood until you get a stable blaze, and then add some small pieces of hardwood. When they have caught, close the covers of the smoking chamber and the firebox. Observe as your first pieces of hardwood burn. You need to have some viable coals underlying smoke production, so make sure of them. Close the air intake vents until the fire is still burning, but not a raging inferno.

When you are ready to smoke, damp the vents down more, and add a couple chunks of your favorite wood. See that they smolder, not ignite. Combustion can be slowed by dipping the wood briefly in water before adding it to the fire, or further reducing the oxygen at the entry. Observe the smoke emerging from the exit vent of the smoking chamber. It need not be copious; subtlety is key. If you are able to check the temperature in the smoking chamber, look for 160 to 180°F. I like the hot end of that spectrum, and I generally find that I get the result I want in somewhere between 1 and 2 hours.

FIRING UP THE SMOKER

1. Start a small fire in the offset firebox. You can use pine or other softwood shavings to get it going, but make sure they are entirely burned away before you introduce food.

2. Have all the vents wide open to establish a good fire.

3. Add a few pieces of hardwood to establish a little coal bed.

4. When you're ready to smoke, start adding chunks of your "tastiest" wood, close down the intake vent, and pop in the food.

SMOKED FISH

Here are a few particulars. Experiment for yourself to find what you like best.

FINFISH

1. Scale, clean, and fillet the fish. Leave the skin on the fillets, but pluck out any bones you perceive.

2. Brine the fish for about 30 minutes, then allow at least an equivalent length of time for drying. Shake off the brine. Dab with a paper towel, and then lay the fillets skin side down to let the upper surface dry naturally. I usually put the fish on cookie racks at this point, and leave them on through the whole process; it makes handling easier and keeps the fish nice and clean and intact. Drying may be advanced with an electric fan.

VARIATION FOR SMALL FISH

Pound 1 teaspoon coriander seed and 1 teaspoon black peppercorns coarsely in a mortar. Add 1 tablespoon kosher salt and 1 teaspoon organic sugar, and 2 tablespoons cold water. Brush on 6 fillets: mackerel or tiny bonito or other super-fresh small fish fillets. After 45 minutes blot with a paper towel without removing spices; dry on rack in a cool breeze in the shade.

SCALLOPS

1. Arrange shucked scallops on cookie racks, and then set the racks on baking pans that fit in the smoker. (Keeps them clean and gives an added layer of security. The only downside is that this apparatus needs a good hot soapy scrubbing after.)

2. Smoke around 180°F until they're the way you want them.

SMOKED TURKEY

This turkey slices beautifully for sandwiches for a very lucky crowd.

1 (12- to 14-pound) turkey, split
  Brine made with 1 cup kosher salt and ½ cup
  sugar per gallon cool water

20 to 30 Servings

1. Submerge turkey in brine. Keep chilled overnight.

2. Smoke at around 190 to 200°F until internal temperature registers 175°F in the thigh joint (in the neighborhood of 3 to 4 hours). Wrap and chill.

PORK BELLY OR JOWL MEAT

Slice the finished pork in thick slabs, and serve it hot from the smoker, accompanied by a crispy pungent salad and a smear of hoisin sauce. (Keep a defibrillator handy.) Leftovers are the best foundation for fried rice, ever.

1 pound pork belly or hog jowl
2 cups cool water
½ cup kosher salt
¼ cup sugar
4 star anise, lightly crushed
1 small dried hot chile
1 tablespoon toasted sesame oil
1 tablespoon canola oil

8 Servings

1. If the pork belly has skin on it (which I prefer), use a very sharp knife to cut a shallow gridwork (at ¼-inch intervals) through the outer rind. (A utility razor knife works great.) Put the meat in a storage container.

2. Stir the water, salt, sugar, star anise, and chile together until the salt is dissolved. Pour onto the pork, seal, and chill 4 to 8 hours.

3. Remove the pork from the brine, quickly rinse, and pat very dry with paper towels. Place on a rack, brush skin with the combination of oils, and smoke at around 180°F for about 3 hours. Repeat the oiling every now and again.

BARBEQUE, TWO WAYS

Essentially barbequing is defined as protracted low-temperature roasting, usually of whole animals or large cuts of meat, and usually on a metal grate, over wood coals. Any meat that is suitable for grilling — quickly cooking at high temperature on a grate over wood coals — would be silly to barbeque; it would be like boiling a lamb chop. That eliminates tender and lean cuts, but indicates the fatty sinewy meat that requires low slow cooking to break down tough bits and melt fat, like pork shoulder or beef brisket.

Our first approach to barbeque will be as it was waged before the metal-fabricating revolution of the mid-twentieth century, as an open-pit super-slow-roasting business, and will seem very familiar after our late experiments in chapter 2 with spits and grills. Then we'll use a purpose-built wood-burning smoker/roaster.

Practicalities of Pit Barbeque

Quite like spit-roasting, pit barbeque requires the manufacturing of coals and the manipulation of the distance between those coals and the meat. Unlike most spit-roasting, though, barbeque usually calls for the cooking of the meat past the point of doneness to near disintegration. The challenge is to keep the temperature low so that the meat doesn't externally char before that tenderness is reached, all without drying the meat out.

The "pit" can be an actual depression dug into the ground — I use a foot-plus-deep stone-lined oval hole in my yard that started life as a clambake pit. Some old-timey pros and dedicated amateurs build permanent above-ground cement block enclosures to corral the burning wood and support the grates.

As well as the depth and area of the pit, the gauge of the grating must be scaled to size of the food to be cooked, from pretty wispy for some racks of ribs to

Barbeque, Two Ways

extra heavy-duty for an ox. If it is a whole animal (the norm for festive barbeques in the past), the carcass is splayed open and seasoned. Because of the weight of the meat and its descending level of body integrity over time, turning the carcass is done once, several hours into the cooking; thereafter it becomes impossible.

Initially a hardwood fire is burned in the pit to form the starting coals; a subsidiary fire is needed nearby to supply coals for replenishing the pit over the hours that the meat is cooking. When setting up your pit, plan exactly where you will burn this extra fire. While this may not be traditional, I've had success with building a sort of a coal dispenser into one end of my pit; I took a foot-diameter heavy steel pipe, about 2½ feet long, and set it on a brick and angle iron support so that coals from a fire in the cylinder would drop down into the pit as they formed. It's definitely more efficient than just an open fire down one end of the pit or nearby, and it's child's play to rake the coals here and there as needed. (Plus it was fun to see my beloved old steel tannur succeed in a new guise.)

The Wood

The type of hardwood you burn will have an effect on the flavor of your barbeque. If you have a special stash of, say, hickory or apple with which you'd like to experiment, use it early in the process. That's when the meat is most susceptible to picking up its nuances.

Mostly I use oak, since I live in an oak forest. It seems silly to me to use fuel "from away" when I go to the trouble to acquire local foods to eat.

The Temperature

This is not mysterious. Water boils at 212°F. If you can cook something a shade under that temperature, it will stay more succulent than if you boil all the moisture out of it. That's why barbeque takes so long, and why it's so darned good.

The internal temperature of the meat will have reached "done" long before it becomes barbeque. It's all that extra time in the low heat after it's cooked, strictly speaking, that matters. Let your own taste on the chewiness/tenderness spectrum be your guide. Make notes for next time.

The Seasonings

As excited as people get about this topic, it is my feeling that applied seasonings run a distant third in determining the outcome of your project.

The quality of the meat and the righteousness of the technique, above all, are what make this stuff worth doing. The rest is hype and marketing. History shows that a lot can be achieved with a little red and black pepper and salt and then a dash of vinegar.

BACK-TO-BASICS SPARERIBS

Spareribs are composed of thin layers of stringy meat, connective tissue, and fat, layered and wrapped around bones. Thinking about your own ribs, and how they work when you breathe and move, may help you understand why this might be a tough cut.

While cooking ribs well is a challenge, handling something of their size is not. Therefore they are a good way to set about gaining some basic understanding of the principles of barbeque before you move on to something unwieldy and high stakes.

Use this as an introductory pit barbeque project and take notes on what you do and how you like the result. Then repeat, changing a variable to see what happens. A few experiments along these lines will give you the confidence to progress to more challenging and time-consuming cuts, including the pork shoulder, which was heaven-sent for barbeque, and eventually perhaps a whole animal.

RIBS

- 2 full racks spareribs (not back ribs, which being just pork chop bones, are tender enough to just grill)
- 2 teaspoons cumin seeds
- 2 teaspoons coriander seeds
- 2 teaspoons peppercorns
- 1 teaspoon kosher salt
- 2 cloves garlic
- Half of your beer

SAUCE

- ¼ cup ketchup, homemade preferably
- 2 tablespoons cider vinegar
- 1 teaspoon hot pepper sauce
- ½ teaspoon prepared mustard
- Freshly ground hot pepper

Serves 4, with appropriate sides

1. Remove the flat membrane that runs inside the ribs. Poke a small pointy knife under the cut edge of the membrane where it runs over one of the rib bones. Poke a chopstick under there, following the bone and separating the membrane as you go. Pull steadily to remove, and discard.

2. Pound the cumin, coriander, and peppercorns together in a mortar. Add the salt and garlic and reduce to a crumbly powder. Rub all over both sides of the ribs. Fold them up and set in a resealable container. Chill till needed (1 to 3 hours).

3. Arrange a fire pit so that your grill may be suspended 10 to 12 inches above the coals; be ready to make adjustments and refinements as the situation develops. Burn a hardwood fire there for about an hour. Start your secondary fire, too.

4. Take your fire shovel and remove any burning wood from the cooking spot; leave behind only glowing coals. Set the grate up, and wait for the dust to settle before laying out the ribs.

5. Keep a sharp eye on things at the beginning. If it looks like you're grilling the meat, that means the situation is too hot. You want to be able to have them on the fire for 4 hours or so, so calibrate your cooking thus by adjusting the amount of coals or, more

effectively, the distance between the meat and the heat. Move the ribs so that they are not directly over the coals, but rather offset to them, and bathed in the smoke and heat wafting from the fire.

6. Because I like to share, I usually pour half a beer into a bowl and brush some of it on the ribs every 30 minutes or so. You can add some aromatics, like some garlic or onion or ginger or a bay leaf if you want to get fancy. The idea is mostly to keep the superficial moisture level up.

7. If you've done your work well, the ribs won't have to come off the grill for three to four hours. The meat will draw back from the bones and look and smell very appetizing. Longer cooking will render it tenderer, to a point; the idea is to get it when the connective tissue has softened and the fat has melted and basted it, but before desiccation sets in.

8. Some people like to offer sauces only at the table, but I admit that I like to apply a modest sauce for the

More Gear

last 15 minutes or so on the grill, so that there's a bit of penetration and caramelization over the low, low heat. Stir together sauce ingredients in a pan and warm it up on the grill. Brush on ribs when hot and leave on grill until absorbed, flipping to get both sides. Transfer racks to cutting board, slice into individual ribs and serve on a hot platter.

VARIATION: SMOKED RIBS

The methods of an earlier era of barbeque still deliver great results when undertaken with skill and care, but a lot of wood is burned in the process. It's probably the inefficiency, plus the fact that it's a long and demanding project, that makes it so rare to see people barbequing in an open pit today. Over the last half-century, barbeque lovers have developed an arsenal of gear designed to reduce the fuel, time, and, dare I say it, the skill, needed to deliver exceptional barbeque — to cook these challenging meats until they balance tenderness and resistance and are delicious through and through.

If pit barbeque is slow roasting with a lot of concomitant smoke, covered barbeque more resembles smoking at low-roast temperatures. This subtle shift results from the fuel-saving technical change of the twentieth-century barbeque that came via the welder's torch: the enclosed firebox and cooking chamber. A metal cover creates a more oven-like atmosphere around the meat, trapping heat and tasty smoke under its dome. While it can have a pernicious effect used when grilling, a cover is a great help for barbeque, and attaches no shame, as long as the fuel is still wood.

Follow the recipe for pit-barbequed spareribs, but fire up the roaster/smoker as in the hot-smoked fish recipe (page 185). Aim to keep the temperature in the 200 to 210°F range for about 4 to 5 hours. Turn and baste every 30 minutes or so, just like in the open pit. You may find that you use a lot less wood than the pit method, and that it's easier to keep the meat from drying out. Sauce and serve as described previously, or as you like.

RETAINED HEAT

As wonderful as roasting before an open fire is, it is simply not the best method for all foods. Sometime in deep prehistory, the technical range of cooks was broadened by the understanding that heat can be stored in something as basic as a rock, then deployed culinarily.

Long before the development of ceramic or metal vessels, the idea of retained heat, made real in the form of hot stones, permitted the simmering of foods in convenient but non-flameproof containers such as hides, stomachs, and wooden or bark boxes. This technique lives on today in the form of the Mongol khorkhog, where heated river stones are layered into a container — for millennia the stomach of an animal, today a sealable milk can — with mutton or goat meat, vegetables, and water.

Entirely taken for granted today, simmering allowed humans to derive nourishment and enjoyment from bones, sinews, hard seeds, fibrous roots, and many other foods that need softening or rendering to be edible.

But what about occasions when ancient cooks faced truly massive cooking operations? Retained heat to the rescue again. For millennia, the pit or earth oven, a precursor to the retained heat masonry oven, allowed cooks to tackle the biggest tasks, according to archaeological evidence from the Pecos River to the Ukraine to the Indus Valley to North Africa. These were *big* tasks, like baking a gigantic heap of agave plants or (seriously) a mammoth.

Current pit-cooking practices from the South Pacific Islands to the Yucatan Peninsula to New England, complemented by documentary material and oral histories, hint at the range of techniques and materials involved over centuries as cooks have fired up a hole in the ground and cooked in the residual heat.

UNDERGROUND INSPIRATION FROM AROUND THE WORLD

Probably the best-known examples of earth ovens originate in the South Pacific among peoples of Papua New Guinea, Fiji, and the Polynesian Islands. There are many subtle variations in the general Pacific Islander school of pit-baking. One common method involves balancing all the stones to be heated atop a huge hardwood pyre before starting the fire — all the fuel and the rocks are stacked up together in a shallow pit and set alight. It's a dramatic technique that advantageously leaves some very hot rocks available to actually stick inside the hard-to-cook parts of whole animal carcasses before they get buried in the steamy leaf-lined pit.

Kalua Pig

Kalua pig is certainly the most familiar of these earth-oven treatments in the United States. The fire is made as just described in a pit called an *imu*, and burned until all that is left is a pile of glowing rocks. Banana tree stalks and leaves and *ti* leaves are variously readied to create steam and enclose and protect the food.

The kalua pig is a living part of the culture of the Hawaiian people, as well as a staple of the tourist luau. It is both performance and celebration, and offers an indelible sense of place. The more I thought about earth ovens, the more this thread came back to me. The basic idea, pit, rocks, fire, pig — could happen almost anywhere. Even the celebratory/touristic nature of pit cooking seems an inevitable part of the package. It's the plant matter — in this case, ti leaves and banana stalks — that offers the sense of locality and really set it apart.

Without those plants, it's impossible to make an "authentic" kalua pig. Sure, these days I could probably have ti leaves overnighted to my door, but that really defeats the idea behind these simplest of foods, which were invented by good cooks who made the very best of the particular situations they were dealt.

But is it foolish to create a Cape Cod kalua? Our temperate New England plants and trees just don't make leaves on a tropical scale: fleshy, juicy, and large and sturdy enough to wrap and protect food. But the native pit-cooking tradition of my own region points the way via the clambake. The ocean provides perfect steam-creating buffering plants in heaps — seaweed is the banana tree of my terroir.

By following the principles of the Pacific Island earth oven, we should all be able to bring some of the excitement of underground cooking into our lives. Adapting the technique to local ingredients and conditions can be half the fun.

Retained Heat

The Maya Pib

It may seem pretentious of me to think of adapting a tradition in this way, but I am not the first. Another classic earth oven is the Maya *pib*. The first people who brought that idea to the Yucatan were bummed to find no suitable stones for pit cooking. Instead of giving up the idea as "inauthentic" to the place, they "made" stones for the purpose out of clay. Archaeologists have discovered oodles of fist-size lumps of fired clay which bear the molecular imprint of repeated heatings in the presence of various foodstuffs, including corn and squash. These finds hint at the latitude of items which may have gotten the pib treatment.

Today, the most famous pib dish is *cochinita pibil* (literally, "little pig cooked in a pit"), usually described in tourist literature as a primordial pre-Columbian food. But everything about this dish, even in its most "authentic" form, displays a brilliant sort of evolution, an ongoing fusion, starting with its half-Spanish, half-Mayan name. When the Spanish arrived with their European hogs, what had once been a preparation for wild peccary was applied to this domestic meat.

The paste smeared on the pig is still redolent of both the Mayan and Spanish kitchens — the Central American *achiote*, or annatto, and allspice pounded with European garlic and citrus. The traditional accompaniments, too, are bicultural — the small corn tortillas of the Yucatan paired with salads of European vegetables: crisp cabbage and wilted onion.

So if this clearly "inauthentic" food can be so wonderful to eat, I am encouraged to apply clambake techniques to "a little pig" next summer and see what comes of it. At least I won't have to make my own rocks.

Cocido das Furnas

And, to close these musings, consider the most exciting underground cooking fire of all — magma from a nearby volcano. Cooks on the Azorean island of San Miguel layer various cuts of pork, beef, and chicken, with cabbage, kale, potatoes, and sausages in huge kettles, and slide them into steamy silos for a six-hour spell by the sulfurous shores of Furnace Lake. The resulting stew, *cocido das furnas*, is a local adaptation of the Iberian favorite mixed meat and vegetable dish. But volcanic gases supply the defining mystery ingredient in place of smoky steaming vegetation.

And rather like the clambake and all the rest of the surviving subterranean cooking traditions, the performance is part of the dish, in a hygienic reenactment for tourists of what was once purely a celebratory mode of marking a festive occasion. But, unlike those traditions, this is one that the rest of us can't just try at home, unless we too happen to live near a convenient steam vent.

THE EARTH OVEN:
COOKING IN A HOLE IN THE GROUND

There's something very exciting about digging into the ground and finding a pip-
ing hot, absolutely delicious meal, even if you are the one who placed the raw
materials down in the hole to begin with. If you've closed things up properly,
there's no aroma, and in some cases, not even any steam or other clue to the magic
that is taking place underground.

Here are a few traditional earth-oven favorites. Once you have tried one or
two, you may want to invent your own.

A Lobster Bake

In the last century or so, commercial operators in the southern New England
clambaking heartland have nestled quite a range of foods under the tarp with
the shellfish — great racks of potatoes, onions, sweet potatoes, linguica, chicken
quarters, fish fillets, sweet corn, whole eggs, and poultry stuffing, to name a few.
Now, one problem with this panoply, beside the loss of focus on the shellfish, will
be obvious to anyone who has ever cooked these items: it takes ten minutes to
cook some of them and an hour to cook others, yet there they all are in the same
sauna together.

It is therefore satisfying to strip away all extraneous matter and get back to
basics. Excluding all but the essentials makes kitchen preparation nonexistent,
keeping everyone outside by the fire and having fun. It also means that advance
planning is kept to the joyous activities of gathering seaweed from the shore and
digging a hole and lining it with stones. Most importantly, this technique surely
produces the most delicious lobster ever eaten.

You may scale down to two lobsters or up to a hundred, but the proportions
I'm giving here will comfortably accommodate 10 to 12.

Advance Preparations

Go to the shore and collect two 5-gallon buckets of seaweed. Rockweed, which
has nice moisture-holding bubbles, is the preferred type but it is not essential.
I like to rinse each clump of seaweed in sea water as I pick it up, swishing away
clinging sand. Keep it moist until zero-hour. If you are unsure about where to get
rockweed, discuss it with the person from whom you are acquiring your lobsters;
it is often used to pack and ship them.

Dig a pit and line its bottom and sides with more or less grapefruit-size stones.
Aim for a finished result about three feet in diameter and about a foot deep. (Scale
all these proportions up for a larger bake.)

The Earth Oven: Cooking in a Hole in the Ground

Six Hours before Dinnertime

Kindle a fire and gradually really stoke it up. You can burn a mixture of wood, but the majority should be hardwood. This type of fire is a good opportunity to clean up branches around the yard and get rid of big, odd-shaped, unsplittable chunks of wood ("logs of shame," a woodstove-owning friend calls them). It's also the kind of fire that pyromaniacs enjoy; there's no control-freak cook yelling at them to quit messing with it. The sole aim is to heat up the surrounding rocks and dirt, so there's no harm in building a big, exciting blaze.

Meanwhile, line up all the gear you'll need for the bake: your fire shovel, the seaweed (make sure it's still wet), the lobsters in a cooler under wet burlap, a pair of scissors, a dampened large clean sheet of cloth (like an old bedsheet), a cotton dropcloth, and then something more steamproof like a chunk of an old sail or, failing that, a vinyl tarp. We have also found a large solid object that fits over the pit (like an upside-down saucer-shaped commercial metal fire pit) to be handy, but not essential.

About Ninety Minutes before Dinnertime

Feed the fire for the last time with a good pile of small-diameter hardwood sticks. When these have burned down to smallish coals, everything should be standing by, ready to go. You'll want an extra pair of hands or two at this point — a great opportunity to involve your guests.

Work swiftly from this stage until the pit is covered. Get two helpers started with the scissors, snipping the rubber bands from the lobsters' claws. With your shovel or a rake, pull out any unburned wood or large embers that might remain in the fire. If any stones have fallen out of place, try to nudge them where they'll do the most good. Spread about three inches of seaweed on the pit evenly. Arrange the lobsters snugly in a single layer on the seaweed. Cover them with seaweed, and ring the whole pit with more seaweed. Fold the damp bedsheet into an arrangement that will cover the pit, and drape it over the whole pile. Follow with the drop cloth and whatever other steam barriers you may have devised. Last goes the vinyl tarp with some logs or other weights around the edges. Set your timer for one hour, have a refreshment, and relax.

(At this point, despite the dramatic tension of the buried lobsters, the emotional vim of your gathering may be subtly sapped by the disappearance of the fire. I recommend removing the large burning chunks you raked out of the pit to another location to start a new fire, if only for recreational purposes and for convenient disposal of lobster shells later.)

When your hour has elapsed, simply excavate, and enjoy. Have an old dishcloth handy to give each lobster a quick wipe before it goes on the plate. Even pre-swished seaweed is bound to shed some sand.

LOBSTER BAKE, STEP BY STEP

1. Start a big fire in a stone-lined pit about six hours before dinnertime. The beach location is splendid but optional; we've had many a fine bake in our woodland backyard.

2. Feed the fire aggressively for the last time about 90 minutes before dinnertime. Gather your ingredients, then rake out any wood, leaving a pit of super-hot stones and coals.

3. Working with alacrity, line the pit with about three inches of wet seaweed. Set on the lobsters, and a bag of clams if you like, in a single layer.

4. Pile on a lot more seaweed. Completely cover all the hot stones surrounding the pit.

CONTINUED ON NEXT PAGE

LOBSTER BAKE, <small>CONTINUED</small>

5. Cover with a damp cotton tarp or folded bed sheet.

6. Follow with whatever other steam barriers you have devised. Here we used a heavy canvas drop cloth, with a handy copper alloy "fire pit" for good measure.

7. Last, deploy your most moisture-proof layer — here a chunk of old sail — but a heavy tarp would do. Tack down the edges with firewood or rocks to seal in the steam.

8. Go swimming, eat hors d'oeuvres, or just lie in the sand and drink beer for an hour, then uncover the bake and enjoy.

Retained Heat

BEAN-HOLE BEANS

If you don't happen to live on the New England shore as I do, putting on a lobster bake may prove unjustifiably expensive and silly. But cooking underground need not be costly. One fun and delicious traditional application of this technique followed loggers all over the northern tier of North America — bean-hole beans. Essentially, logging camp cooks adapted the traditional staple of baked beans to the transient life by using an earth oven as a stand-in for the accustomed brick oven.

Bean-hole beans involve a long timetable, but the work is enjoyable and punctuated with long stretches of passive waiting. The beans are great for breakfast — all the work is long over by then, but for the excavation — and can't fail to provide a dramatic morning diversion for overnight guests.

You'll need a large cast-iron pot with a bail and a very snug-fitting lid. Consider explicitly how you will keep dirt from finding its way into this pot when it is buried. Heavy-duty foil can provide a helpful barrier. Some bean-hole devotees go so far as to have fabricated a steel lid that fits down an inch or two over the rim of the pot, completely protecting the contents from shifting sands and careless shovel work. (We have successfully used yet another cast-off part from a burnt-out Weber grill — the very light-duty aluminum ash-catcher that hangs beneath the lower vents — as a sort of a helmet placed upside-down over our securely lidded pot of beans.)

Prepare the bean-hole while the beans are soaking, or ahead, if you'd rather. Make a cylindrical pit, about three feet deep, about twice the diameter of your bean-kettle. Line the bottom and the perimeter of the lowest portion of the pit with stones. Make sure your pot will have plenty of elbow room.

There are a few other oddments you may want to have in hand. A long-handled hook of some sort is helpful for lowering in, and almost essential for hauling out, the pot. Gather some leafy material — ferns or bracken, tall grass or reeds or rushes — to pack over the pot.

The Earth Oven: Cooking in a Hole in the Ground

BEAN-HOLE BEANS

The following recipe features ingredients and proportions authentic to nineteenth-century usage. The finished beans are savory, brothy, and complex, flavored with, more than sweetened by, molasses. They are a revelation of essential beaniness, in terms of both texture and flavor, compared to the syrupy article usually on offer. Go out of your way to find good quality dry beans. Traditional for this purpose, and for good reason, are a few heirloom varieties with excellent flavor and texture: Jacob's Cattle, Yellow Eye, Soldier, and Marfax. Salt pork made at home, or by a trusted butcher, elevates these beans yet further.

2 pounds dry beans
½ teaspoon salt, or more
1 teaspoon freshly ground black pepper
1 teaspoon dry mustard (optional)
3 tablespoons molasses
1 medium onion
8–12 ounces salt pork

Serves 8

1. Twenty-four hours before you want to dig the beans up, rinse the dry beans and put in the pot you intend to bake them in. Cover them with abundant cool water and let soak for 4 to 8 hours.

2. About 18 hours before you wish to serve the beans, kindle a nice fire down in your prepared bean-hole. Starting a fire in a clammy narrow pit can be challenging, so make it easy for yourself by having plenty of nice dry tinder and kindling wood. Once it has caught, feed it to keep a steady moderate fire going for 5 or 6 hours.

3. Parboil the soaked beans. Add more water to the beans, if necessary, so that they have at least an inch of coverage. Place them over a medium flame and bring to a very gentle simmer. Cover and cook very gently until the skins of the beans wrinkle when you dredge up a few and blow on them. This generally takes at least an hour, the time required depending entirely on the age and quality of the beans.

4. Place the salt, pepper, optional mustard, and molasses in a small bowl. Ladle in some of the bean broth and stir to combine. Add the mixture back to the beans and stir well. Add the onion either chopped or whole. Cut into the rind of the salt pork in a cross-hatched pattern. Bury it just below the surface of the liquid. Heat over a low fire so that it is at a good simmer as it goes into the ground.

5. Meanwhile, gather everything you'll need to get the kettle cleanly into the hole and covered up (see page 203). If you plan to use a foil barrier under your pot lid, apply that now.

6. When all is in readiness, use a long shovel or fire tongs to pluck out any large chunks of unburned wood remaining. Push smaller coals and embers to the perimeter of the pit, so that the kettle will rest securely upright at the bottom. Carefully lower it in so that it rests in the center. If you are using some sort of protective helmet like our Weber ash catcher or something of your own devising, deploy that now. Quickly pack the plant material rather loosely all around and over the pot. We add a layer of wooden clapboards at this point, and then cover with earth, mounding it up as necessary.

7. Let the beans cook at least 12 hours; longer is fine in our experience. When you dig it up, try to be mindful of the dirt at each turn. Carefully avoid disturbing your protective barriers prematurely. A small hand broom is helpful.

8. As good as these beans are right away, they're even better reheated if there are any left over.

Retained Heat

THE MASONRY OVEN

The wood-fired masonry oven, at only a few thousand years old, is a relative newcomer. The general type of oven familiar to us today came to us via classical Greece and Rome; its design driven by the baking needs of risen loaves of bread. The griddle and the tannur are all very well for flatbreads, but the front-loading vaulted oven allows for the slower, even heat required for the vast family of breads descended from the risen loaves of antiquity. This particular oven technology arose at an intersection in human understanding of fermentation (the process whereby microorganisms create carbon dioxide) and of gluten (the protein abundant in wheat that allows a dough to capture that gas). The subtle interplay of these forces (and their microscopic allies and antagonists) still delight and bedevil bakers to this day.

Thanks to the expansiveness of the Roman Empire, and all those military mouths to feed in far-flung locales, Roman oven remains are very widespread. Europeans did not stop baking in the post-Roman era, so the technology has endured and spread through conquest and colony over the last 1,500 years. Wherever masons and bakers have gone, ovens have sprung up.

Do You Really Need an Oven?

In earlier chapters, we considered a range of techniques for wood-fired cooking and baking that spare you the expense, trouble, and commitment of building or buying an actual oven. After all, if you can make a great pizza on a grill, roast a luscious chicken on a string, and bake a perfect loaf of bread in a campfire, do you really need to spend the time and money on a big chunk of masonry that will take up space in your yard or kitchen for years to come? If, on the other hand, you have mastered and enjoyed baking in the ashes, against a plank, on a griddle, in a cast-iron pot, or in a tannur, and yet your urge for wood-fired baking is unfulfilled, well, alright — rest assured that you have come by this self-knowledge honestly.

If you have decided that you *need* to have a wood-fired oven of your own, nothing I can say is liable to dissuade you. I understand this because when I left the living history museum where I had enjoyed building and baking in wood-fired ovens sporadically for a couple of decades, I could not rest until I had built one to use at home. I was surprised myself by the fervor with which I plotted this course over a winter, and the obsessive speed with which I achieved my goal as soon as spring thaw allowed. So it would be hypocritical for me to pooh-pooh your conviction.

Indeed, there is much to appreciate about a wood-fired oven in your yard or house. Even the humblest little mud oven will elevate your bread-baking abilities and will bake the best pizza you've ever eaten. No matter where you are as a baker — from newbie to master — having your own wood-fired oven will spark your learning and drive you to enjoy baking more.

Retained Heat

And, of course, the oven goes way beyond bread and pizza. So many other foods can be cooked as the oven heats and cools. I outline a few recipes to follow to acquaint you with some basic techniques. No doubt you'll be quick to add to them with adaptations from your own cooking repertoire.

I also take back that "taking up space" slander. The oven should be beautiful and pleasing to look at even cold. And during gatherings, it becomes a natural centerpiece independent of its cooking ability, just by virtue of containing a raging fire so attractively.

Choosing Your Oven

Selecting the type of oven right for you requires yet more self-reflection. Know the answers to the following questions before embarking on a decision: What do you think you'd like to bake, and on what scale? Will it be important to you to bake batch after batch of bread at one firing, or are your aims more modest? What is your level of DIY inclination? Are you interested in the oven-building as much as the baking, or do you just want to bake as soon as possible? What kind of budget can you commit? What are your location options?

There's an oven for every budget. The home-baker's little mud oven shown on the facing page can be built for about $50-100 in supplies. Or a much more considerable investment pays Maine Wood Heat Company to outfit you beautifully with the custom Le Panyol oven seen here.

Building versus Buying

Building your own oven can be tremendously satisfying, but it's not to be entered into lightly. Conceptually and physically simple as it may be, an oven nonetheless benefits from careful planning and entails a bit of heavy labor. You can build a mud oven with excellent baking qualities ridiculously cheaply if you are a dedicated scrounger like me. If you are a perfectionist and would like to build a brick-and-mortar oven for the ages, you may spend a few years and quite a bit of money on materials and plans. (I actually have met some oven enthusiasts who are all about the construction; to them the baking seems almost incidental.)

Paying someone else to build your oven will relieve you of many burdens but not that of decision-making; there are many options here as well. You may buy a refractory clay oven core (for anywhere between $1,000 and $8,000), which takes a lot of the guesswork out of providing yourself with an efficient baking chamber. But then you (or your mason) will need to ensconce that core in at least an outer veneer, if not additional thermal mass and/or insulation.

Choosing a core manufacturer, if you go that route, is only getting more confusing with time as wood-fired ovens become more popular. The number of manufacturers selling precast dome sections and other kit options has increased significantly in the last decade, with many new entries onto the field undercutting the prices of the more venerable French, Spanish, and Italian producers. The old-guard companies counter by questioning the quality of the upstart brands.

Finding a Mason

It can be a game changer to hire a mason from the very outset. A tradesperson can certainly install and finish a purchased core, but, more importantly, he or she might tempt you away from the core by underbidding it with a sweet custom brick-and-mortar oven. The Masonry Heater Association of North America maintains a large directory of professionals who are experienced with safely and efficiently accommodating fire. Over the course of decades, this organization has fostered the commitment of its members to wood-fired baking as well as heating.

The bottom line? It's all up to you. If you can afford it, a gorgeous, big, top-of-the-line Le Panyol is absolutely dreamy to use, indoors or out; but it is way beyond the means of many of us. (The aggregate costs of a beauty I recently baked in came to more than four times the value of the car I arrived in — or about 250 times the materials cost for one of my mud ovens!)

Oven Characteristics

A few important factors determine an oven's basic baking characteristics.

For the purpose of this discussion, an "oven" is a hollow shell of masonry, basically a strategically shaped, mostly enclosed space, intended to be heated by

THE OVEN ALREADY IN YOUR HOUSE

If you are lucky enough to have an old brick oven in your chimney, count your blessings and find a good mason. You want someone who is knowledgeable about and accomplished in the use of lime and clay mortars, and who is enthusiastic about your rehabilitation project. (It's most ideal if the mason is small or has a small apprentice — I'm not joking! These things are a lot easier and cheaper to repair from the inside.)

At the very least, have a mason inspect the oven and any associated flues and dampers for safety. I have seen ovens opened that had been paneled over for more than a century and found to be in pristine, perfectly usable-today condition. I have also seen piles of rubble, char, and spider webs so confusing that it was impossible to tell where the oven's mouth had been or what pattern the bricklayer had used so many years ago. Unfortunately, many twentieth-century homeowners found the "empty" space next to the fireplace in their old house to be a handy place to run ductwork for the central heating. I have been delighted to see some folks haul that stuff out, restore the masonry, and get back down to baking.

fire for the purpose of baking. The materials from which it is made must endure extreme heating and cooling and the occasional poke with a stick or worse.

Strictly speaking, this defines a "black oven"; one in which the baking chamber is heated directly, and then the fire removed, and the baking effected by retained heat only. The other sort — yes, a "white oven" — is heated by means of a fire in a remote chamber, with flues and dampers controlling the passage of heat. Thus, the baker may fire the oven and bake simultaneously rather than sequentially, obviating the need for stopping and recharging the masonry every so many batches. While a luxurious idea, the white oven is beyond the needs of most home-bakers, but very helpful for a commercial operation. If you are interested in a white oven, take it up with a Masonry Heater Association member mason; he or she will be delighted to hear from you. (See Resources, page 309.)

Ensuring Proper Proportions

An oven's proportions — the relationships among the baking chamber's height, breadth, and depth — contribute to how it will draw and heat. In chimneyless models, one easily determined factor does the most to make or break an oven's bakeability: the height of the door opening should equal 63% of the interior height of the dome. The authors of a masterful study of the bread ovens of Quebec found that the older mud ovens that cleaved most closely to a key ratio between dome height and door height (preserving the sacred geometry, as it were) consistently drew and heated better than newer, sometimes concrete, ovens whose builders neglected that ratio. Some of the poor performers had been retrofitted with chimneys as compensation, spoiling the inherent elegance of the original design.

Thermal mass is a description of the heat-storage capacity of the masonry of the oven, but can't be fully understood without its partner, **insulation**. Grasping this interplay is critical to understanding ovens, so I'll belabor it a bit in the following model.

For the sake of visuals, imagine the interior space of an oven is a semi-dome. Putting building principles aside for the moment, let's consider that hypothetical oven chamber in three versions: surrounded by ordinary masonry one inch thick, versus 10 inches thick, versus 10 feet thick. We'll make exactly equivalent fires in the three theoretical ovens, burning each for three hours. What will be the result?

Oven A, at one inch of thickness, will have absorbed all the heat it is capable of absorbing long before the three hours heating time is up. The surplus heat, that which is beyond its capacity to absorb, is just radiating through the oven's shell, warming the air around the oven. If you were to take the temperature of the interior oven walls after the fire was removed, they'd be very hot, and the exterior would not be very much cooler. A few loaves of room-temperature dough introduced to bake in this oven might start well, but the oven's temperature would fall rapidly as the heat stored in the thin shell of masonry moved inward into the relatively cold, wet dough and dissipated outward into the surrounding air. Even if those loaves baked, a second batch from that heating would be impossible.

Oven B, at 10 inches of thickness, is the "just right" straw man in this example. The masonry will have absorbed a lot of heat, although the exterior temperature will lag considerably behind the interior after three hours of firing, and the air around the oven will not be very much heated by the fire in the oven. The hypothetical baker should be able to bake a full range of bread, and many other good things, as the oven gradually falls back to ambient temperature over the course of hours.

Oven C, at 10 feet of thickness, has so much thermal mass that three hours of firing can't touch it. The temperature of the masonry in the baking chamber may seem perfect right after heating, but that perfection is as short-lived as that of Oven A. Once the fire has been removed from the chamber, the heat that has been stored in the inner masonry continues to radiate outward, into the cold stuff. The heat available for baking is sapped quickly of its intensity.

But where, you ask, is the insulation in this model? Wouldn't insulation help? In this experiment so far, all three ovens have the same insulation: the air outside the masonry. Air is not the best insulator, but that is how it functions in these models, as the ovens' thermal break, since air cannot absorb heat as well as masonry can. So, would it improve these ovens to insulate them?

SEVENTEENTH-CENTURY OVENS ON THE EDGE

Organizers of English colonies from Ireland to Newfoundland to Virginia furnished their colonists with oven cores manufactured at a few potteries in North Devon. These so-called cloam ovens were set into the hearth walls of houses, at a convenient height for baking, and presumably given a bit more thermal mass in the form of some surrounding daub or rubble to hold more heat than could the oven core's thin clay shell. This strategy provided colonists an almost instant baking capacity, no expertise in masonry required.

Archaeologists at Jamestown have found several examples of rudimentary ovens just dug into the suitably clayey earth of basements. If properly proportioned, such ovens are perfectly functional except that they are difficult to keep at sustained heat. (Too much thermal mass, not enough insulation.)

French colonies, on the other hand, tended to be staffed with masons who built ovens of stone, clay, brick, and tile, as materials were available. The archaeological record shows these ovens to be good-sized and well-built. In one instance, when the colony's oven was built, the masons put down their trowels and took up baking, since no men following that profession had yet emigrated.

Oven A would perform differently with insulation, but not entirely desirably so. Right after the firing, it would be fiercely hot and pretty hard to use. True, it would later spend more time in the perfect zone than in its uninsulated iteration, but it would remain a touchy, sensitive creature.

Oven B would make very good use of some applied insulation, retaining its heat longer to provide more production to the baker. It would lose more heat into the bread, and each time the door was opened, than it would to the air around it.

Oven C would not profit from insulation at all, unless a fire were burned many hours longer — long enough to saturate the masonry. Then, and only then, would the insulation really kick in, and that oven would remain at baking temperature for many, many batches of bread. Professional bakers historically used this kind of huge thermal mass to keep their ovens at a steady heat, with occasional firings to sharpen it. Only continual baking renders this sort of oven efficient; it might take days to get the oven fully heated, and likewise days for it to thoroughly cool.

Choosing Materials

A variable glossed in the above scenarios pertains to materials. The way heat moves through different substances matters. Think about this: heat flows quickly into some materials and tends to pool there, and is sort of rebuffed by others. So by this shorthand reckoning, soapstone and refractory firebrick would be at one end of the spectrum, sucking up the heat, and commercial insulation would be at the other end, resisting it. Most building materials — clay, ordinary rocks, bricks, cement, sand — hold heat, but just less efficiently than special refractory products. And unless you utilize a commercial insulator around (or in) the masonry, it will probably be the first air touching your oven that supplies the thermal break. As you plan your oven, think about surrounding the baking space with heat absorbers, and then surrounding those materials with heat resistors. The less efficient the materials in each category, the more you need of them.

Today's oven builders have access to far more efficient materials than ever before, and they are a boon to commercial bakers and the masons who build for them. Through online forums, home bakers and DIY masons can tap into the expertise wielded by these generous and passionate professionals, and learn how to use these materials to build really amazing, super-efficient ovens. (See Resources, page 309.)

That being said, most of us don't need our ovens to stay at 460°F for eight hours. In fact, we're okay with the gentle cooling curve of our ovens, and love the challenge of using up as much of that heat as possible to prepare food.

Considering Aesthetics

Just because this is the most personal aspect of planning your oven does not demote it from a level of concern equivalent to the laws of thermodynamics. In fact, understanding the physical properties of the oven and its heating is really just a tool to help you get the oven that will delight you most. We're not talking about a coat of stucco here. Your aesthetic conviction is a major determinant of your choice of design and materials. It will affect your decision-making from the ground up and the core out.

So look at as many oven images as you can, both recent and historic. What really grabs you? If it is within your means and makes sense for the level of baking you anticipate, follow your bliss. Online resources are such that, if you are in love with an authentic adobe *horno*, full instructions are out there. If you are a history buff and you have room in your house for a new chimney stack, you can find a mason to build a reproduction of a colonial-era brick oven right in your living room. If your aesthetic sense is horrified by inefficiency, refractory materials and super-insulation will be the way to go.

The ovens I build and enjoy arise from my own particular circumstances. I see in retrospect that I have chosen materials that I love based on my work as an archaeologist and food historian, at an efficiency level that works for me as a home baker. Even the most pragmatic decisions must sort within an aesthetic framework that is comfortable to me. For example, I feel it is critical to insulate beneath the hearth of an oven. Flat rigid materials like insulating firebrick or cellular glass insulation are easily plunked down beneath the refractory firebrick that I favor for the hearth surface. The huge improvement in efficiency wrought by this addition has absolutely zero impact on the final aesthetic of the oven; the only other aspect to balance is cost. On the other hand, I love the finished look of a mud oven; while I know that putting it inside a box and filling that with perlite would really increase my efficiency, I'm simply not interested in looking at that every day.

Determining the Size and Shape

The size of the baking chamber may be varied according to the needs of the baker; carefully consider your preferences early on. Arrange favorite pans or actual loaves of bread on a surface you are pretending is the inside of your oven-to-be. Measure how much room they take up (with a bit of space between), then add a few inches to the total. Ovens can be built to almost any crazy size; I have used one measuring 16 inches, and another 16 feet, across their interiors. These dimensions are extremes; for most home bakers a diameter in the ballpark of 34 to 38 inches is a happy medium. Too large makes heating a chore; too small is just frustrating to an avid baker.

The interior shape of ovens is also quite variable, but mostly determined by the overall style of construction. The vault of a mud oven, like that of old-fashioned brick and stone ovens, is dome-shaped. Most precast oven cores follow the dome tradition. Many of today's masons, however, gravitate toward building an arched vault atop short, plumb brick side walls: home-oven-size versions of nineteenth-century commercial ovens. Many do-it-yourselfers emulate this style in the Alan Scott oven. (See Resources, page 310.)

Selecting Hearth Materials

The oven's hearth, the horizontal baking surface, must sink plenty of heat. It also should be both highly durable and easily replaceable, since even a careful baker gives it a real beating between firing, sweeping, loading, and unloading. Most oven-builders use heavy refractory clay firebrick for their hearths. I follow suit in ovens that are not meant as historic reproductions (typically thereby incurring my greatest materials expense). Building reproductions and archaeologically experimental ovens has given me occasion to lay hearths in clay, cobble, and old-fashioned soft brick. (All beautiful but not bulletproof.) The hearths of precast oven cores are usually cast of the same refractory clay as the dome, and are very durable.

If you reject mortaring the hearth bricks in favor of simply laying them in a bed of fine sand, replacing a few worn bricks several years and hundreds of loaves down the road will be easy. You only have to repair an oven hearth once to be grateful to yourself for this choice.

Incidentally, don't be tempted to use slabs of marble or granite for your oven's hearth; they simply can't take the heat. Even heat-loving soapstone may spall at pizza temperatures, and tends to release its heat so violently that it is difficult to bake bread without charring.

Incorporating a Flue

A flue, to carry smoke out of the house, is essential in indoor ovens. For the last few centuries, the average New England brick oven was provided with a small flue just inside its mouth to provide draft and convey smoke up into the main kitchen fireplace stack. In earlier years, ovens, inset in the rear or side walls of fireplaces, simply took advantage of that one wide flue. Both types work equally well in my experience, but the more modern version allows for simultaneous full-scale cooking and baking.

Outdoors, a chimney is optional in a well-proportioned oven. On the plus side, a chimney keeps your oven mouth's arch from being besmirched by soot, if such things trouble you. In the negative column, a chimney creates an opportunity for wear and moisture at a weak spot in the oven. One could argue that, as a needless elaboration — just one more thing to build and maintain — the chimney robs the oven of some of its elegance and simplicity. Worse, it deprives the baker of the opportunity to broil food under the dramatic sheet of flame that can be produced in the entryway of the oven as it heats.

Siting Your Oven

Locating an oven in just the right spot on your site can present a bit of a challenge. Consider each of the following variables and how they might balance in your own situation.

Let's start with the natural world. Which is the predominant wind direction during the season you anticipate using your oven most? The easiest course, in terms of ease of firing, is to point the back of the oven into the prevailing wind. If other factors persuade you against this choice, you may need to curtail baking on windy days, or employ a windbreak in front of the oven and then expect both firing and baking to take a bit longer than usual.

While you're thinking about wind, consider your near neighbors. Anticipate how smoke might travel. Once your oven catches alight and is blazing away, combustion becomes more thorough and the smoke is minimal; but sometimes the wrong breeze or the wrong kindling will cause fire-making time to be a tad smoky. Pizza parties go a long way toward easing neighborhood relations; but better yet is to anticipate trouble, and try to head it off at the pass, by thoughtfully siting your oven to start with.

Shade or sun? Siting your oven near a pleasant shade tree may incline you more toward baking on otherwise lazy dog days. The only dangerous heat that should emanate from your oven shoots out the top of its mouth. So a nearby tree is not necessarily a red flag. But do avoid overhanging fire hazards and recall that trees fall down sometimes. A rather sickly red oak standing to one side of one of my favorite ovens has made me a bit nervous for years. This winter, an ice storm blew down the apparently healthy pitch pine five times its size growing next to it. Thankfully, that real crusher went the other way, and the oak still stands, sickly as ever.

Siting for a Stable Foundation

Your oven wants a well-drained location. Avoid places that hold water after a rain or that sit too near a runoff area. While you're looking at topography, notice if you may have a spot that already contains many advantages. A little patch of bedrock showing above the soil may make a naturally dry and solid foundation for your oven. A waist-high heavy-duty retaining wall, a frequent feature of old farms in my part of the world, could supply a handsome ready-made base for your oven.

A mason, if you bring one in to build a large brick-and-mortar oven, or to install a precast core, will probably want to excavate to pour a footing. With that investment of time and money, you may agree that you don't want your heavy oven to sink or tilt. However, I have always been able to site my mud or stone ovens on solid stony or gravelly ground, sometimes augmenting the gravel beneath to improve drainage and stability, and none of them have budged yet.

Siting for Fun!

What location factors make your oven more fun and easier to use? No matter how well organized you are, you will be running between your oven and your kitchen or other food prep area more than you would have thought possible, so proximity is helpful. Balance your convenience with fire safety and smoke issues.

Don't feel that you must incorporate the oven into existing outdoor entertainment areas. First, during its construction period, it'll be nice just to return to

This little oven faces away from the prevailing wind, stands between an established outdoor entertainment area and the kitchen door, and, most critically, is sheltered from the weather by a decent roof.

your old fire pit and make flatbread and grill kebabs and ignore your new project. Second, when it is finished, the oven will create its own focus, as your spatial use of it evolves. You may find that you prefer a work table diagonally across from it, rather than next to it, and find that your guests unconsciously gravitate to sitting so that they can see right into it . . . In short, it's an opportunity to transform a little used and undistinguished area of your yard into a focal point and a gathering place.

PORTABLE OPTIONS

What if you don't have a yard? Many non-homeowners have built ovens on trailers so they can take them with them when they move. In fact, I have seen as wide a spectrum of ovens on wheels as on terra firma — from the cruddiest mud oven to the most sparkling, copper-clad Le Panyol. (See Resources, page 310.)

Providing Cover

Don't neglect to plan for the roof. Protect your oven from the elements, especially if it is built with clay-based mortar. Saturation followed by freezing is your dread enemy. And a tarp is not a real solution. When you're designing your roof, think about how nice it would be to have a covered work table or shelf so that your proofing loaves can stand by, sheltered from the sun and rain.

BUILDING A BASIC WOOD-FIRED OVEN

Whether you plan to build in clay, brick, or stone, most of the principles are the same. Plan how you will protect your oven from moisture creeping up from the ground and falling from the sky. Locate your oven (and elevate it on a base) so it will be comfortable, convenient, and safe to use. Use forms to support masonry elements until they can support themselves. Preserve proper proportions for efficient firing; remember, the more functional your oven, the more innately beautiful it will be.

I am comfortable building mostly in natural materials. As a result, my ovens are cheap and biodegradable. I know that this is individual, but I find them beautiful to look at and am thrilled to use tools built from such deep and long traditions. I am fascinated to think of the future archaeological footprint of each of them.

Base Ideas

Unless you want to spend a lot of time crouching or lying on your belly when baking, it's a great idea to build your oven on a base. For those of us who live in frosty climates, the base also provides a moisture barrier from the ground beneath, protecting clay mortar from freezing injury in winter.

Prepare a level, well-drained site about 4 feet square and wide. In most cases, unless you are building on a very well-drained surface, it's a good idea to bring in about a half-yard of coarse gravel, and smooth and tamp it down well as a pad.

Stone

A Combination of Block and Stone

My favorite way to make an attractive, durable, and cheap base for a small-to-medium oven: a core of 12 concrete blocks provides stability to the body of the oven, and is encircled by a ring of dry-laid stone. Set three blocks on edge on your gravel pad, forming a rectangle. The long axis of the rectangle should be oriented from front to back of your oven, to support the oven's mouth. Seat very securely and levelly. Add the next course, also on edge, staggering the arrangement of the blocks. Build up courses of stone around, to make a finished circumference of at least 40 inches at the top. As you go, fill the inside of the ring and blocks entirely with small stones and loose gravel. Continue with two more courses of blocks, stone and gravel. (Four courses of blocks all told make a comfortable work height for most people; vary as you like.) Make the front face of the base as plumb as possible for ease in baking.

Concrete block

Blocks, Rebar, and Rubble

If you don't have access to stone, you can make a very stable, strong, boxy base out of 48 concrete blocks. Set blocks on edge, level. Offset courses, then drive down a few 3-foot lengths of rebar to keep the base from spreading at all. Fill gaps loosely with rubble, stones, or gravel (nothing that will wick up moisture). At right, center, on the finished base, we're seeing if we will have enough insulating firebrick for two layers beneath the hearth bricks.

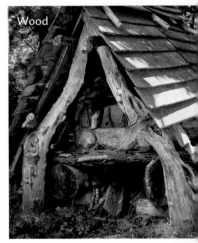

Wood

Wood

A wooden base works, too, as long as it is heavily built and you use insulation between it and the oven. (Note also the alternative, henge-style oven mouth. No bricks, no forms.)

BUILDING THE OVEN

This is a basic oven type that has worked well for me; it is functional if not super-efficient, durable despite being made of mud, and at least to its creator, aesthetically pleasing. The monetary investment is minimal. And though there's quite a bit of work involved, most of it is pretty fun. For best results, plot your ideal oven on graph paper; a plan will help you calculate important factors like how many hearth bricks you need. Be advised that the oven must be thoroughly dry before the onset of freezing weather.

MATERIALS

- 15 or so 5-gallon buckets (about 35 pounds each) of raw clay (ask farmers, excavators, and landscape contractors for leads in your area)

- one yard of masons' sand

- one 30-gallon trash can of manure (equine okay, bovine best)

- one bale of straw (old and rotted is fine)

- insulating firebrick for under hearth (30–60 depending on how many courses you use. You may also use a slab of cellular glass insulation.)

- refractory firebrick for hearth (32–40 standard-size bricks. Hint: To give your oven just a bit more heat-storage capacity, buy extra brick and lay them on edge instead of flat.)

- plywood arch form for oven mouth (The one pictured on page 224 is 14 inches wide. Size for your particular baking needs and equipment.)

- bricks and/or pavers for oven mouth (I've used anywhere from 10 to 20, depending on their thickness and the size of the oven's mouth.)

EQUIPMENT

- machine to chop straw
- mortar tub
- 5-gallon buckets
- measuring tape and levels
- rubber mallet
- trowel, shovel, hoe
- 2–3 heavy tarps (Old sails or rubber roofing are both great options. They don't have to be huge; 8 by 10 feet is fine.)
- wheelbarrow

SITE REQUIREMENTS

- access to water
- pop-up tent for shelter and until your roof is finished

MIX THE MUD

Also known as daub, "mud" in the construction context refers to a mortar made of clay combined with sand and water, usually with the admixture of some organic material like manure and chopped straw. Because the main ingredient — clay from the earth — is so variable in purity, it would be misleading to give an exact recipe; but I'll demonstrate my favorite way to mix it.

Unlike lime- or cement-based mortars, daub is on a relaxed schedule, and is infinitely adjustable. If you end up with too much sand in the composition, say, just add more of the other ingredients to balance. Worst-case scenario: you build something you don't like, you take it down, break it up and remix it, and start anew.

You'll need a lot of daub to build an oven; if you're working alone, mixing will take up most of your time. That's just one more reason why oven-building is a nice group project — someone can always be starting a new batch.

1. MIX THE DRY INGREDIENTS. You can mix in a mortar tub, on a tarp or just in a hole or depression in the ground. Throw in equal volumes of broken up clay, manure, and sand. (If your clay is very silty, hold back on about half the sand until you get a sense of the strength of the mix. You can always add more later.) Mix this up dry with a hoe, chopping and tossing.

2. MOISTEN GRADUALLY. Add water to one end of the pile and start mashing the clay into the other ingredients. You can continue with a hoe for a while, but sooner or later, the feet, with the weight of the body to back them up, are the best tools for the job. It's easy to overdo the water, so be stingy at first. For huge jobs and no fun, you can use a gas-powered tiller or cement mixer.

3. ADD STRAW. Chopped straw adds structural stability and dries it out a bit. I find it's easiest to scatter a bed of straw on a heavy-duty tarp, then turn the mix out onto that.

4. MIX WELL. Tread it up and down, continuing to work out lumps, and use the tarp to help flip the pile over. Thorough mixing now saves work later. You can also mix the daub a bit on the wet side the day before you want to use it and cover lightly overnight. The resting period only improves it.

LAY THE HEARTH

1. ISOLATE THE HEARTH THERMALLY FROM THE BASE. Insulation — a course or two of insulating firebrick (or a slab of cellular glass insulation) — is a must here. Top with a smooth layer of fine sand to make it easier to bed the hearth brick levelly and without gaps. Use a thicker layer of sand if you want to create more of a heat sink under the hearth.

2. SET THE BRICKS. Constant application of the level, the occasional tap from a rubber mallet, and a bit of patience are needed to get your hearth laid just right. Lay the bricks straight down, without pushing sideways, to avoid kicking sand up between them.

The hearth is made of refractory firebrick, a very durable baking surface. They are most commonly available in a size close to that of standard bricks, but we scored these wonderful huge ones while working on an oven for an art center. (They once were part of a potter's kiln.) Note, toward the rear of the first photo at left, the firebrick that will lie under the oven's mouth. It forms an apron emerging from the front of the oven.

3. LAY THE FIRST COURSE OF DAUB.
Knead in some extra straw to
make the first course of daub
stronger and drier. Since it is destined to surround and lock in the
hearth arrangement, it needs to be
structurally stable. This is the first
mortar used in the oven, basically
stabilizing the layers of insulating
bricks. Note how distant it is from
any ground moisture.

NOTE: If you've used a lot of insulation and sand to prepare for your
hearth bricks, you may find that
you want to apply a ring of this
nice, stiff daub to stabilize that
base before you set up the hearth.

CREATE THE ARCH

1. MOCK IT UP. Mock up the oven's mouth with the form and the bricks you intend to use flat on the ground so you are ready to go. The bricks need not all be the same size or sort, but their arrangement should be harmonious, since they will be the face of your oven. If you don't happen to be given keystone-shaped bricks, as I was for this oven, it's a good idea to create one for the top of the arch, using a wet saw. Talk to a masonry supply outfit for help.

2. PLACE THE FORM. Center the form for the arch on the hearth apron at the front of the oven. Place shims beneath the form so that you'll be able to remove it easily when the time comes, and get it nice and level.

3. LAY THE ARCH BRICKS. Make a small amount of mortar (about a gallon) of equal parts clay and sand while you soak the arch bricks for a minute or two. Lay bricks up using minimal mortar, especially on the inner edge, where the bricks should virtually touch. Keep the work wet with a brush as you go, as the bricks will suck the moisture right out of the mortar.

4. EVEN UP THE BRICKS AS YOU GO.
Make sure all the brick faces on the front of the oven are flush, and try to space the bricks evenly. If you get a pretty even coat of mortar in between the bricks in the middle, you can go back and fill in from the sides later. Note how we used a wood shaving as a shim at about 11 o'clock on this arch, to make a wayward brick line up correctly.

5. FILL THE CRACKS. Once the bricks are more or less in place, press mortar in the cracks to fill in all the spaces.

CREATE THE OVEN FORM

HOW TO FIGURE THE HEIGHT OF THE OVEN'S CENTER. Start by measuring the height of the oven's mouth. That figure is 63% of the ideal height of the oven's center interior. In the oven pictured, the height of the arch was 8½ inches. To find the ideal height for the ceiling, we multiplied 8½ times 100 and then divided by 63, giving us 13½ inches. Cut a stick to that length and use it to gauge the height of your form.

1. FILL THE SPACE. Chalk a line to mark the inside of the oven. Unless you have tons of sand, pile objects on the hearth floor that will easily fit through the oven's mouth. An inflatable (and, more importantly, *deflatable*) beach ball might work too! Notice the stick placed in the center of the oven, demarking the ideal finished height.

2. ADD DAMP SAND. Imagining the negative space of the oven, build up damp sand to the level indicated by the stick. Make the oven shapely and as large as you can, as long as you leave room on the perimeter for walls at least 8 inches thick.

Retained Heat

3. FIRM UP THE SAND. Pat the sand into a firm and smooth form, spraying with water if it should dry out, and slapping with a clapboard or shingle to finish. Try to make the bottom of the form as plumb as possible, so that your oven can accommodate pan loaves near the edges.

4. ADD A LAYER OF NEWSPAPER. Dampen some newspaper and layer it over the completed form. This parting layer makes it easier to remove the form without damaging the oven. I forgot it one time, and the sand still came out, but not as cleanly.

FORM THE CORE OF THE OVEN

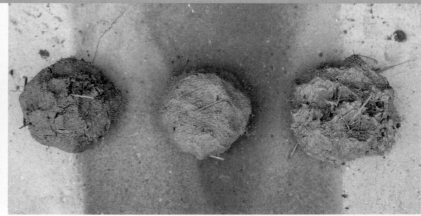

1. MIX MORE DAUB. If you haven't already been doing it, make a large batch of daub out of clay, sand, and straw as before. It should be a bit wetter than the batch we made earlier — more moldable, but not the slightest bit saggy.

The cracks in the mix on the left say "too dry"; the surface moisture and sagginess of the mix on the right say "too wet"; the mix in the middle says "just right."

2. FORM THE FIRST COURSE. Work the daub into compact "bricks" and slam them into place as a first course of oven wall around the form.

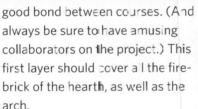

3. FORM THE OVEN CORE. Work your way around and over, trying to keep the same thickness throughout. This will form the inner core of the oven. If any areas dry out a bit, just dampen with a brush or spray bottle to make sure you get a good bond between courses. (And always be sure to have amusing collaborators on the project.) This first layer should cover all the firebrick of the hearth, as well as the arch.

4. APPLY ANOTHER LAYER OF DAUB The second layer of daub should be applied at an even thickness; dampen the exterior of the first layer for a good bond. The oven's shape begins to emerge.

5. REMOVE THE ARCH FORM AND SAND. Pull out the internal form and clean up the arch bricks with a trowel and a damp sponge. As soon as your work is stable, you can remove the supporting forms so that the mortar may begin to dry from the inside as well as the outside.

Building a Basic Wood-Fired Oven

FINISH WITH PLASTER

A nice protective plaster can be made by breaking up clay, wetting it to a slurry, and mixing up some finely broken dry cow or horse manure. Be sure to go easy on the water if your manure is fresh! For best results, let this plaster sit overnight before applying it. Apply a coat of the plaster and smooth into final shape. If the oven is ever injured, just dampen the area and reapply.

LIGHT IT UP

 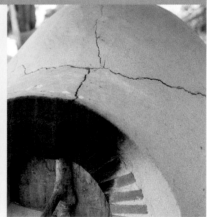

Try a first fire of small, light, dry sticks, right near the mouth of the oven. Even a wispy little fire gives your oven the opportunity to show off its drawing capacity. Cold air goes in along the bottom; hot air comes out along the top. This is a pretty good fire for a soaking wet oven. A few small fires over the course of drying helps to drive out the moisture.

Be prepared for some cracking the first time you heat your oven. Think of the cracks as added character rather than disfigurement. Do not fill them; they simply want to open and close each time you fire the oven.

GETTING READY TO BAKE

Every oven is different, and, especially if you have built your own, you will be your oven's expert. Every baking session will increase your proficiency in that oven's particular characteristics.

Fuel

Wood for your oven should be three things: dry, dry, and dry. Beyond that, I'm flexible and usually burn a promiscuous mixture of scrounged wood. Since many people don't like to burn pine in their woodstoves or fireplaces, it's often available as a giveaway in my area. Softwoods are perfectly serviceable for heating an oven for baking bread, so I rely on them a lot. Pine is easy to split into the relatively small diameters that make firing easy.

When I am planning to use the oven for a live-fire application like pizza, I will make a transition from pine to oak or maple about halfway through firing. The hardwood will provide a bed of hardwood coals that will quickly ignite new hardwood fuel to both spike the heat and provide a bit of smoky savor.

Oven Tools

Again, scrounging may serve you well here, and is my default mode. Nowadays, if you prefer, tools made just for each purpose are available with a quick online search. While I learned some by looking around at what is sold on the Internet and generally at what other bakers use, I realize that a lot of my baking practice was established by my training at a living history museum, in the seventeenth-century English tradition. Old habits die hard; archaic habits die even harder.

MANIPULATING THE FIRE. You'll need something to poke the fire with, and as often as not I find myself just using a random stick. I am careful enough with the masonry of my ovens that I think twice before levering things around with a metal tool. The downside of a stick is flammability, but that's one of the reasons you have a tub of water standing by.

Sometimes it's nice to have a metal poker with a hook on the end. Used with care, such a tool is great for dragging coals and embers forward, or removing them from the oven. A chunk of rebar with the last inch or two bent at ninety degrees isn't pretty, but gets the job done. Make it long enough that you can reach to the back of the oven, but not so long that you are a hazard to yourself, the oven, and all around you.

A once-common tool among European bakers was a long-hafted iron fork (*fourgon* in French, which collapsed, amusingly, into "fruggin" in English), used to manipulate the fuel in the oven. These implements were especially handy when bundles of small sticks or gorse were the primary fuel.

MOVING SMALL COALS, EMBERS, AND ASHES. When it's time to clean the hearth for baking, I use a lightweight wooden tool I call a rake to drag hot stuff out of the oven. It's really just a trapezoidal board (shaped to get into the corners of my ovens) mounted on the end of a stick. (To be honest, it's based on an illustration from an English work of 1688.) It doesn't burst into flame if I wet it then let it drip pretty dry before using.

Modern bakers use a rake-like scraper with a steel blade for the same purpose. I do not covet this tool for my ovens because, as I mentioned above, I am leery of damaging the masonry with too much harsh metallic scraping, and I love how the custom-made wooden rake nestles right into the edges of the hearth, sweeping the coals and ashes from the base of the oven walls.

SWEEPING/SWABBING THE HEARTH. Once again, I admit to seventeenth-century influence here, in that I will occasionally resort to using a damp swab, made of linen or hemp canvas strips tied on a stick, to sweep out the oven. In seventeenth-century England, this tool (along with a raggedy hag-like woman) was called a "malkin"; Dr. Johnson reported "scovel" in his dictionary (endearingly pronounced "scuffle" by twentieth-century English bakers). In any case, if necessary, I deploy a malkin to swiftly brush out still-burning embers that the rake misses. Then, to avoid wear on the hearth from the wet swab, I resort to a light natural bristle brush (like a gigantic soft toothbrush on a long wooden handle), the gentlest possible sweeper. Mine have been cast off from a local wood-fired pizza restaurant, seemingly discarded because of a little wear on the end or because they had been on fire. (I saw the defective part off.)

You can buy brass brushes from pizza-tool dealers, which of course will not ignite, but may be a bit rough on the masonry if you are a nervous nelly like me. Sometimes people will follow the brass brush with a damp towel. Do be sure to squeeze excess moisture out of anything you use for swabbing the oven clean.

I have also gotten in the habit of dry-sweeping the oven clean just before and after the "soaking" period (the roughly 20-minute rest period between firing and baking). This practice really seems to minimize the need for introducing any wet tools.

PEELS. I use a variety of peels, depending on the work. First, I use a lovely handmade wooden one, just the right size for my needs, for introducing the raw foods into the oven.

OVEN TOOLS

Left to right: Two kinds
of peel (aluminum and
wooden), a light natural
bristle brush, a wooden coal
rake, a malkin, an iron poker,
and a galvanized tub for
catching coals and ashes.

Getting Ready to Bake

Then, I use an old aluminum pizza peel (that's right, cast off from the same pizza place) to retrieve things. Its finer edge makes it easier to slide under everything, especially, naturally, pizza.

It's important to have a narrow peel-like tool you can use to turn or move pizzas deftly or peer underneath them while they bake. They make a cute steel lollipop-shaped tool for this purpose, but I get by with a long clapboard with a very fine edge on it. (I also use that clapboard peel for loading couche-risen baguettes into the oven one at a time.)

HEATING AN OVEN

A new oven's first heating is likely to be its trickiest, all other factors being equal. Some new ovens just take right off, but it is not unusual for a new oven — especially a good-sized earthen one, which can hold a lot of moisture — to be a bit sluggish to heat. Even persuading oxygen to enter the oven to keep the fire blazing can seem difficult in a wet oven. A couple of firings may be in order before such an oven is ready for baking.

Make sure the area directly in front of the oven is clear of combustibles, and have a bucket of water handy, so that you can extinguish any small stray fires on the ground. These are most liable to occur when you scrape live coals out of the oven, preparatory to baking, but it's a nice idea to be thinking about safety before you strike a match.

Use a knife to make a good pile of light pine shavings.

Have plenty of nice light, dry pine, split up small (about an inch square on the end).

If you are planning to do some live-fire cooking, and not just to use the residual heat to bake bread, have some small hardwood on hand for later.

Remembering that oxygen is a key ingredient here, kindle a small fire using an airy stack of the above ingredients directly inside the mouth of the oven. Feed it to establish some good combustion. When all seems well, use a stick to push the fire back several inches. Push on the lowest fuel in the fire, and try not to collapse the whole structure. Usually, this takes the fire aback a bit, but arrange things as best you can, adding small amounts of fuel gently.

Now is a good time to notice how your oven draws in air at the bottom, and exhausts through the top of the doorway. (Or exhausts through the chimney if you have one.) When a fire is operating on the edge of oxygen debt, think about any little thing you can do that may help. For instance, structuring your fuel as openly as possible atop two supporting sticks running from front to back under the fire leaves an opening below and plenty of air room throughout.

Continue to inch the fire back until you can get strong combustion in the center of the oven. This slow approach may not prove necessary, but patience at

HOW TO HEAT AN OVEN

1. Start a small fire toward the front of the oven, bearing in mind the need for airflow beneath. Gradually build it up into a good, stable blaze in the center of the oven.

2. Add more fuel when you can and burn a smart fire until the ceiling of your oven looks nice and clean. And then burn it for a while more. The specifics of timing vary radically among ovens.

3. Let the last fuel burn down pretty well, then rake out any remaining coals. Dampen a malkin and sweep lightly to get the edges. (Don't sweat the small stuff now; rather, give it a quick sweep with a dry brush after the heat has equalized.)

4. Right after firing, the temperature of the masonry is very uneven. Close up the empty oven to rest or "soak" for a spell and balance it all out. (If you ever seriously overheat an oven, give it a few minutes with the door open to release some heat.)

this point can save a lot of frustration if your oven is balky. Once you have a bright stable fire in the center of the oven, it's usually just a matter of feeding it one or two pieces of larger wood at proper intervals. At this point you can leave it alone to do its thing while you go about some other business. You'll get a feel for when it's time to add new fuel.

After a while (in a dry oven, maybe an hour or so; in a clammy new oven, much longer), you'll notice that the ceiling of the oven over the hottest part of the fire is nice and clean. The soot from the fire has burred right off, the first indication that your oven is taking some heat. By this time, the fire is burning differently and very aggressively. Newly introduced fuel catches almost before it touches down. Give the fire a final push right to the rear of the oven. Keep burning this sprightly fire until the entire ceiling is clear of soot.

Check in with the timetable for your bread. With my ovens, I assume that from this point — when the fire is burning sweetly and the masonry is clear of soot — it will still be close to an hour before the bread goes into the oven. That includes about half an hour for the wood burning in the oven to be consumed, and then about 20 minutes of "soaking," allowing the heat to equalize throughout the cleared-out oven with the door closed. The fire can be fed and extended if need be to accommodate your bread's schedule; it's dicier to rush things.

When the last fuel is mostly burned, rake out the majority of the coals into a fireproof container. I sometimes use a metal hook for larger items, but prefer wooden tools as a rule, as they are less liable to damage the oven. Naturally, wooden tools are also quick to catch on fire if you let them, so it's a good habit to immerse them in water while the oven is heating. Likewise, I start soaking my pine oven door as soon as I start my fire; a thoroughly wet door is not only less likely to smoke and smolder from the heat of the oven, it also provides a lovely steamy atmosphere for the bread to enjoy. Moisture early in the bake promotes open cuts, prodigious oven spring, and thin crispy crusts in your loaves.

Once the coals have been raked out of the oven, I have a look inside. If it's really pretty clean, which is often the case if softwoods, which leave no coals, have been used for fuel, I'll just close the oven door. Only if many small coals remain in the oven at this point, will I use the malkin or scuffle. This tool must also be soaked to keep from igniting; but never just slop it into the oven soaking wet. For the preservation of your masonry, and to keep the best heat in your oven, allow the malkin a few minutes drip dry, or squeeze it out, before use. Quickly swab out the coals. Don't worry about every last ash at this point, and mind the malkin doesn't flip burning coals at you on the out-stroke.

During the "soaking" phase which follows (20 minutes in my ovens; you'll discover the correct interval for yours), the oven undergoes an essential balancing activity — the ceiling drops from blazing hot, and the floor creeps up from a bit too cool, and ideally they meet at around 500°F. This period is also useful to the baker. This is the time when I make sure that everything required for getting bread into the oven is right at hand and ready to go. Aside from a peel and a hearth brush, you may need a lame, razor blade, or small sharp serrated knife for slashing the bread; some semolina or fine cornmeal to ease the bread off the peel; and, of course, the proofed loaves.

When the time is up, if you have a wooden door, place it back in water to continue soaking, or, quite possibly, to quench any incipient ignition. Use the dry hearth brush to sweep the entire oven clean, swiftly zipping along the edges where ashes and coals can hide. The second that the dust has settled, load in your loaves, slashing them on the way in. (If there is any delay here, simply reclose the door.)

VARIABLES THAT AFFECT THE HEATING TIME

The sequence of oven-heating events I describe on page 234 proves similar across a range of disparate oven types, with the main variable — how long it takes to get from one stage to another — being just that: highly variable.

The circumstances that make an oven heat quickly are these: being warm from a previous baking, being thoroughly dry, having less thermal mass to heat, being perfectly proportioned, and having good insulation.

An oven's heating is slowed down, not prevented, by moisture, cold, wind, mass, poor insulation, and design flaws.

Gauging Temperature

You are facing down the mouth of a freshly cleaned out oven after its 20-minute "soaking" period; how do you know the temperature? Historically, many accounts describe bakers judging heat by introducing objects into the oven and then counting to see how long it takes them to burn. Pieces of paper and handfuls of flour are frequent candidates for this treatment, but the all-time most-popular choice is the baker's hand or arm. In most accounts, oven heat that could be tolerated for 10 seconds of arm-time was judged suitable for baking.

However, most good bakers of the past probably also observed subtle and hard-to-describe signs the oven and fuel gave during firing; my interpretation is that these frequently quoted "how-long-it-takes-for-ignition" rules — which do work, after all — were great to fall back on when distracted by extraneous issues, like strangers and children asking questions about how you know when the oven is hot enough.

With experience, you will learn to read your oven's signs during firing and see that the way it takes heat influences the way it gives it back during the bake.

Thinking about it in retrospect, I realize that I initially learned to judge the temperature of an oven by observing food cooking in it. For example, if a big apple pie baked in under an hour, I'd know there was still plenty of heat left for something else.

THERMOMETERS. I once tried to test for hot and cool spots in a masonry oven with a standard bimetal coil oven thermometer. It didn't take long until it was fried beyond all using. Our ovens just get too hot for the "classic" oven thermometer to handle — and that's even after the fire has been taken out.

Today's laser infrared thermometer, which can be used to measure the temperature of even a remote object, has made this kind of testing easy. These toys are tons of fun to mess around with and really take the guesswork out of learning how your oven fires, where it loses heat, and so forth.

Remember, though, that as awesome as your laser thermometer is at showing you the current temperature of any surface at any one moment, it does not entirely render obsolete your own senses and experiences. Your oven has its own particular heat-retention characteristics, and will tell you with subtle cues how long it is likely to linger at a certain temperature.

Further, each firing of your oven will have a distinctive cooling curve, depending on how long the oven was heated, the ambient conditions, and other variables. It's useful to think of an oven's heating as "deep" or "shallow"; each one has its place, but it's unfortunate to mistake one for the other. The infrared thermometer is a great tool. Use it to learn your oven's characteristics and develop an understanding that will allow you to anticipate your oven's next move.

COOKING WITH AN OVEN FULL OF FIRE

Way before the oven is heated enough for pizza, let alone bread, you can cook all sorts of foods right in the mouth of the oven, or just inside, near the fire. Fun to do and beautiful to watch, this technique makes efficient use of the fire you have to burn anyway, and so feels virtuous to boot. When I'm planning to make pizza, this is how I deal with any toppings that want pre-cooking, like roasted peppers or Italian sausage. It's also a good way to entertain or keep busy any early guests.

As it heats, the oven passes through a few phases that make it more suitable for one food than another. I'll try to describe them. But as with so much having to do with your wood-fired oven, there's a lot of latitude, and once you know the temper of your own oven, let your own expertise and imagination be your guide.

STAGE 1: THE BROILER SETTING

As soon as a fire is steadily burning in the center of the oven, you have what I think of as "the broiler setting"; that is, a great deal of heat is washing over the ceiling of the oven and out the top of the mouth. This phenomenon is especially pronounced in ovens built without chimneys (like all of mine); when the oven starts to crank, it's possible to get a sheet of flame to pass within a few inches of your food. This intense heat is not beneficial for every food item, but if you choose wisely, you can develop some very wonderful flavors through its application.

Vegetables that you want to char and peel, like tomatoes, peppers, garlic, and onions, work very well this way. Or quick-sear asparagus or green beans tossed with olive oil and salt.

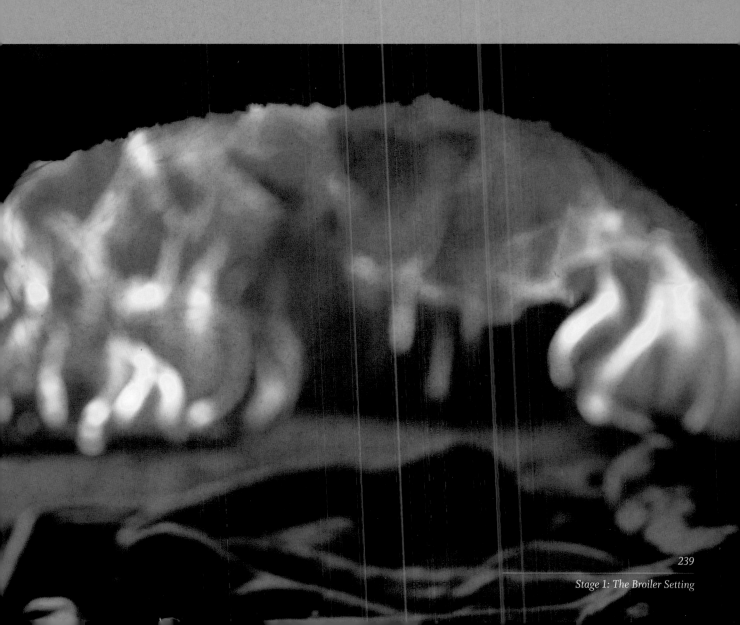

BROILED MIXED PEPPERS

These are money in the bank. I make them every time I bake throughout our all-too-short New England pepper season. They are wonderful on pizza, or in pasta dishes, soups, appetizers, or even virtually straight-up as a salad.

Most peppers are suitable for this treatment, depending on how much *picante* you like in your life. I like a mix of sweet (Italian frying peppers like Marconi or Jimmy Nardello) and medium to medium-hot peppers (poblano, New Mexico, Hungarian wax, and jalapeno); much as I love scorchers like scotch bonnets or habaneros, their thin walls and subtle flavors make them better, and easier to modulate, as a raw addition to a dish.

I. Arrange the peppers in a single layer on a baking sheet. Slide it partway into the oven and don't go too far away; this usually doesn't take very long. When some of the peppers begin to char, pull the baking sheet out with an oven mitt, and use tongs to make adjustments. Turn the whole sheet around if it's helpful. Remove the peppers that are thoroughly charred to a stainless bowl with a cover. Add new peppers as you can. When they are all roasted, keep them covered until cool enough to handle.

2. Slip the skins off the peppers. Sometimes a scrap of paper towel helps make this slippery/sticky job easier. If you have roasted some hot ones, you might wish to use silicone or latex gloves. With a small knife, slit the pepper lengthwise, pull out the stem end and most of the seeds will follow. A wipe with a towel helps get the rest.

3. Leave the peppers whole for stuffing or cut in strips for pizza or salad.

ROAST PEPPER SALAD

Toss 1½ to 2 cups roasted pepper strips with a tablespoon of olive oil and a tablespoon of balsamic vinegar, and kosher salt and freshly ground black pepper to taste. Add nothing else or maybe a few tablespoons of minced parsley, cilantro, or tarragon. Or a clove of crushed garlic and ½ to 1 cup feta cubes or sliced goat cheese and a sprinkle of fresh thyme leaves. Or some kalamata olives.

SALSA RANCHERA

This very mellow salsa is great for *huevos rancheros* or ladled into a bean burrito.

6 poblano chiles

6 jalapenos

2 medium tomatoes

2 cloves garlic, minced

¼ teaspoon kosher salt

2 tablespoons neutral oil

1 medium white onion, finely chopped

Makes about 1¾ cups

1. Roast, skin, and seed the peppers as described in Broiled Mixed Peppers (page 241). Chop finely.

2. Roast the tomatoes in the same way, leaving them whole and turning them in the great heat at the oven's mouth until they are blistered all over. You may peel the tomatoes thoroughly, a little bit, or not at all, depending on your inclination. At any rate, chop them fine, catching the juice; combine with the peppers, garlic, and salt.

3. Heat the oil in a 10-inch frying pan over a medium-high flame. Add the onion and sauté just until soft and translucent. Add the pepper mixture all at once, being careful of spattering. Stir and cook rapidly for a few minutes until reduced a bit. Check for salt.

NOTE: For quick *huevos rancheros,* crack 4 fresh eggs gently right into the sauce to poach over low heat. If you like, grate some cheese over them and cover for 3 minutes. Meanwhile, quickly fry 4 corn tortillas in a small amount of oil to make them pliable. Arrange 2 tortillas on each of 2 plates and carefully scoop out the soft-cooked eggs and their sauce to top. Scatter chopped cilantro and scallions or sliced white onion over. Serves 2.

GREEN SAUCE

This is an intensely flavored sauce, a tasty spark for grilled lamb chops or flank steak. If you find its bitter note too much, balance it with a little pomegranate molasses.

¼ cup unblanched almonds

2 cloves garlic

½ teaspoon salt

4 poblano or other favorite peppers, roasted as described in Broiled Mixed Peppers (page 241), seeded, skinned, and chopped

1 cup parsley leaves and tender upper stems, minced

¾ cup cilantro leaves and stems, minced
Freshly ground black pepper

¼ cup extra-virgin olive oil

2 tablespoons balsamic vinegar

1–2 tablespoons pomegranate molasses (optional)

Makes 1¾ cups

I. Toast the almonds. You may accomplish this either on a baking pan in the wood-fired oven after you roast the peppers, or on a dry griddle or skillet over a medium flame. In either case, do not permit your attention to stray; keep them moving and remove the pan from the heat source as soon as the nuts begin to brown and smell toasty, about 3 minutes. Remember that they will continue to roast in the pan, especially if it is of heavy-gauge iron.

2. I like to make this sauce either in a food processor (don't forget ear protection — almonds are LOUD) or on a large cutting board with a big knife (safe decibel level). Mince the garlic and salt together finely. Add the almonds and chop well. Add the peppers, parsley, and cilantro, and keep chopping. If you're using a food processor, use the pulse function to keep it chunky.

3. Scrape the mixture into a mixing bowl if you are using the knife method. Add the olive oil, vinegar, and black pepper, and taste for salt. Add pomegranate molasses if desired.

STAGE 2: SUPER-HOT ROASTING

Once you have pushed the fire all the way to the rear of the oven, and it is burning viciously, there should be lots of heat and plenty of room in front of the blaze to cook. The heat at this stage is less flame-y than the earlier phase, but still delivers a powerful sear on one side of the food. Many sorts of vegetables can be roasted in this heat. Small-diameter meats like sausage, poultry livers, shellfish, and finfish all thrive in these conditions.

So let the oven do your prep work; this is the time to pop in things that have a little more bulk and need more than superficial searing. It is also an opportunity to make a pretty effortless tasty appetizer.

Retained Heat

SPICY LITTLE NECKS

Southeastern Massachusetts is blessed with many great Portuguese restaurants. This simple recipe is inspired by their great way with clams.

4 medium tomatoes
1 pound chorizo (optional)
24 littleneck clams, scrubbed
2 large white onions, thinly sliced pole-to-pole
1 head chicory, chopped
6 cloves garlic, minced
4 jalapeno chiles, seeded and chopped
2 Anaheim chiles, seeded and chopped
2 Hungarian wax chiles, seeded and chopped
8 tablespoons butter, chopped
1 cup dry white wine
1 loaf stale bread, thickly sliced for toast

Serves 5 to 6 as a robust appetizer

1. Have the fire burning smartly toward the rear of the oven. Put the whole tomatoes in a pie pan into the center of the oven, and roast, turning occasionally, until blistered. Remove and as soon as you can handle them, chop them up, discarding the skins if they upset you. If you are using the chorizo, give it a quick roast in the same way, and then slice it ½-inch thick on the diagonal.

2. Select a large enamel-coated cast-iron baking dish, or failing that, a heavy-duty lasagne pan. Arrange the little necks in a single layer in the dish. Pile all the rest of the ingredients on. Slide the dish into the center of the oven and roast about 7 minutes. Pull the pan out and use tongs to give the whole mess a little stir. Return to the oven, placing it on a slightly different spot. Check it again in another 7 minutes, turning things over again. Return to the oven until most of the clams are open, another 3 to 7 minutes. Use a knife to help clams that may have gotten stuck.

3. While the clams are deep in the oven, make toast closer to the mouth. Just arrange the sliced bread on a cooling rack on a baking pan and slide it into the mouth of the oven. Turn the pan end-for-end and the bread slices individually as necessary. Keep warm and serve with the clams when they are ready.

CAJUN SHRIMP

My mother's been cooking this great recipe for about 30 years, since she clipped it from a newspaper column touting a Providence, Rhode Island, eatery that has long since disappeared. The original was a sauté, but it's also a natural for the wood-fired oven. Choose a beer that is neither too sweet nor too hoppy.

½ teaspoon hot pepper flakes

½ teaspoon freshly ground black pepper

¼ teaspoon salt

½ teaspoon flavorful powdered red pepper, like New Mexico, Aleppo, or hot Hungarian paprika

2 teaspoons minced fresh thyme or ¼ teaspoon dried

2 teaspoons minced fresh rosemary or ¼ teaspoon dried

2 teaspoons minced fresh oregano or ¼ teaspoon dried

4 tablespoons butter

4 cloves garlic, minced

½ teaspoon Worcestershire sauce

2 pounds medium or large shrimp, shells on

1 cup beer

1 cup clam juice (optional, but contributes a lot to the sauce)

Serves 6 people who like to eat with their fingers

I. Have the fire burning smartly toward the rear of the oven. Mix the herbs and spices in a small bowl, and have all the rest of the ingredients ready to go. Put the butter in a large flat enamel-coated cast-iron or ceramic baking dish; slide it into the oven for a minute to melt the butter. Pull it out of the oven without letting it brown, and add the garlic and Worcestershire sauce. Top with the shrimp and toss to coat thoroughly. Pour over the beer and clam juice if using. Place in the center of the oven. Roast 5 minutes. Draw from the oven and toss shrimp all about. If the shrimp are not pink and curling up, return the dish to the oven until they are. They will also continue to cook in the residual heat of the pan after they're drawn.

2. Serve with rice or toast to sop up the juices.

STAGE 3: PIZZA TIME

Clever bakers have long taken advantage of the tremendous heat available toward the end of the firing period, when the oven is already radiating what it has stored, yet is still hosting a mini-inferno within. At this point the entire vault of the oven has cleared of soot, signifying that the masonry has reached a temperature suitable for more critical live-fire baking.

Some of the most attractive uses of a wood-fired oven, the pizza and its family, fall into this category: foods originating as treats or snacks for those working around the oven on baking day. Previous to the development of the wood-fired oven, the ancestors of the pizza family were breads baked on a griddle or directly on a hot hearth, covered in embers, like those described in previous chapters. The names of these breads point us toward their origins, with pizza looking eastward to the *pide* and pita lands of Greece and Turkey, perhaps indicating a griddle- or *tannur*-baked origin. *Focaccia* and *fougasse* reveal the spread of the Roman versions of the flatbread originally cooked right on the hearth (Latin, *focus*) throughout the Italian peninsula and southern France. Strasbourg's *flammekeuche* recalls the Roman past; the descendants of the Allemani and Franks there still insist on the proper Roman-style oven and live fire to bake it.

Pizza, of course, has perversely made the leap from a secondary to the primary use for a wood-fired oven in many people's minds. I have met many folks who were very surprised that you could use a wood-fired oven to bake bread! But, as a tail-wagging-the-dog scenario, one could do a lot worse. The intense heat of a well-fired oven with live flames still curling under the vault does set the ideal stage for the lightest, crispest, most delicious pizza imaginable.

GETTING READY FOR PIZZA

For me, live-fire baking, great as it is, is virtually always just a detour in the path to baking bread, so I bear in mind from the beginning that I want a thoroughly and evenly heated oven waiting for my loaves after we've had fun with pizza. Ultimately, I think that you wind up with a better oven for pizza by holding that thought as you fire it up. (Also on the few occasions that I have heated the oven just for a pizza party, I find myself scrounging around the kitchen for something to bake in all that perfect heat after the fun is over. It just isn't right to let that go for nothing! At least plan to make *clafoutis* or bread pudding or a cobbler or a pie for dessert.)

So, to heat the oven for members of the pizza family of foods, follow the general method for heating the oven for bread outlined on page 231. Once the soot has burned off the oven's vault, transition to all hardwood if you have been heating with softwood or a mix thus far. Continue to maintain a good fire in the middle-rear of the oven. Have on hand plenty of small dry hardwood in stick or chunk form.

Line up all the ingredients and equipment you will need for working and topping and maneuvering the dough, including a clean work surface, your preshaped dough, rolling pin if you like, semolina flour, wheat flour, all your prepared toppings, a wooden peel, a metal peel, cutting boards to receive the baked pies, and a pizza wheel or big knife to cut them.

Make the final adjustment to your fire. Using a metal scraper or hook or poker, push the whole fire off to one side, right against the side wall of the oven. With a scraper and then a nonflammable brush, clean the rest of the oven of all coals and ashes. Arrange the fire on the side so that it continues to burn smartly. Throughout the live-fire baking process, manage the fire with the occasional addition of hardwood pieces. You can continue producing pizzas if it burns down to coals intermittently, but ideally you want to effect the constant licking of flames on the ceiling of the oven.

Shaping Dough for Live-Fire Baking

These last steps must be done immediately before baking. Once toppings are applied, especially, delays on the way to the oven are unwelcome.

Like so much having to do with baking, stretching dough can be fun or frustrating depending on your preparation and attitude. I look at it as something I'll be improving at for the rest of my life, with hundreds of delicious treats to practice on.

248

Retained Heat

Here are a few pointers for shaping dough:

- While you never want to incorporate any more flour into your dough after the initial mix, have plenty of flour and semolina flour on hand when stretching the dough.

- Have a clean, dry work surface. Take one ball of nicely relaxed dough and dip it lightly in a tub of flour. Pat it into a flattish disk on your work surface. Continue patting the dough outward from the center with flat open fingers, while quickly pivoting the disk with the other hand. Now pick up the dough and gently and quickly make small stretching motions all around the edges. The middle of the dough tends to stretch itself; it's mostly the edges you need to help along.

- Feeling adventuresome? Try tossing your dough at this point like a Neapolitan pizza baker. The spinning motion draws the dough out from the center perfectly evenly with as little contact as possible (until you have to catch it). Since the edges of the dough are moving more rapidly than the middle, the perimeter stretches thinly and uniformly. In theory. No time like the present to start practicing.

- Avoid holes at all costs when toppings will be used; thin untopped flatbreads can cope with raggedy edges or a tear or two, but even a pinhole can cause trouble in a pizza with moisture in the filling.

- Try a rolling pin. A short uncambered rolling pin can be very helpful if you get frustrated with stretching. It helps consolidate the dough into an even disk, preparatory to any heroic airborne stretching you might want to venture.

- Let the dough rest if you get resistance. The long final proofing time on the pizza dough recipe to follow should make your dough very extensible. But whenever you perceive a tendency in dough to snap back, a few minutes rest is indicated.

- Look upon this aspect of your live-fire baking as an enjoyable long-term project; remember that a pizza's scrumptiousness does not rely on roundness. (Pi is not essential to some pretty good pie.)

TIPS FOR TOPPING PIZZAS

1. Scatter semolina on a wooden peel.

2. Center the stretched dough on peel and apply toppings with restraint. You can bowl people over with just a scatter of sage leaves, a drizzle of olive oil, and a sprinkle of salt.

3. Two or three tablespoons of sauce and a couple of well-chosen accents will stand up better than a pile of all your favorite things. Too much moisture and too many flavors and textures weigh down the whole experience.

4. Peel the pizza instantly into the oven.

Baking the Pizza

This is the best part. Launch your pizza or flatbread into the center of the clean part of the hearth. Don't expect the oven to bake evenly in a live-fire application; you must turn the food part way through to expose the "cool" side to the heat. About a minute after contact, the bottom of the dough should be sufficiently baked for you to use a small peel to spin the pizza and move it to a hotter or cooler spot if necessary.

In a properly heated oven, you may observe the baking process as if it were a time-lapse film, a great learning experience. The crust inflates and browns, the toppings steam and collapse, the cheese becomes a molten pool. The hearth and vault will each be delivering a blast of heat in its own way; ideally the bottom and top of the food will be done at the same moment. Use the peel to pick up the pizza at the last minute and hold it close to the vault if the top surface is lagging behind the crust.

Use a peel to scoop the pizza or flatbread out of the oven and deposit it on a serving board. Cut it into sections but remind your guests that the food just spent a formative 90 seconds in a 900-degree environment.

Depending on the size of your oven, there may be plenty of room to bake more than one pizza at a time. The baking time is so quick, though, that it's seldom important to rush to load the oven up. It's nicer to take your time, and keep the heat up, and produce sequential perfect pizzas.

I like to brush the floor of the oven clean when I have the opportunity; scorched semolina is not a great addition to any food.

PIZZA DOUGH

This base recipe will serve eight people as an appetizer. This estimate takes into account the tendency of most people to really dive into these, even if they know another course is coming. It might serve six as the entree, depending on the richness of the toppings. Leftovers are welcome if you can manage to keep them, but usually guests just keep eating them until they are all gone, even if it takes all night. The recipe multiplies easily to make vast amounts of dough as needed.

If you do not maintain a leavening culture, simply omit it from the recipe. It serves to create flavor and texture as much as to leaven this dough, but perfectly fine pizza may be made without it.

2	cups warm water
22	ounces bread flour
5	ounces white leaven (or whole wheat, if you prefer), optional
1	teaspoon dry yeast
1	tablespoon kosher or sea salt
1½	tablespoons olive oil

1. In the bowl of a standing mixer (or in any large bowl if you will work by hand), stir the water into the flour with a fork, mixing just until there are no dry spots left. Cover the bowl airtight and let sit about 30 minutes.

2. Chop the leaven in a few chunks and drop on top of the flour mixture, along with the yeast and salt. Mix on slow speed with the dough hook (or a wooden spoon or your hand) until completely combined. Mix one step faster and add the olive oil. Work two minutes or so, until the dough feels strong and smooth. Compose the dough into a nice ball in the bowl and cover airtight.

3. Allow to ferment two hours, stretching and folding the dough twice at 40-minute intervals, as follows: scrape it out onto a lightly floured counter, pull it gently into an oblong, and fold it in thirds. Repeat on the opposite axis.

4. Divide the dough into ten 4.2-ounce blobs for smallish pizzas, or six 7-ounce blobs for medium. (You have about 42 ounces of dough, so you may deploy your mastery of the multiplication table in any way you like.) Knead each little blob up into a smooth round

ball, incorporating as little new flour as possible. Dust it with flour and set aside for between 1 and 2 hours, covered up to keep it from drying out. The ideal way to manage these dough balls is to set them in broad, flat plastic storage boxes; they are airtight, stackable, and easy to transport.

SLOWING THE RISE

The schedule on page 252 describes the minimum amount of fermentation time for great pizza dough. But you can make your life easier, and your dough even better, by stretching out the process over a longer period, as long as you have a cold place to store the dough to retard the pace of fermentation. Here are two techniques that may be helpful to slow fermentation:

RETARD THE DOUGH IN BULK OVERNIGHT, OR FOR UP TO TWO DAYS. After the second stretch-and-fold, place the dough in a big plastic storage tub (twice the size of the dough — it will still rise) and put it in the fridge. Slow, cool fermentation provides for a great improvement for the dough and lots of flexibility for your schedule. Take out at least 3 hours before pizza-making time. Gather up and neaten the chilly dough, and press back down into a ball. Cover and let warm up for about an hour. Then divide and shape the dough as in the main Pizza Dough recipe.

RETARD THE SHAPED DOUGH. Place the boxes of preshaped dough in the fridge for up to 4 hours; they may be rolled or stretched cold, or allowed to warm up some before final shaping. The dough becomes very extensible, and the additional fermentation develops deeper flavor. Equally important if you are entertaining, retarding the dough at this point buys you time when you might be busy with other things like heating your oven, preparing toppings, or enjoying a cocktail with your guests.

The major downside of this useful technique is that it takes a lot of refrigerator room; tricky for many of us. Since I live in a cool climate, I often take advantage of the great outdoors to retard fermentation. Even a summer evening with the temperature in the 60s slows things down a bit compared to a hot kitchen.

These two techniques may be used separately or in tandem. Experiment to find what works for you.

Retained Heat

PIZZA TOPPING COMBINATIONS

To be honest, many of our favorite toppings have evolved from the "there's nothing in the house" scenario. For some reason I rarely plan ahead about pizza making, so I seldom have mozzarella around to make the always great classic, pizza margherita (tomato reduction, nice fresh mozzarella, basil leaves, a thread of olive oil). But there is always *parmigiano* in the cheese drawer, and bits and bobs of other nice cheeses to combine with a few key ingredients. And some of our favorites eschew cheese altogether in favor of other savory ingredients.

ARUGULA, BLUE CHEESE, AND PEPITAS

Even very strong-flavored mature arugula is great this way. We like to use our local Great Hill Blue; perhaps you have a favorite from your neighborhood. It is important that the pepitas are raw; toasted ones will burn.

- 1 large bunch arugula, washed and trimmed, or 5 cups baby arugula
- 2 tablespoons extra-virgin olive oil
  Pinch kosher or sea salt
  Ample freshly ground black pepper
- 3 ounces blue cheese, in chunks
- ¼ cup raw pepitas

Enough topping for 3 medium pizzas

---

1. Put the arugula in a large work bowl, tearing it up if large. Toss with the remaining ingredients.

2. Pile as much of the mixture as physically possible on stretched pizza dough, making sure to dredge up some of the good stuff from the bottom of the bowl for the very top.

3. Bake as described on page 251.

ANCHOVIES, WALNUTS, AND PARSLEY

The underappreciated flavor of parsley takes center stage. Substitute pecans or almonds for the walnuts if you prefer.

- 2 cloves garlic
  Pinch of salt
  Copious freshly ground black pepper
- 6 anchovy fillets or more
- ½ cup raw walnuts
- 1 bunch broad-leaved parsley, leaves and smallest stems
- 2 tablespoons extra-virgin olive oil

Enough topping for 3 medium pizzas

---

1. Use a chef's knife on a large cutting board to reduce the garlic and salt to a fine mince. Chop in the pepper and anchovies. When that is reduced to pulp, add the walnuts and parsley, chopping until mostly finely minced: a few chunky bits are pleasant.

2. Scrape the mixture into a bowl, and stir in the olive oil.

3. Use a large soup spoon to dollop onto stretched dough and spread into an even skim coat.

4. Bake as described on page 251.

SALT COD, CAPERS, AND RED ONION

Here we use the southwestern French salt cod and potato mixture called *brandade de morue* as the base for a very delicious, if unexpected, white pizza.

½ pound piece of salt cod
1 large potato
   Pinch of salt
2 cloves garlic
⅓ cup cream, heated to steaming
¼ cup extra-virgin olive oil, warmed
   Freshly ground black pepper
¼ of a red onion, sliced very thinly
¼ cup capers

Enough topping for 3 medium pizzas

1. One day ahead, rinse the salt cod in cold water, and then put in a container, covered with cold water, to soak. Change the water frequently at the beginning; place the container in the fridge with fresh water when you go to bed.

2. Next day, peel the potato and cover with cold, lightly salted water in a saucepan. Bring to a simmer and cook until tender. Drain the water, let the last moisture evaporate, and mash. Keep warm, lid ajar.

3. Meanwhile, cover the cod with fresh cold water and bring to a point just below a simmer. Do not boil. Turn off the heat and let it stand 5 minutes, then drain. As soon as it's cool enough to handle, use your fingers to pull it into as many small pieces as you have patience for.

4. Do the next part while the fish and potato are still warm. Use a large mortar and pestle to crush the garlic with a pinch of salt. Add the salt cod gradually, crushing it as you go. When it is reduced to a thready-looking pulp, work in the potatoes, transitioning to a circular mashing motion.

5. Once the cod and potatoes are well combined, gradually work in the hot cream. When that is amalgamated, start pouring in the warm oil, stirring it in as a fine thread.

6. Grind in plenty of pepper, and taste for salt. (This is a delicious appetizer in its own right served warm on toast with a handful of olives.)

7. You may close it airtight in a container and chill for a few days until needed. No need to reheat before applying to pizzas unless it is too thick to spread, in which case, stir over very low heat until warm.

8. Spread ¼- to ½-inch thick on stretched pizza dough. Top with red onion slices and capers, pressing down a bit on the latter to keep them in place when the pizzas are peeled into the oven.

9. Bake as described on page 251.

FLAMMEKEUCHE

This Alsatian specialty is incontrovertibly a member of the extended pizza family, but the toppings — bacon, onions, fresh cheese, and cream — belie its home in the borderlands between France and Germany. Here is my ultra-mellow version.

1 cup heavy cream

1 cup minced leek, white lower part only (about 6 inches of a fat leek)

Kosher salt

Fresh pepper

Part of a nutmeg

6 ounces (¾ cup) *fromage frais* or quark or *labne*

4 ounces bacon, minced

2 2-inch piece of palest green leek, shredded into fine strips lengthwise

12–15 button mushrooms, thinly sliced

6 4-ounce lumps of pizza dough

Makes 6 smallish flammekeuchen, a substantial appetizer for 6

---

1. Put the cream and minced leek into a saucepan and bring to a simmer, uncovered. Add a pinch of salt and cook on a medium-low flame for 10 to 15 minutes, until sauce has reduced to about 1 cup and the leeks are thoroughly tender. Grind in fresh pepper and grate in nutmeg to taste. Check for salt.

2. Stir in the fromage frais. This base may be stored in a jar in the refrigerator for up to two days if you like.

3. To make the flammekeuchen, have the oven heated as for pizza. In a medium bowl, toss together the minced bacon, the leek shreds, and the sliced mushrooms. Add a pinch of salt and grind on some pepper and mix well.

4. Stretch the dough exactly as for pizza. Spread a few tablespoonsful of the creamy leek base on the dough, and top with a small heap of the leek and mushroom mixture.

5. Bake just as for pizza.

Getting Ready for Pizza

PIDE

I almost never set out to make a batch of pide on purpose. Rather, it is a great fallback when I have leftover pizza dough, as I most always have some odds and ends of cheese and fresh eggs in the house. We'll happily eat it for breakfast, lunch, or supper. This is our home-style version.

24 ounces pizza dough (page 252)
4 ounces mixed cheese: definitely some crumbled feta or goat cheese, but can include grated *manchego*, *parmigiano*, or cheddar, and a bit of cream cheese
2 scallions or a small handful of chives, minced
A few sprigs of parsley or cilantro, minced
2 tablespoons plain yogurt
Pinch salt
Aleppo or other flavorful powdered hot red pepper
4 fresh eggs

4 servings

1. You'll want the oven fired as for pizza.

2. Divide the dough in four, and preshape into smooth balls. Hold in an airtight box at room temperature between 1 and 2 hours, or retard as long as overnight.

3. In a small bowl, stir together the cheeses, herbs, yogurt, and pinch of salt, remembering that the need for salt will vary depending on the cheeses in your mix. Leave at room temperature for a few minutes so that it will be easy to spread. (If it is still very stodgy, add a bit more yogurt or a dab of soft butter.)

4. Prepare a work surface with a scattering of flour. Use a rolling pin to flatten one ball of dough into foot-long oval about 6 inches wide in the middle.

5. Leaving an inch-wide border clear all around, spread one quarter of the filling over the remainder of the oval. Sprinkle with Aleppo pepper to taste. Turning the sides of the dough upright and a bit over the filling, pinch each end of the oval firmly together to make a gondola or canoe shape.

6. Transfer to a peel prepared with semolina. Just before peeling the pide into the oven, crack an egg into the very center. Keep your movements nice and smooth and level thereafter.

7. Bake as you would pizza, turning partway through.

VARIATION

If you prefer a soft-cooked egg, launch the boat into the oven without it, making sure there will be room later (using a spoon to create a shallow divot in the filling in the center is helpful). When it's time to turn the pide, slide the egg in then.

PIDE: A PIZZA COUSIN

When I first saw the word *pide* on bakers' signs in towns on the Anatolian plateau of Turkey, I expected a regional variant on the flat pocket breads (pita in Israel; *khubz* in Arabic-speaking Levant) so familiar to Americans. While all manner of flatbreads suitable for baking on griddles or tannurs are to be found in Turkey, it turned out that this pide is not really one of them. It is baked in a front-opening, classical-style oven, and is filled with delicious cheesy toppings. Except for its distinctive boat shape, pide recalls the pizza, of which it is certainly a close relative if not progenitor. The Italian peninsula is home to a baffling array of pizza variants. Two from Sicily, *piduni* and *pizzolu*, calzone-like stuffed breads, share etymological and culinary roots with Turkish pide, and suggest the connection was made sometime during the Byzantine rule of Sicily, between the seventh and ninth centuries.

Pide is part of the richly developed bread tradition that happens to occupy the region of wheat's domestication. It is a dead ringer for the Georgian *khachapuri*, which in turn has siblings and cousins across central Asia.

STAGE 4: THE DYING FIRE

The dying fire in the heated oven — when your final sticks of wood are burning down to coals and ash — presents a mellower scenario. This heat can be used to cook larger, denser foods that would scorch on the outside in a flamier oven.

One caveat here: be conscious that placing a large cold item on the hearth will definitely drain heat from at least that one spot for at least a little while. Compensate by shifting the food from one place to another at least once during the cooking, and by allowing plenty of time for the heat to equalize during the "soaking" period. An infrared thermometer is very helpful in learning how your oven reacts when used in this admittedly unorthodox fashion.

DYING FIRE CHICKEN ROAST

This is a pretty effortless way to get a fabulous dinner made on a busy baking day. Because you're really heating the oven to bake bread, it's necessary to move the chicken around to accommodate proper oven heating, but in reality all this maneuvering is not half as fussy as it sounds.

¼ cup kosher salt

3 cups cold water

8 chicken thighs

4 garlic cloves or 3 big scapes, finely chopped, plus 1 or 2 cloves for the optional toast

1 sprig each rosemary, marjoram, parsley, thyme; tender parts minced

1 small fresh red hot pepper, minced

2 tablespoons olive oil
  Freshly ground black pepper

1 stale loaf rustic bread for toast (optional)

1 poblano chile, cut in short strips

1 large potato, peeled and cut in large dice

10 green olives

½ cup dry white wine

1 bunch chard or other tender greens, sliced across in ½-inch ribbons

---

4 to 5 servings

---

1. Put the salt and water in a lidded container large enough to accommodate the chicken thighs. Stir until the salt has dissolved, then immerse the chicken. Refrigerate the brined chicken for at least an hour and up to a day.

2. Assemble the dish while the oven is firing. Select a shallow enamel-coated cast-iron or ceramic baking dish. Toss in the garlic, herbs, and red pepper. Add the olive oil and combine, oiling the sides of the dish as you do so. Remove the chicken from the brine and shake off; add to the baking dish along with plenty of pepper. Toss to coat with the herb mixture, then arrange the chicken pieces skin side up.

3. When the last wood you added to the fire has begun to burn down, push the fire along the back of the oven, and slide in the baking pan. Roast 15 minutes, turning and shifting the dish every 5 minutes.

(If you intend to serve the chicken on toast, this is a good time to make it. Just arrange the sliced stale bread on a cooling rack on a baking pan and pop it in the oven alongside the chicken. Turn the pan end-for-end and the bread slices individually as necessary. Rub each toast with a half clove of garlic and set aside until serving time.)

4. Remove the chicken dish from the oven. Add the poblano chile, potato, olives, and wine, stirring things about with a wooden spoon. Consolidate your coals, then return the dish to the oven for 15 more minutes.

5. At this point, you should be ready to clear out the coals to prepare the oven for your bread (remember your bread?). Remove the chicken and set aside in a safe place while you clean the oven. (I set mine right on the top of my oven, and since it's none-too-well insulated, it keeps warm there. This may work for you.) Close the door of the oven for a few minutes to let the dust settle. Meanwhile, add the chard to the chicken, stirring it into the sauce as best you can. When the coast is clear in the oven, pop the chicken back in to finish. Roast about 20 minutes more, shifting location once partway through.

6. Serve in flat soup plates, piled on toast, if desired, and don't forget to pop your bread in the oven in the excitement.

ROASTED EGGPLANT

Large Italian-style eggplant chars and roasts perfectly by the dying fire. The delicious pulp can be put to use in *baba ghanoush* and other mixtures like the recipes that follow.

1. When the last wood of your fire is burning actively — just after pizza making is ideal — sweep off a place on the hearth and use long tongs to place eggplants directly on it. Roast, turning this way and that, until skin is entirely blackened and eggplant deflates, about 15 minutes.

2. Remove and set aside in a bowl for about 10 minutes. When you have a chance, cut off the stems and peel off the skin and discard. Place the eggplant meat on a cutting board and run a large knife over it once or twice.

BABA GHANOUSH

You'll never eat store-bought again.

    1 clove garlic
    1 fat pinch kosher or coarse sea salt
 1¾ cup (13 ounces) roasted eggplant pulp, chopped
    3 tablespoons tahini
    1 tablespoon fresh lemon juice
    1 tablespoon fresh parsley, minced (optional garnish)

Serves 3 to 4 as an appetizer

1. Use a large mortar and pestle to mash the garlic and salt to a pulp. Using the pestle in a circular, stirring motion, work in the eggplant pulp, crushing it to a rough puree. Once the eggplant is of a uniform texture, stir in the tahini followed by the lemon juice. Scrape the mixture up from the bottom with a spatula, mix again, and taste for salt.

2. Spread the *baba ghanoush* into a flattish dish and serve right away, with the optional scatter of parsley and the obligatory stack of fresh pita.

Retained Heat

ROASTED EGGPLANT APPETIZER

Roast the peppers along with the eggplants, then peel, seed, and chop. After that, the whole thing mixes up in seconds with a mortar and pestle.

½ teaspoon cumin seeds

½ teaspoon coriander seeds

½ teaspoon peppercorns

2 cloves garlic

½ teaspoon kosher or coarse sea salt

1 tablespoon extra-virgin olive oil

1 tablespoon balsamic vinegar

2½ cups chopped roasted eggplant pulp (from 1 large eggplant)

½ cup roasted poblano, Anaheim, or Italian frying peppers, chopped

⅓ cup walnuts, chopped, plus a few whole to garnish

1 tablespoon minced cilantro stems and leaves, plus more for garnish

Serves 6 to 8 as an appetizer

1. On an iron griddle over a medium flame, toast the cumin and coriander seeds until a shade darker and fragrant. Toss them into a large mortar and grind them to powder along with the peppercorns. Add the garlic and salt and crush into an aromatic paste. Work in the oil and vinegar. When all is emulsified together, add the eggplant, crushing it a bit, then the peppers, walnuts, and cilantro.

2. Stir it up from the bottom to make sure it is well combined, and taste for salt. Serve in a flat dish, garnished with cilantro and a whole walnut or two (a flag for the walnut-allergic), with a fresh stack of pita, shrak, or other flatbread.

USING RETAINED HEAT — THE COOLING CURVE

The oven proves its mettle when the fire is gone. Gracefully returning the heat you've piled into it is the heart of the oven's work.

Any oven that bakes using retained heat is gradually cooling from the time combustion ceases, regardless of its design sophistication in general or its mass-to-insulation ratio in particular. The baking chamber may actually get hotter after you take out a batch of bread and close the door for a few minutes. That's because you've removed the thing that was cooler than the masonry, the bread. Overall, though, the temperature of the masonry can go only one way, and that's down, until it rejoins the ambient temperature of its neighborhood.

For home bakers this is not a bad thing. Most days I can only use so many loaves of intense-heat-loving bread; the fun becomes using as much of the stored heat as possible for other purposes.

Not only does it seem a waste to let all those hard-won BTUs just dissipate into our already warming world, but also the fact is that pretty much anything baked in your wood-fired oven will taste better than the same thing baked in the metal box in your kitchen. And, fortunately, many foods benefit from baking at lower temperatures than those favored by unsweetened yeast-raised breads.

Following are some sequences I use to absorb the retained heat from my ovens — you may need to adapt them to work in the special circumstances of yours. The challenge is to learn the cooling curve of your oven and to attune yourself to how long you have in the various temperature ranges. Each batch of cold food you place in the oven draws down the temperature, of course, and any time you open the door has an effect; always close it any time you can.

Temperature is not the only factor to consider when planning a baking strategy. Some of the following schemes are mutually exclusive — for example, a moisture-exuding heat-sink like roasted tomatoes will not leave an atmosphere enjoyed by meringues. Granola takes up a lot of room and time. Baked beans should enter the oven while it's pretty hot and then just sit there unmolested all night; they're incredible for breakfast.

BAKING WITH FALLING HEAT

≥500°F

The first and most intense retained heat of each firing is almost always used to bake unsweetened yeast- or naturally leavened breads. Many ovens with better insulation than mine will allow several batches of this primary bread.

425-450°F

Yeast-raised breads and cakes that are enriched with dairy products, eggs, or sweeteners bake nicely in this temperature. These need some heat to achieve a good rise, but those enriching ingredients all contribute to a tendency toward rapid browning. They will bake more quickly than in your gas or electric oven, so be alert! Chemically leavened breads like biscuits, scones, and cornbread are also good choices for this temperature range, as are casseroles and roasted vegetables.

400-425°F

Fruit pastries large and small, from apple pie to blueberry cobbler to pear tarts, bake well in this heat. Pastry in general does not benefit from moisture in the oven. This oven temperature is also great for baked beans, which will use up the rest of the heat and may remain in the oven overnight.

375-400°F

Most anything else you can think of — sponge and butter cakes, cookies, bars — are worthy candidates for this oven temperature.

350-375°F

A batch of granola will use up the rest of the heat. Or try reducing apple or pear sauce to "butter" in a wide non-reactive baking dish.

325-375°F

If the oven is good and dry, meringue-based treats will use up the rest of the heat.

265

BREAD FOR THE WOOD-FIRED OVEN

If you are already a bread-baker, plunging right into wood-fired baking with your own favorite recipes is the best way to start learning new skills. Formulas you know intimately may have surprising results when they hit the bricks of a wood-fired oven's hearth. Observing these differences will teach you a lot about your oven's temper.

If you don't have a lot of baking experience, you may want to start out with some loaves risen with commercial yeast, like Vienna bread, before diving into the world of natural leavening. And, congratulations on taking your first steps; there's never been a better time to learn to bake!

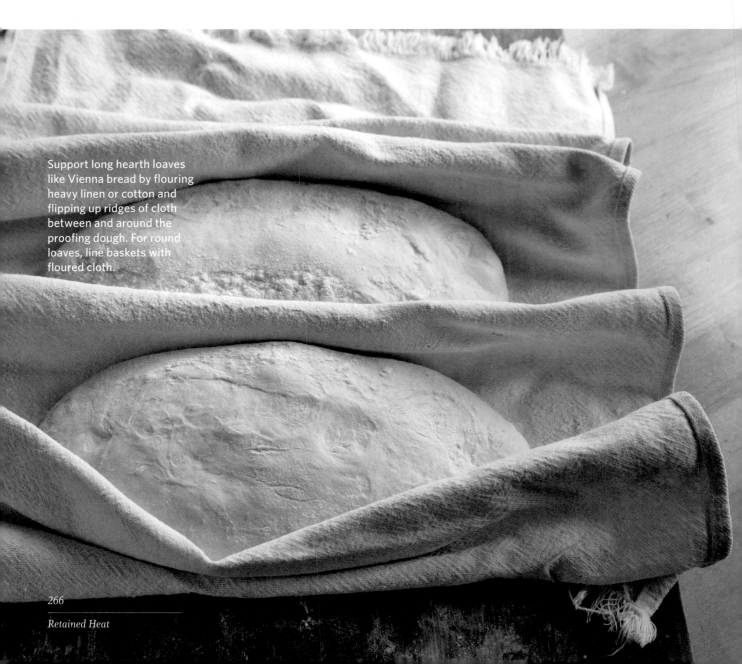

Support long hearth loaves like Vienna bread by flouring heavy linen or cotton and flipping up ridges of cloth between and around the proofing dough. For round loaves, line baskets with floured cloth.

VIENNA BREAD OR ROLLS

Austro-Hungarian bakers, scientists, and farmers revolutionized bread in the 19th century, bringing in technical advances that swept the bread-eating world and became the baking norm. High-protein wheat, commercial yeast, and steam injection all made their international debuts in the loaf we still call Vienna.

FOR THE PREFERMENT
- 1 cup milk
- 1 cup boiling water
- 16 ounces unbleached white bread or all-purpose flour
- 1 pinch dry yeast

FOR THE FINAL DOUGH
- 16 ounces unbleached white bread or all-purpose flour
- 1 cup warm water
- 1 teaspoon dry yeast
- 1 tablespoon kosher salt

Makes 2 large loaves or 32 rolls

1. Make the preferment. In a large bowl, combine the milk and boiling water; stir in the flour, and then the yeast. Cover and let sit in a warmish place 12-16 hours.

2. The final dough, step one. Stir the warm water and flour into the preferment, just until no dry flour remains. Cover and rest 20 to 30 minutes.

3. The final dough, step two. Toss the yeast and salt on top of the dough and mix it up in earnest, either by hand for 7 or 8 minutes, or in a mixer with a dough hook for 3 minutes on lowest speed, followed by 3 minutes on the next speed up. Cover the bowl and set in a warm place to ferment for 2 hours, folding the dough every 30 minutes, as shown on pages 276–277.

4. Meanwhile figure out your timetable and heat your oven so that it will be cleaned out, equalized, and in the neighborhood of 500°F when your loaves are ready to hop in. (See page 234.) Tricky, yes, but that's what the learning is all about.

5. Divide the dough into 2 loaves or 32 rolls. Preshape by drawing the outer floury part of each dough ball up to enclose the wetter inside surface, very lightly pulling them into smooth balls. Allow the dough to rest for a few minutes, smooth side down on the floured counter and lightly covered, while you lay out a piece of bakers' linen or other hefty canvas on a flat surface and dust and rub it with flour.

6. To shape, lay a preshaped round, rough side up, on your very lightly floured counter. Stretch and flatten a bit, then fold up one long edge and then the opposite one over the center. Elongate the resulting oblong loaf by pulling it crosswise along a not-very-floury part of the counter, seam side down. Place on the well-floured linen, good side up. Pull ridges of cloth up to gently support the rising dough. Lightly cover, and proof in a warm place for about an hour for loaves; about half an hour for rolls.

7. When both dough and oven are ready, dust the peel with fine semolina. In transferring rolls, pick them up by their ends and give them a little stretch, even pinching the ends to a point if you like. Slash from end to end. For loaves, which will bake in 30 to 40 minutes, transfer gently from beneath to the semolina-dusted peel and slash with a blade in one long cut from end to end. For best oven-spring and crust, spritz a lot of fine mist into the oven using a pump sprayer or atomizing bottle before and after loading.

NATURAL LEAVENING FOR YOUR WOOD-FIRED BREAD

Of course you can use your wood-fired oven to bake any sort of bread that you would bake in a conventional oven, and, as long as the oven is appropriately heated, the wood-fired loaf will way outshine the ordinary one. But the rhythm of wood firing cries out for breads with long, slow fermentation. And if you've taken enough control of your bread to free it from electric or gas baking, fermenting it with your own wild yeast is the next logical liberation.

Maintaining a nice leaven embroils you much more intimately in the interior life of your bread. For those who bake only occasionally, keeping a sourdough culture going may not make sense, but for anyone who bakes a lot or most of their bread, the practice will not only broaden your repertoire, opening the door to some great traditional European bread styles, but draw you deeper into an understanding of the whole baking process.

How to Start and Maintain a Leavening Culture

Frankly a lot of baloney has been written over the years about sourdough, obfuscating a process that bakers have understood implicitly for many centuries. When I started down this path some years ago, I did some reading and thinking before jumping in. As a home baker, I needed to have a sustainable leavening process — one that I could rely on year in and year out, and that would take no more work than, say, owning a guppy. I was enthusiastic to learn and willing to apply myself, but turned off by common approaches that involved either a lot of opaque mumbo-jumbo or wasteful discarding of great blobs of leaven. In the end, I used a mix of contemporary and historic ideas to come up with a simple system that works in my life. When I started out, I thought it was important to understand every last thing about enzymes and proteins and acidity, and it's wonderful if you do *but,* it turns out that this process is far more intuitive than that. Most times, the dough is happy to ferment productively, and when it isn't, it's not too hard to figure out why and set it back on track.

You don't need any fancy equipment, but you will want some organic wholewheat flour at the beginning. Eventually you can maintain your culture using the unbleached flour of your choosing, but at the start, it's critical to have the clean complex carbohydrates and naturally occurring microorganisms found in whole grains. The other absolutely indispensible ingredient is pure, unchlorinated, water. If you have your own good well water, you're all set. If not, use a good water filter to remove residual chlorine from treated water. In the recent past, another option was to let the water sit for several hours in an open pitcher, allowing the chlorine to dissipate. However, some of today's water delivery systems use new chlorine compounds designed to resist dissipation; filtration may be essential.

Day 1

Put about 2 tablespoons pure, unchlorinated water in a small bowl. Use a fork to stir in as much organic whole-wheat flour as it takes to make a dough (less than an ounce). Put a bit more organic whole-wheat flour on a clean work surface and knead this teeny blob, incorporating as much flour as necessary, until it's a fairly stiff little ball that holds its shape.

Take a wide-mouthed container (with a lid) of 2 cups or so capacity. (Glass is great; you'll be able to spy on progress without disturbing things.) Fill it roughly ⅔ full of organic whole-wheat flour. Bury the little lump of dough in the flour, less than an inch below the surface. Place the lid on the container and set aside at cool room temperature (60 to 68°F).

Once a Day for the Next Few Days

Peek at your experiment. If nothing has changed, leave it alone for another 24 hours. If, however, cracks have appeared in the flour above the dough ball — eureka! life! — you may move to the next step.

The Next Step

Retrieve the little dough-blob — now your leaven — from its floury resting-place. Cut away the crusty outside of the dough and discard. Place the spongy inner bit in a small bowl. Stir in roughly a tablespoon of pure, unchlorinated water, and then as much organic whole wheat flour as it takes to make it back into a dough, then once again, knead it until stiff with more flour. Place your refreshed starter in a small airtight container, like a yogurt tub. Let stand at room temperature overnight.

The Next Few Days

Inspect the leaven to judge its "ripeness." It is said to be ripe — meaning that it is the perfect time to either bake with it or refresh it — when the leaven has puffed up to a dome, and just begun to give out in the center. Apply your nose to this question, too. The leaven gives plenty of olfactory cues, and you will learn to interpret them as your friendship deepens.

Ripeness also indicates that the yeast in your leaven has consumed everything it can get from its last refreshment. Refresh it by stirring in a splash of pure, unchlorinated water and as much organic whole-wheat flour as it takes to make it back into a firm stirrable dough.

Depending on kitchen conditions, you'll probably find that daily refreshments are favored by your leaven (it may become quite exuberant in warm weather and prefer attention twice daily). Graduate the leaven to a larger container as necessary.

Natural Leavening for Your Wood-Fired Bread

About "Refreshment"

You and your leavening culture have entered into a cyclical relationship. You add some water and flour to the ripe culture. This "refreshment" transforms it instantly from an aromatic, collapsingly risen state to a firm, neutral-smelling ball of dough. Then, in a matter of hours, it will rise and fill with bubbles again, and redevelop the complex set of aromas that are the signature of your particular leaven.

You and Your New Friend

I initially entered the world of natural leavening with the idea that baking bread was the ultimate goal, but came to discover that each loaf of bread — whether splendid or mediocre — has been really just an offshoot, a branch, a trial. I was surprised to find that the leavening culture — and maintaining it in a way that is sustainable in my life — is actually itself the project. The adventure of this relationship reminds me that the food I cook and eat and offer to others is literally part of a much larger natural and cultural web, most of it only visible under a microscope. Working with natural leavening has added a task to each day, to be sure, but its benefits to me are far more than just getting loaves of bread to rise.

In each refreshment cycle, the fermenting leaven increases in volume and develops complex aromas and flavors.

Using Rye and Other Flours to Vary the Leaven

Once you have a flourishing starter, you can experiment with other flours. Your leavening culture may be capable of a great diversity of expression, given changes to its diet. Although I have experimented with other flours, I generally maintain a wheat leaven (either white or whole wheat) and a rye leaven. Even these two pets can occasionally overwhelm me and my kitchen, but the breads they make are so different and each so wonderful in their own way, that their maintenance seems justified. Every baker must decide for herself.

To start an offshoot leaven, simply take a small piece of your current one, and refresh separately using the new flour.

Prefermenting rye flour brings out its best baking characteristics, so, as a rye bread lover, it's easy for me to find the time to maintain that particular leaven. In fact, I find that it moves rather slowly, and I refresh it only every other day. Be warned that it can become shockingly strong smelling if neglected for a day too long. Don't panic; just refresh.

Using Natural Leavening in Your Baking

Time your bread-making so that you are able to use your leaven at optimal ripeness. Fortunately, since these cultures are slow-moving, this window is usually nice and wide. Just remove the appropriate weight of ripe leaven from the container and add to the bread dough as instructed. Refresh the remaining culture and set aside as usual.

Following are a few recipes for some household standbys. These will get you started, but experiment with adding soaked grains, dried fruits, and seeds and nuts to your liking. Also try adding a dollop of leaven to breads you're accustomed to making with commercial yeast — cut back the dry yeast some and stretch out the fermentation times a bit. You'll be struck by the improvements to moisture and depth of flavor in everything from oatmeal bread to hot cross buns. Keep a notebook of your experiments, tracking time and temperature, as well as proportions, so that you can replicate your results.

NATURAL LEAVENING Q&A

Why use a stiff dough, instead of a wet batter?

Many people maintain a yeast culture in a batter-like slurry, but I prefer the stiff-dough method, which has distinct advantages for home bakers. The process is slower and more controlled, and the activity of the culture is easier for the baker to perceive. The stiffer texture is also slower to respond to temperature spikes, a boon in an active kitchen during hot weather. In fact, during heat waves, I maintain the culture in a kneadable, rather than stirrable, state, to further arrest its action.

How much water should I use?

Naturally, each time you refresh your leaven it grows in size. Determining how much leaven you will need and when you'll need it is important so that you calibrate your refreshments to produce the right amount of ripe leaven at the right time.

If you happen to bake every day, it will be easy for you to find a rhythm and regimen for maintaining your leaven. Those of us who bake more irregularly — say, only once or a few times a week — will have to use a bit more judgment in refreshing. The leaven enjoys radical refreshment — nothing makes it hum along like being reduced to a couple tablespoons and then being flooded with new water and flour. It's easy to make a lot of leaven in a reasonably short time. What is harder is to grow your leaven incrementally, controlling each addition so that by the weekend, when you finally have time to bake, you have enough starter for your bread, but are not reenacting a science fiction film on your kitchen counter.

At those times, when I'm not baking very much, when I just want my leaven to be healthy but not to grow in size very much, I'm very chintzy with the refreshments: a tiny splash of cold water and a kneading of whatever amount of flour it takes to make a stiff dough. This skinflint regimen will not keep the leaven in the most flourishing condition, but it gets it through times when you are not baking enough for its liking.

Another strategy I've developed to help manage the volume of leaven in the house is to have a variety of baking strategies up my sleeve — including a few recipes that consume a large amount of leaven.

What if I must neglect my leaven?

In the real world of my kitchen, my poor leaven has to get by on the attention I am able to give it; it competes with a great range of other daily concerns, and sometimes loses. Fortunately, these cultures are as tough as they are forgiving. When life conspires against my paying proper attention to my leaven — I know it only takes two minutes, but sometimes there aren't two minutes left in the day — it will fall into a sullen, literally alcoholic, state. It will sag, and look grayish, and smell sour — really, it could not seem more like a drunk after a huge bender.

Some simple ministrations, though, no more than proper refreshments for a couple of days, and the thing is usually back up to snuff and ready for action.

Can I go on vacation?

If I plan on being away from home for two to ten days, I merely refresh the leaven, perhaps a bit stiffer than usual, place it into an airtight container with plenty of headroom, and refrigerate. This is cruel, but the leaven will survive, and recovery will be a matter of days with regular refreshments.

It pays to plan your baking so that the leaven is quite reduced in size before this sort of treatment. It's always nice to show up on vacation with a bagful of crusty sourdough bread, anyway.

What about longer storage?

You can freeze a small piece of your culture, and then revive it through regular refreshments. I have also had success following a seventeeth-century method that achieves immortality through mummification rather than cryogenics. Simply knead up a tough little marble-sized beanie of your culture as dry as possible and bury it in a jar full of kosher salt. Label it, because, take it from me, it'll be hard to identify years later when you return from your adventure. To revivify, rinse off the salty crust and crumble the lump into about a half-cup of warm water. Massage it into a slurry and strain it to remove the chunks. Knead it up to a stiff dough and proceed as usual. No guarantees, but I've had it come to life in 24 hours — I've never felt more like Dr. Frankenstein!

The ultimate hedge against losing a wild yeast culture you value is generosity: the more friends and acquaintances you get started in sourdough baking with a piece of your leaven, the more insurance you have that you'll never lose it!

NATURALLY LEAVENED BREAD

Consider this a simple master recipe for naturally leavened baking; infinite variations are possible, using different flours and different proportions of leaven. My current favorite employs a good proportion of whole-wheat flour and half rye leaven and half wheat leaven.

Loaves like these that spend a long time proofing benefit from the support of a basket. I use the world's cheapest split-bamboo baskets, lined with a loose light cotton or linen cloth. If you feel flush, you can spend the equivalent of a dozen loaves of bread to buy one purpose-made basket (a *brotform* or *banneton*). It's up to you, if you are a home baker. I've been using the same mismatched chintzy baskets for many years, and when my bread is subpar I wish I could blame them; but, sorry to say, it's all me.

These proportions make one medium-sized loaf of bread but can be scaled up to fill your oven easily.

10 ounces unbleached white bread flour

6 ounces whole-wheat flour

1½ cups (plus possibly a bit more) warm water (100 to 105°F)

5 ounces ripe leaven

2 teaspoons kosher salt

Makes 1 two-pound loaf

---

1. Mix the flours with a fork in a medium bowl. Stir in the water to form a shaggy ball of dough. Add drops of additional water as necessary if dry spots remain. Cover and let rest 20 to 30 minutes in a warm spot.

2. Add the other ingredients and mix until well combined and the dough has begun to develop some strength — by hand for 7 or 8 minutes, or in a mixer with a dough hook for 3 minutes on lowest speed, followed by 3 minutes on second. Cover the bowl and set in a warm place to ferment for 2 to 2½ hours, folding the dough every 30 minutes, as shown on pages 276–277.

3. Turn the dough out on a lightly floured surface and round up into a ball with a few light kneads. Let it sit on a floury spot, round side down, covered lightly with a scrap of plastic, while you ready a rising basket by dusting the cloth lightly, but thoroughly, with flour.

4. Lightly knead your loaf two or three strokes, increasing the surface tension of the outer skin, without tearing and without incorporating undue flour. Put it on a flourless part of the counter, smooth side up, and, using both hands, pull it gently along the surface to increase the tension a bit more, and to seal the loose flaps of dough on what will be the bottom of the loaf. Dust the smooth skin of the dough with flour and invert it into the basket. Cover lightly with the loose part of the cloth, and put the whole thing into a large plastic bag.

5. The final proofing of this bread takes 2 to 3 hours; kindle a fire in your oven accordingly. When it is ready to bake, the bread will feel puffed, but still a bit muscular — not at all in a state of collapse.

6. Have handy by your oven a peel, some semolina or corn meal to release the bread from the peel, and a lame, razor blade, or small sharp serrated knife. When your oven is ready to load, dust the peel with the semolina or corn meal and invert the loaf onto it gently. Score the loaf quickly and decisively, then load it into the oven. Keep the door closed whenever you can.

7. Peek in after about 30 minutes to see if it would be advantageous to turn the bread — the rear of the oven is almost always hotter than the mouth. In a few more minutes, the bread should be done, sounding a bit hollow when rapped on the bottom. Remove to a rack to cool.

Retained Heat

FOLDING DOUGH

Gently stretching and folding the dough during fermentation develops structure without incorporating superfluous flour. Let the dough ferment for 2 hours overall, but twice during that period, at 40-minute intervals, you will develop the dough by stretching and folding it. Use a timer to keep you on schedule, and have a bench knife or dough scraper at hand.

1. Flour a patch of clean counter about 16 inches square fairly thoroughly. Use a spatula to scrape all of the dough from the bowl out onto the flour. Use the bench knife and your fingertips to pull the dough into a rough rectangle about an inch thick. Imagine that this rectangle is a business letter that must be folded in thirds, picking up one end of the "letter" and shaking or brushing off any extraneous flour before folding over the middle section of dough. Follow suit with the other end. You're half done.

2. Stretch the dough gently — no tearing! — into a rectangle again, and repeat the folding exercise, this time along the other axis. Scoop the blob up and place it back in the bowl, seam-side-down, and cover airtight. (Don't forget to set the timer again. And the second time you stretch and fold, take note of how different the dough seems.)

SHAPING FOR THE FINAL PROOF

Create a taut outer skin on each loaf, while incorporating the least amount of additional flour humanly possible.

1. Tighten up the preshaped dough.

2. Lightly drag the dough on an unfloured part of the counter to tauten the skin.

3. Use the outer edge of the left hand to seal the bottom of the loaf.

4. Place the dough, bottom side up, into a basket lined with a floured cloth, to support it as it rises.

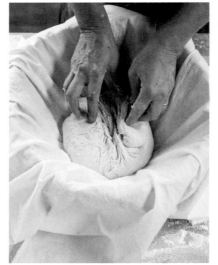

5. Make sure the bottom edges are nicely sealed together.

6. Cover the dough for warmth, then place the basket in a plastic bag.

LAHMAJOON

A favorite from the Armenian bakeries of the Rhode Island mill town of my childhood. You may bake these either with a small live fire or with retained heat while the oven is still plenty hot.

½ recipe pizza dough, page 252
1 tablespoon olive oil
1 cup chopped onion
1 tablespoon butter
¼ cup pine nuts
1 pound lean leg of lamb, coarsely ground
1 medium green pepper, minced
2 cloves garlic
3 scallions, minced
1 teaspoon kosher or sea salt
¼ teaspoon cayenne, or to taste
½ teaspoon freshly ground black pepper
½ cup parsley, minced
1 tablespoon dry mint, crumbled
½ cup crushed or diced tomatoes
2 teaspoons pomegranate molasses
1 teaspoon ground allspice
1 teaspoon lemon juice

Makes sixteen 5- to 6-inch lahmajoon

---

1. Heat the olive oil in a frying pan over medium heat. Soften the onion in it without browning. Let it cool.

2. In a small pan, melt the butter. Add the pine nuts and cook gently a few minutes until they take the faintest color. Transfer to a bowl and set aside.

3. Place all the remaining ingredients in a large bowl. Add the mellowed onions and stir and knead together. If you want to taste the filling for salt level and flavor balance, fry up a pinch in the pan that just held the pine nuts.

4. Have your oven fired as for pizza, but on the cool side. (Alternatively, you may bake these by retained heat while the oven is still pretty hot, if that's more convenient.)

5. Divide the dough into 16 walnut-sized blobs, pre-shape them round and cover them lightly with plastic for 15 to 30 minutes of resting.

6. Roll out thinly on a lightly floured surface, then spread each with about ¼ cup of filling, working it to within ¼ inch of the perimeter. Sprinkle over a few of the pine nuts and press them in, so you won't lose them when peeling the lahmajoon in and out of the oven.

7. Bake, turning back to front once, until dough is crisp and golden, and filling is sizzling and browned.

8. Serve with yogurt, lettuce, parsley, and olives.

SIMSUM

If you have a little extra lahmajoon dough, use it for these home-style Lebanese tea-time or breakfast treats.

FOR EACH SIMSUM

1 tablespoon sesame seeds
1 teaspoon sugar
1 tablespoon extra-virgin olive oil
1 walnut-sized lump of dough, rolled out thinly as for lahmajoon (see above)

Stir together the sesame seeds, sugar, and olive oil in a small bowl. Spread the mixture thinly on the rolled-out dough, and bake live-fire as for pizza or in a hot retained heat oven.

CARAWAY RYE BREAD

I take the trouble to maintain my rye-based leaven because I simply have to eat this bread once a fortnight. Thinly sliced under smoked fish, in slabs with butter, or as a hunk with a bracing bowl of borscht, this hefty loaf features really complex flavor, plenty of chew, and excellent keeping qualities. The addition of caraway seeds to the mix brings me back to my Providence childhood and the seeded rye at the late, lamented Korb's Bakery.

Note that the fermentation time is very brief. Be sure to take the compact schedule — around two and a half hours, all told — into account in planning the heating of your oven.

16	ounces ripe rye leaven
1	cup plus 2 tablespoons very warm water (90°F), plus a tablespoon more, if necessary
16	ounces unbleached bread flour
2–3	tablespoons caraway seeds
1	tablespoon kosher salt
2	teaspoons dry yeast

Makes 1 large loaf

1. Put the leaven, water, and bread flour in the bowl of a stand mixer (or other large bowl if you'll work by hand). Mix with a fork until combined but rough looking, adding a splash of water if persistent dry spots remain. Cover airtight and let rest at warm room temperature for 30 to 45 minutes.

2. Add the rest of the ingredients, and mix on slow speed with a dough hook in a stand mixer, or by hand, until the dough has come together and developed some strength, 3 to 4 minutes. Cover airtight and ferment 80 minutes, turning the dough out onto a floured counter when half the time has elapsed for a stretch and fold. (See pages 276–277.)

3. Scrape the dough out onto a lightly floured surface. Using a light touch, round it up into a blob and shape it into a tight cylinder. Transfer to a sheet of baking parchment, and neaten it into a flattish oval or oblong. Pat it with a wet hand and sprinkle with a few more caraway seeds if desired. Cover very lightly and let proof 60 to 75 minutes.

4. This loaf wants a hot, steamy oven — it can go in right after the heat has equalized in the "soaking" period (see page 232). When all is ready, slide your peel under the parchment to ease its delivery into the oven. Slash deeply from one end to the other or repeatedly crosswise (the Korb's look). Check after 30 to 40 minutes.

BROWN BREAD

Brown bread is one of the few breads that simply cannot be approximated in a standard oven. It is a great illustration of the alchemy of time — the three or four hours spent slowly setting up from a pallid, quaking batter to a deeply caramelized, mahogany, fragrant, crevassed slab. During that long period the bread spends baking, the ambient temperature and moisture levels of the oven slowly equalizing with those of the bread, a transformation occurs that perfectly illustrates the magical power of the wood-fired oven.

It's a challenging bread to get to know, however. When it is first drawn from the cooling oven, the crust is impressively flinty and sharp — you're more liable to cut yourself, than burn yourself, on it. Taking a cue from the ripening process employed on some European ryes, I wrap the loaves in linen and set them aside for two or three days before trying to slice them. Then, sliced thinly and spread with good butter, this brown bread is like nothing else — deep and complex and wonderful. And it keeps improving for a week.

13 ounces stone-ground cornmeal
 2 tablespoons kosher or coarse sea salt
38 ounces boiling water
 6 ounces molasses (optional)
13 ounces whole-rye flour
13 ounces whole-wheat flour
 1 pound leaven (whole wheat and/or rye)

Makes one very large or two large flattish loaves

---

1. Place the cornmeal in a very large mixing bowl. Whisk in the salt, followed by 32 ounces of the boiling water. Stir thoroughly and rapidly to eliminate lumps. Whisk in the molasses, if using. Pour the remaining 6 ounces of boiling water on top, and set aside until cool.

2. When the bowl feels lukewarm, whisk the water from the top down into the mixture. With a fork or a wooden spoon, stir in the rye and wheat flours, then the chopped up leaven. Stir very well together. Cover airtight, and allow to ferment for 3 hours at warm room temperature. Halfway through the fermentation, thickly strew a work surface with rye flour. Have a dough scraper standing by. Scrape the dough out onto the counter, and quickly and deftly fold it up from the four sides as in the master recipe on pags 276–277. You probably won't have to do much stretching — the dough stretches itself by oozing. Do the best you can to toss it all back into the bowl, and cover it up again.

3. Prepare one very large or two medium-large cloth-lined baskets in which to proof the bread. Dust them thoroughly with rye flour.

4. Prepare the work surface again. Dump the dough out onto it, and with the help of the scraper, either divide the dough for two loaves or just round up the bread as best you can. Dust each loaf with rye flour and set, better side down, into the baskets to proof. Cover the loaves and place the baskets inside large plastic bags.

5. Let proof at room temperature about 4 hours. Have the oven fairly hot, but let it soak unoccupied long enough that hot spots have dissipated. Reading between 475 and 500°F is fine, especially if you have made enough of this to fill your oven — these loaves have a lot of cold and wet in them.

6. Bake around 3 hours — loaves will be a deep brown and hard as granite, top and bottom, by the time the center has baked through. Cool on racks, wrap in linen or smooth cotton toweling, and store for a few days before trying to get in. Slice as thinly as possible, setting aside any impossible bits for brown bread brewis — essentially a hasty pudding made out of the otherwise inedible crusts of brown bread simmered in milk. This was a common breakfast and supper that disappeared along with brown bread by the middle of the nineteenth century.

THE BYGONE STAFF OF NEW ENGLAND LIFE

This brown bread was southern New England's daily bread for literally centuries. Wheat, the preferred grain of English bread lovers, simply refused to thrive in the region. But rye, the European fallback grain for marginal agricultural situations, performed reasonably well. Corn, bred into countless varieties by America's indigenous peoples for success in many microclimates, was of course best suited to the region; the immigrants quickly accepted it as their principal crop, too, and adapted their cooking and baking to its particular characteristics.

Equal parts cornmeal, rye meal and, sometimes, whole-wheat flour, comprise this naturally-leavened loaf. In the middle of the nineteenth century, a drop of molasses made its way into some folks' brown bread. As cast-iron cookstoves came in, and brick ovens were left by the wayside, baked brown bread disappeared from all but rueful nostalgic descriptions of the good old bygone days of real food. The corn/rye/optional wheat mixture made its way, chemically leavened, from the oven to the stovetop to become steamed "Boston Brown Bread" — good, but child's play to appreciate and eat compared to the more austere and nuanced brick oven ancestor.

REAL CRACKERS FOR CHOWDER

Using a pasta-rolling machine is the best way I've found for the home cook to approximate old-fashioned chowder crackers. You'll want your oven fairly hot — between 400 and 450°F — for the first baking. Then use the last heat — from just above 200°F — to finish drying them down.

1 pound unbleached bread or all-purpose flour
½ teaspoon salt
¼ teaspoon instant yeast
¼ teaspoon baking soda
½ teaspoon cream of tartar
1 ounce (2 tablespoons) butter or lard
About ⅔ cup cold water

Makes 2 or 3 dozen crackers

I. Combine all the dry ingredients in a bowl or food processor. By hand or with a food processor, work the butter into the dry ingredients. Mix in just enough water so that the dough can be pinched together. You needn't fear overworking this dough, but you do need to mix it as dry as physically possible.

2. Turn the crumbly lump of dough out on the counter and use a long straight rolling pin to crush the dough into coherence. (Work the pin like a seesaw over the dough, pushing down vigorously. Fold in the dry corners of the mass, adding a few molecules of water only if necessary.) Once the dough is a solid homogeneous lump, wrap it in plastic, or put it in an airtight tub, to rest for 45 minutes.

3. Work with about one-third of the dough at a time; keep the portion you're not handling airtight. Set the rollers of the pasta-rolling machine on the widest setting, and pass one lump of the dough through, working it into a long strip. Fold the strip and pass it through the machine several times. Finished strips should look glossy and even, and have plenty of strength and snap. Set the rollers closer together to thin it out a bit

more; I go to the third thickest notch for my crackers. Remember that these crackers are supposed to be hefty and sturdy and almost impossible to eat without soaking. Cut into desired shapes (pilot crackers were about the size of a playing card, but round crackers are cute, too) and prick all over with a fork. Toss the trimmings in the airtight container. When you're done with the lumps of dough, all the leftover bits easily work back together for rerolling.

4. You may bake the crackers on pans, on parchment, or just loose in the oven if you don't mind chasing them around with the peel to retrieve them. If this works in your oven, I find it's a great shortcut to place cookie racks on pans and load the unbaked crackers right on the racks from the get-go. Just turn them over after the first baking.

5. Watch carefully and remove from the oven when they are just beginning to color, about 15 minutes. Set the crackers on cooling racks. When the oven's cooled down quite a bit, pop them back inside, and let them sit there with the oven door slightly cracked, for at least an hour or as long as it takes for them to become bone dry. (When they are cool, they should be entirely crisp and hard, with no flexibility whatsoever. Err on the side of overdrying; the flavor deepens and the keeping quality improves.) Store in an airtight container when cold.

Retained Heat

LIMPA

When I was young, our family was lucky to be invited to the annual Christmas Eve smorgasbord at the home of our friends the Johnsons. Highlights were listening to Swedish singing both raucous and sacred, sipping grown-up glögg, and sampling pickled herring and crackerbread, meatbals, and Christmas *limpa*, an aromatic rye bread. Kristina Johnson Guadagni recently revealed a family limpa secret — using potato water in the mix.

½ teaspoon cardamom seeds, cleaned of shells and papery skin

1 teaspoon anise seeds

1 teaspoon fennel seeds

16 ounces bread flour

2 ounces rye flour

1 ounce (3 tablespoons) vital wheat gluten

1 tablespoon kosher salt

1½ teaspoon dry yeast

1¼ cup warm water (90°F), preferably from boiling potatoes

the zest of 1 orange, finely grated

1½ ounces (2 tablespoons) molasses

12 ounces mature rye leaven

4 ounces (1 cup) raisins, preferably golden

Makes 2 medium loaves

---

1. Use a mortar and pestle or spice grinder to reduce the cardamom to powder. Add the anise and fennel seeds and bruise, but do not pulverize.

2. Combine the flours, wheat gluten, salt, and yeast in the bowl of a stand mixer or other large bowl f you intend to work by hand. Add the water, molasses, orange zest, and leaven, and mix a few minutes until all ingredients seem uniformly combined. Mix in the raisins.

3. Cover dough airtight and ferment 80 minutes at warm room temperature.

4. Divide dough in half and shape each into a taut round. Set in floured-cloth–lined baskets, good side down.

5. Overturn each loaf onto a peel dusted with semolina or cornmeal, slash, and bake after the first heat of the oven has been used, at between 450 and 425°F.

CLAY POT VEGETABLES

From the Mediterranean to the Balkans to Anatolia, innumerable variations occur on this theme — likewise, from season to season, between my own garden and oven. Here's a seat-of-the-pants version from late summer New England; vary the ingredients any way you like — shell beans, tomatoes, and piles of red peppers are some of our favorites. For greater depth of flavor, roast some of the juicy vegetables — peppers, tomatoes, eggplants — in front of the live fire as the oven is heating.

If you trust your clay pot for sautéing purposes, start right out in it. If you are frightened of cracking the pot, cook the onions in a cast-iron pan and transfer to the pot with the rest of the ingredients.

1 tablespoon olive oil

1 tablespoon butter

2 medium onions, sliced

8 cloves garlic, sliced

1½ teaspoons salt

Freshly ground pepper

¾ pound freshly dug tiny potatoes, scrubbed, but left whole

2 very thin eggplant, sliced ½-inch thick

1 small mature crookneck squash, seeded and cut bite-size

1 jalapeno, chopped

2 cups chard stalks, cut crosswise to ¾-inch lengths

Boiling water or broth to cover

A handful of chopped parsley, basil, chives, or marjoram

OPTIONAL TOPPING:

1 egg

½ cup whole milk yogurt

1 cup crumbled feta

A dash of flavorful powdered red pepper

4 to 6 servings

I. Put the olive oil and butter in the clay pot or cast-iron pan over a medium flame. Add the onions and sauté until just beginning to brown. Add the garlic; stir, and remove from the heat.

2. Everything goes into the clay pot at this point. Close it up and put it into the wood-fired oven after the bread has been drawn, anywhere from 450 to 325°F. Cook it at least an hour, or much longer if you want everything to melt together (especially if the oven is on the cool side) When you check on doneness, taste for salt and correct. Stir in handful of optional fresh herbs when it is done.

3. For optional topping, beat the egg in a small bowl, adding the yogurt and cheese. Pour over the vegetables and sprinkle with red pepper. Place back in the mouth of the oven, uncovered, for a few minutes, until set. Serve hot, warm, or room temperature.

Retained Heat

ROASTED TOMATOES

This is a great use for the inevitable blemished tomatoes at the height of the season. Scoop roasted tomatoes when cool into zip-lock bags and freeze for the rest of the year, as a great base for pasta sauce, salsa, and many other dishes.

   3 pounds garden tomatoes
   1 teaspoon kosher salt
3–4 cloves garlic, chopped
  ¼ cup extra-virgin olive oil

Makes about 1½ pounds

1. Find a half-sheet pan or other shallow baking or roasting pan that looks like it will both accommodate the tomatoes and fit through the door of your oven. Pop it into the hot oven to preheat for a few minutes.

2. Trim the core and any blemishes away from the tomatoes and cut in big chunks. Cherry tomatoes may be left whole; small plum tomatoes halved. Put them in a large bowl with the rest of the ingredients and toss together well.

3. Pull the pan out of the oven and dump the tomatoes on it, scraping in all the garlic and oil. Quickly return it to the oven.

4. After 40 minutes, draw out the pan and have a look. When they are done, the tomatoes are thoroughly condensed and even blackened on the edges. If they are almost done, give them a good shake or stir and return to the oven. Most likely, more time will be needed, depending on the heat and the tomatoes. Very juicy tomatoes may take much longer.

ROASTED TOMATO BUTTER

This is a mellow and sumptuous treat on fresh bread or toast, in a baked potato, with grilled shrimp . . . like a savory buttercream frosting.

   3 ounces roasted tomatoes
   3 ounces lightly salted butter, cut into 8 chunks

Makes 1 pound

1. Bring both ingredients to room temperature.

2. Place the tomatoes in the bowl of a food processor. Purée. With the motor running, drop in the butter, and process until streaks disappear. You should find that you've made an irresistible pastel-colored emulsion. Don't overdo it or the heat of the food processor will melt the butter. Use soon or pack into airtight containers and chill or freeze. Return to room temperature before using.

CLAY POT CHICKEN WITH GARLIC

Put this into the oven to sop up the heat after baking some crusty rustic bread for an incredible supper. You must have a top-quality small chicken and the best, freshest new garlic, and a clay pot that just fits it all with little room to spare. The "luting," the flour-and-water seal for the pot, is a useful technique to extend to other clay pot cookery.

4–5 heads crisp new garlic

3 tablespoons extra-virgin olive oil

A few sprigs fresh thyme or savory

1 small chicken, rinsed and patted dry

Kosher or sea salt

Freshly ground black pepper

1 cup all-purpose flour, or more

2 to 3 servings

I. Break up the heads of garlic gently, leaving each clove unpeeled, but discarding the outer wrappings and core.

2. Pour about half the olive oil into the bottom of the clay pot and rub it around the sides. (Avoid oiling the rim of the pot, where it will contact the lid.) Toss in about a third of the garlic cloves and a sprig or two of the thyme.

3. Season the chicken inside and out with salt and pepper. Place a handful of the garlic cloves in the body cavity, plus another herb sprig. Tuck the chicken into the pot snugly, filling gaps with the remaining garlic cloves, and topping with a final herb sprig. Drizzle the remaining oil over the chicken.

4. Put the flour in a bowl and stir in cool water gradually until you have a gluey, smooth paste. Plaster a ribbon of the paste neatly around the rim of the pot and fit the lid on firmly. Run a finger around the outside edge for neatness and a better seal.

5. Pop the pot into a medium-hot oven, after bread baking is done (around 400 to 425°F), and leave it alone for 90 minutes or so. Ideally, if you've sealed the pot perfectly, you won't smell anything cooking at all. But even if the seal cracks and some aroma begins to trickle out of the oven, it's hard to feel like you've failed, because it is just so wonderful.

6. Have a loaf of your bread, a green salad, and a bottle of crisp white wine on the table. Pry the pot lid off carefully with a butter knife, and enjoy the sensation. Tear off a crust of bread, squeeze those garlic cloves, and tuck in.

Retained Heat

289

Clay Pot Chicken with Garlic

MUSSAKHAN

I first tasted possibly the most luscious chicken dish ever devised at a dim and nameless East Jerusalem restaurant. One visit, and we became regulars at the place known to us linguistically overwhelmed American archaeology students as the home of Chicken-in-a-Tent.

An ancient Palestinian dish, Mussakhan is composed of tender chicken impressively swaddled in shrak, basted in oniony roasting juices braced with sumac, then finished in the oven until crisp on top, succulent beneath.

1   (4 to 5 pound) free-range chicken
12   cups water, divided
½   teaspoon whole allspice
½   teaspoon peppercorns
2   cardamom pods
1   whole onion
3   whole garlic cloves
¼   cup plus ¾ teaspoon salt, divided
5   tablespoons olive oil
4   cups chopped onions (about 6 medium)
½   teaspoon ground pepper
     Pinch ground cloves
½   teaspoon ground allspice
5   tablespoons sumac
4   large shrak (or more), baked on a saj or
     upside-down wok
¼   cup pine nuts

4 servings

1. Cut the spine out of the chicken and cut off the wing-tips, and put these spare parts in a small pot to make stock. Cover with 4 cups cold water, add the whole spices and whole onion and garlic. Simmer over low heat some hours, until reduced by at least half, then strain the stock and season with salt.

2. Meanwhile place the main part of the chicken in a sealable container, cover with a brine made by stirring ¼ cup of salt into 8 cups of cold water, and chill for 1 to 4 hours.

3. Heat 3 tablespoons of the olive oil in a heavy frying pan; add chopped onions and a pinch of salt and cook slowly for at least 30 minutes, until mellowed out. Add ground pepper, cloves, and allspice, and 4 tablespoons of the sumac. Spread mixture in a heavy roasting pan big enough for the chicken. (Make sure it fits through your oven door.) Shake the brine off the chicken, pat dry, and arrange in a flattish manner on the onions. Rub a little olive oil on the skin.

4. Set the chicken into a medium-hot oven (falling from 425°F is fine). While the chicken roasts, arrange shrak to cover a large serving dish or tray (heatproof and also must fit through oven door). The bread can hang way off the edges because you will be flipping it up to mostly cover the whole chicken. Stir the remaining 1 tablespoon of olive oil and the pine nuts around in a small frying pan over medium heat until the nuts turn the palest tan, then dump them on a plate.

5. When the chicken is just done (165°F, or juice runs clear from thigh joint), transfer the chicken and the onion bed onto the prepared shrak. Scatter on the pine nuts, and fold up the shrak like a tent. Deglaze the roasting pan with a cup or so of the stock, scraping up any browned bits. Stir in another tablespoon of sumac. Pour this sauce all over the bread and chicken and put the whole thing back into the oven to crisp up the tent a bit. Serves four, but if you use twice as much shrak and a little more broth you can really stretch it out and it's no less luscious.

BAKING IN ANTIQUITY — THE TABUN

What about retained heat baking in the Middle East? Open-fire installations like the saj and the tannur — and the masterful array of flatbreads and layered breads they produce — come to mind when we think about baking in and around wheat's homeland. But a little more inquiry shows that retained heat may have long factored into the Middle Eastern baking equation, but as part of a mixed strategy arising long before the first "Roman" ovens.

Archaeological evidence attests to the use of an array of baking technologies, but study has not been rigorous enough to suggest reasons for ancient bakers' choices. Sad to say, archaeologically excavated baking installations the world over are generally scantily analyzed and poorly understood. Lacking good evidence, we can only theorize in lame generalizations that the prevalence of a certain type of baking in any particular place and time was influenced by many factors — the raw materials to be baked, the type of fuel that could be gathered, whether the people were nomadic or settled, the availability of ceramics and iron, and, for the baker, both training in local tradition and exposure to outside ideas.

Because lame generalizations are so hateful, it's fortunate that some techniques of great antiquity are still in use by bakers today. For example, the tabun is a type of oven dating back to at least the Bronze Age in the Levant; it is still built and used by some Palestinian home bakers. And that's a very good thing! Without the continuity of bakers in a living tradition, I am doubtful that archaeologists (including this one) would really understand the functioning of this singular oven.

The tabun is hand built of tempered clay like its cousin the tannur; its shape, though, is like a little Superdome but with a round hole in the top. The baker heats the tabun in two phases. First, she tends a fire within the dome through the hole on top, heating up the baking surface below — a hearth of special heat-retaining river stones. Once that interior hearth is swept clean and the food has been introduced, a supplementary live fire is kindled on the outside of the dome to keep heat radiating downward and inward toward the food. Archaeologists have not focused on this question sufficiently, but, functionally, it seems logical that the tabun is one missing link between the live-fire tannur and the later retained-heat "Roman" oven. It is also just one step removed from the "baking under ashes" technique investigated in Chapter 1.

One more great thing about the tabun is that long ago, certain brilliant cooks used it to invent mussakhan, one of the best chicken dishes ever (see facing page for the recipe). Since I haven't built myself a tabun yet, I've been using a saj to bake the bread and a front-loading oven for the rest to make a pretty creditable version. Seems involved, but so worth it.

AUSTIN CAKE

This is just a great cake from mid-19th-century New England. It keeps really well in a tin for a week or more. Bake it in the wood-fired oven after the sharpest heat has dissipated, ideally as the temperature falls from 375°F to 325°F.

2½ cups (12 ounces) flour
½ of a nutmeg, grated
¼ teaspoon ground cloves
¼ teaspoon salt
½ teaspoon baking soda
¾ cup milk
½ cup (4 ounces) butter, soft
1½ cups (10 ounces) sugar or dehydrated cane juice
1 egg
2 tablespoons molasses
1 cup raisins

Makes 1 loaf cake

1. Line the bottom of a standard (9- by 5-inch) loaf pan with waxed paper, and grease and flour the pan.

2. Whisk together the flour, spices, and salt. Separately, dissolve the baking soda in the milk.

3. Using a mixer, cream the butter thoroughly. Add the sugar gradually, and beat until fluffy. Beat in the egg and the molasses.

4. Working quickly, add the flour mixture and the milk mixture alternately, mixing until it is almost combined. Scrape down the sides of the bowl and the beaters, and then beat for 10 to 20 seconds more. Stir in the raisins and scrape the batter into the prepared pan.

5. Bake for about 90 to 100 minutes, or until a skewer poked into the center of the cake emerges clean.

6. Cool in the pan on a rack for 10 to 15 minutes. Run a knife around the cake to free the sides and turn it out of the pan. Cool upright completely before cutting, or better yet, store in an airtight tin to ripen a day or two. Serve thinly sliced.

Austin Cake

Retained Heat

GRANOLA

Groovy, crunchy oat granola was invented when I was a small child, and somehow I learned to make it by the time I was a teenager. I wish I could give credit to the source. Since I didn't run with any real hippies back then, I must have gotten the recipe from a hippie cookbook. At any rate, this version, which we've eaten for breakfast at our house most every weekday of the 21st century, probably doesn't bear much resemblance to the recipe I learned in 1971. Try this one, and vary it to your liking, adding, subtracting, and substituting as you like. If you want to add dried fruit, wait until it has finished baking.

It is perfectly suited to baking, almost toasting, really, in a cool falling oven. Be sure that your pans fit through your oven door before you commit. It's a good use for a foil baking pan, since you can squish it through the door if necessary.

 4 ounces butter (real hippies use oil)
4½ ounces maple syrup
 2 ounces evaporated cane juice or organic sugar
 5 ounces whole unblanched almonds
 5 ounces walnut halves and pieces
 4 ounces coconut
 3 ounces wheat germ
24 ounces regular or thick rolled oats (not quick oats)

1. In a large pot over a low flame, melt the butter. Meanwhile, weigh or measure out the remainder of the ingredients — it's best if they enter the pot in quick succession.

2. Stir the maple syrup and sugar into the butter. When the sugar has mostly dissolved, remove the pot from the heat. Stir in the nuts, followed by the rest of the ingredients. Combine thoroughly.

3. Spread the granola mix out to about a half-inch thickness, pressing down a bit if you like it in chunks. This quantity takes up two half-sheet pans, if they'll fit through your oven door.

4. Bake in a slack but dry oven for about two hours. Look at it after an hour to see if it needs stirring or turning. Ideally, it acquires a deep toastiness from long slow baking. Allow to cool thoroughly, then store airtight.

5. Fills a 1-gallon jar — enough to keep two middle-aged hippies alive for weeks.

ALMOND MERINGUE COOKIES

These are meringues with soul. They want to use the last heat in a bone-dry oven, but you can make and pipe the cookies 3 to 5 hours ahead so that their surface dries before baking. Do not attempt in humid weather.

5 ounces (1 cup) unblanched almonds, plus 36 more for garnish

4 ounces (⅔ cup) dehydrated cane juice or other flavorful sugar

2 egg whites

Pinch of cream of tartar, if you have it

Makes 36 small cookies

I. Use a food processor to grind the almonds finely — don't forget to protect your ears. Add half of the sugar, and grind a bit more until powdery.

2. Place the egg whites in the bowl of an electric mixer. Beat on medium-high until broken up, then add the cream of tartar. Keep beating until soft peaks begin to form. Increase the speed of the mixer and begin to add the remaining sugar gradually. Keep beating until all the sugar has been added, then increase the speed to the highest setting, beating another minute or so, or until the mixture is very white, stiff, and glossy.

3. Remove the beater and sprinkle the almond mixture over the top of the egg whites. Use a flat-bladed whisk to fold it together quickly and thoroughly.

4. Either use a pastry bag to extrude thirty-six 1-inch-diameter globs on 2 sheets of baking parchment, or drop by teaspoons. Place an almond neatly into the center of each, and place out of harm's way in a dry, and even sunny, spot.

5. When the rest of your baking is long done, and the oven temperature has dropped below 300°F, slide the cookies carefully into the oven. Leave them in until they have taken a little color; they are shatteringly, meltingly crisp; and the almonds have developed an irresistible toasty flavor, between 2 and 3 hours.

OVERNIGHT COOKING TRADITIONS

Some foods, like a whole pig in an earth oven, are traditionally left to bake overnight because that's how long they take to cook thoroughly and to tenderness. But other dishes that traditionally call for long baking were originally the product of cultural, specifically religious, restrictions. For example, the biblical injunction against working on the Sabbath day instigated some great cooking both thousands of years ago in the Bible's homeland, and, culinarily independently, hundreds of years ago in Protestant New England. In both cultures, religiously observant cooks came up with dishes for which all the prep work could be done on the day preceding the Sabbath. An earthen pot containing the meal would be set overnight in a preheated earthen or masonry oven or buried among embers and ashes on a hearth, making fresh, hot food available on the Sabbath without violation of any holy laws. Dishes from both of these traditions have gone on to popularity outside of their original communities.

Even today, some popular, simple, and delicious dishes reveal their overnight-baking heritage in their names only. The modern version may commonly be cooked in metal pots on a propane stove, but dishes whose names translate as "buried" or "hidden" usually have a heritage that goes back to long baking in a clay pot in retained heat. For example, Egypt's *ful medames* is a lowly but delicious dish of broad beans served with garlic, oil, lemon, and, tellingly, *hamine* eggs. Its heritage is ancient, older than its current Coptic name, which means, literally, "buried favas." If a religious injunction was once behind its technique, it has long since faded; the popularity of the beans, however, abides.

Not every "hidden" food has a religious origin story. For example, some Balkan dishes are purported to relate to events in the quite recent past — thieves roasting lamb underground to hide their culpability as rustlers, World War II partisans hiding their cooking from discovery by the enemy, and others. My suspicion is that these dishes are far older than these stories allow.

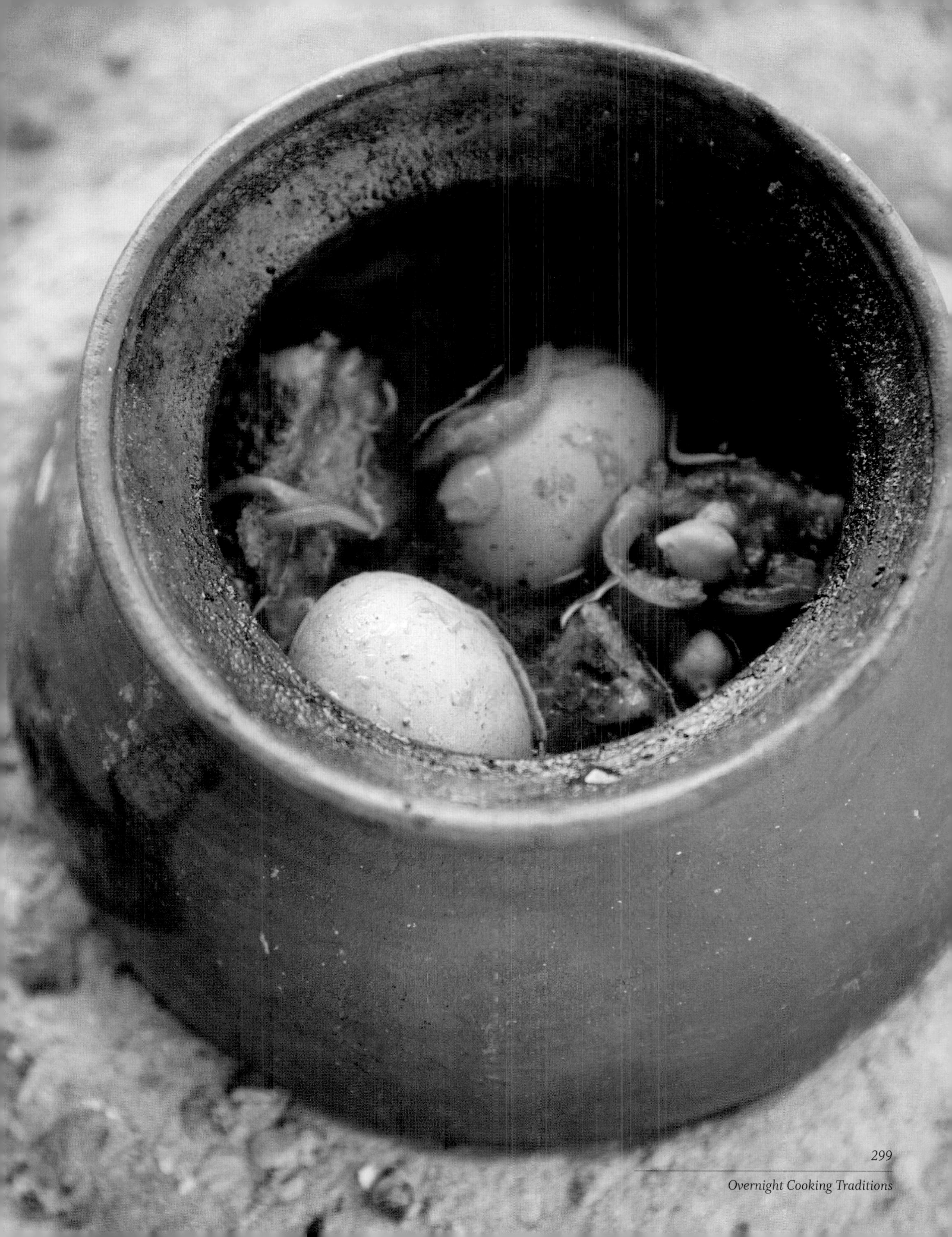

ADAFINA

Jewish overnight Sabbath dishes are found all over Europe and the Middle East; their names are various, but often carry the implication of being preheated, buried, hidden, or sealed away. Today, they are more likely to be simmered on the stovetop, or kept hot in a slow cooker; a shame, given their ancient clay pot heritage.

In this *adafina*, some of the Middle East's oldest cultivars — chickpeas and barley or farro — mellow down with subtle flavors of North Africa. We ate a pot of this after it had baked a mere four hours, and it was very tasty; the second pot, sampled the following morning after 17 hours in the oven, was out of this world.

If you wish to omit the meat, increase the olive oil to three tablespoons when cooking the onions, and add the spice paste to the onions 30 seconds before removing them from the heat. Increase the barley or wheat to ¼ cup.

The eggs are also optional, but they are really one of the highlights of this dish, existing as a dish in themselves, *hamine* eggs. Counterintuitive to anyone who has ever boiled an egg too long, the texture of these eggs after, say, 18 hours of cooking, is soft and creamy. The yolks and whites have almost merged in distinctive, subtly marbled shades of tan, and the flavor is smoky and rich and unfamiliar.

6	ounces dry chickpeas
5	cups cold water
½	teaspoon peppercorns
2	teaspoons cumin seeds
2	teaspoons coriander seeds
6	cloves garlic
1	teaspoon salt, or to taste
1	teaspoon turmeric
1	teaspoon ground hot red pepper
1	tablespoon olive oil
1	medium onion, halved lengthwise and sliced thinly
1½	pounds lamb shanks or lean meaty beef ribs, cut in 2-inch lengths
2	tablespoons pearled barley, farro, or wheat berries
1	inch-long piece of cinnamon stick
4	medium eggs (optional)

3 or 4 servings, and doubles or triples easily depending on your clay pots

1. Four to six hours before you want to assemble the *adafina*, rinse the chickpeas and cover with 5 cups of cold water to soak.

2. Use a mortar and pestle to crush the peppercorns, cumin, and coriander. Toss in the garlic and salt and pulverize. Add the turmeric and red pepper. Rub this paste all over the meat.

3. Warm the olive oil in your clay pot over gentle heat. Cook the onion until wilted and golden. Remove the pot from the heat and let it cool for a few minutes.

4. Place the spiced meat on the onions. Sprinkle in the barley. Add the chickpeas and their soaking water and the cinnamon stick.

5. Wash the eggs, rinse well, and submerge in the top layer of the adafina. Cover the pot and place in the oven after the bread is drawn and the oven is falling from around 400°F. Close the oven securely, and ignore the incredible aromas until tomorrow.

6. Retrieve the eggs and shell them before serving.

Overnight Cooking Traditions

HAMINE EGGS

When your oven has cooled below 300°F, slide in a batch of hamine eggs for breakfast.

Eggs
Onion skins from a few yellow or red onions
1–2 tablespoons olive oil

1. Wash, rinse, and dry the eggs. Place them in a clay pot, surrounded by the onion skins. Cover with ample cold water. Pour the oil on top. Cover the pot and place in the middle or rear of an oven for at least 8 hours. Longer is fine.

2. To serve, dry the eggs, shell and serve with fresh pita, cucumbers, and tomatoes.

FUL MEDAMES

Fava beans have very thick skins and take a ridiculously long time to soften up enough to cook. Aside from thinking ahead to soak the beans, there's not a lot of complication here. You can cook the hamine eggs right in the bean pot if it's big enough; just make sure you start out with plenty of water, and add a skim of olive oil to the top as in the previous recipe.

1 pound dry broad or fava beans
The cloves from 1 head garlic, chopped
Salt
A few sprigs flat-leafed parsley, chopped
Drizzle of olive oil
1 lemon
Fresh pita or other flatbread
Hamine eggs (see this page)

1. Rinse the beans and soak in copious cool water for 2 days, changing the water once or twice.

2. Place the beans, the garlic, and a fat pinch of salt in a clay pot and cover with at least an inch of water. Put the pot into a still-hot wood-fired oven, say, 375–350°F to bake overnight after the bread has been drawn. (Feel free to bring the pot to a simmer first if you are not sure about having sufficient heat. You know your oven best.)

3. In the morning, use a slotted spoon to serve the beans. Sprinkle with parsley, drizzle with olive oil, and offer lemon wedges, pita, and hamine eggs. Some like more chopped garlic to mash in; breakfast thus, and you'll be ready to build the pyramids all day. When not eating strictly from the menu of the second millennium BCE, we enjoy the more modern condiment *harissa* — red pepper paste — with our ful.

OVERNIGHT IN A NEW ENGLAND BRICK OVEN

The predominant religious strain among seventeenth-century English immigrants to New England was a radical or fundamentalist Protestantism, featuring a renewal of interest in and commitment to ancient biblical laws. The official position was that the Sabbath must be kept free of labor (and entertainment, for that matter), and thus free of cooking. Records show that this injunction seems to have been upheld in most households throughout orthodox New England until the early nineteenth century.

New England houses, even modest ones, were generally furnished with masonry ovens, probably beginning in the 1630s. Home baking, as opposed to a reliance on professional bakers, or the use of communal ovens, was the norm for most households in both country and city. Leaving food "buried" overnight in the center of the huge pile of masonry that was the chimney stack assured at least one hot meal on Sunday morning. While a great variety of foods might have been cooked in this way, only a few were well documented, including baked beans and Indian pudding.

Baked Beans

Beans or peas simmered, typically with fatty salt pork or beef until soft and seasoned, were a mainstay of the average English person's diet in the seventeenth and eighteenth centuries. Cheap, easy to cook, and satisfying, legumes were a staple for working people on land and at sea. Tender, kidney-shaped American bean varieties, in a variety of sizes and colors, had been introduced to England well before the English inserted themselves into North America, and they were an instant hit. Easier and quicker to cook and more delicate in flavor than the broad beans available in Europe, they were adopted without the hesitation that accompanied the introduction of other American crops.

Documentation does not exist to inform us when beans first made the jump from the kettle on the hearth to the earthenware pot in the oven, but they probably did so with little change in recipe. Pork and beans survived for a couple hundred years as little more than that: pork and beans. Optional additions by the nineteenth century might be some ground black pepper, an onion, a bit of mustard, and a spoonful of molasses. (Even as late as 1900, recipes commonly called for only one tablespoon of molasses for a quart of dried beans, and that only optionally.)

The New England Protestant Sabbath began at sundown on Saturday night (in some towns, seemingly arbitrarily, a bell rang at 4 p.m. to signal its beginning). It was not unusual for baked beans to be a fixture for Saturday supper as well as for Sunday breakfast. As long as the Saturday baking was in the oven by early afternoon, a pot of beans would be ready to eat by suppertime. Ready, in that they are tender and tasty, but not as sublime as the overnight beans, which turn out super intense and almost caramelized.

For baked beans, make a half recipe of the basic bean-hole beans (page 204), and put it in an earthenware pot with a lid. They should have plenty of liquid over them — add more boiling water if necessary. Put them in the oven hot and leave them overnight, or until they have drunk up all the liquid and become incredibly savory.

INDIAN PUDDING

This very simple Indian pudding is a late nineteenth-century recipe from Plymouth, Massachusetts. It is sweeter than many older recipes, so feel free to experiment with reducing the molasses if you like. These proportions, though, yield a very intense Indian pudding experience; a friend of mine referred to this dish as "the French roast of Indian puddings."

  6 cups whole milk
  ⅓ cup cornmeal, preferably stone-ground jonny-cake meal
  1 teaspoon salt
  1 cup molasses ("old-fashioned," not blackstrap)
  1 tablespoon butter

1. Heat 2 cups of the milk to a simmer. Whisk in the cornmeal gradually. Cook, stirring constantly, until thickened. Add the salt and remove from the heat. Stir in 2 cups cold milk and the molasses.

2. Use the tablespoon of butter to grease a deep large casserole. Scrape in the cornmeal mixture. Pour the remaining 2 cups milk on top.

3. Bake as the temperature falls from the neighborhood of 375–350°F for at least four hours. Overnight is not too long unless your oven is super-insulated.

OVERNIGHT OATMEAL

This can go into the oven after it has lost a good deal of heat, and depending on the heat-retention characteristics of your oven, may bake all night for a delicious treat in the morning. Experiment and you will find a pattern that works for you.

  1 cup steel-cut oats
  4 cups cold water
  ½ teaspoon salt
  2 cups milk
  1 tablespoon butter
    Maple syrup or honey, for serving
    Milk or cream, for serving

1. Select a 6-cup baking dish and stir together the oats and water in it. Let stand for an hour or two at room temperature while you're busy getting the bread into and out of the oven.

2. When you're finished with your other baking, and the temperature is around 300 to 350°F, stir in the salt and milk, drop the butter on top, and slide the dish into the middle of the oven. If you know your oven will cool rapidly, close the door up, and check on things in an hour or so, just to make sure. If your oven retains heat very well, try leaving the door off or ajar; otherwise it may prove too hot to leave the oats in overnight.

RESOURCES, REFERENCES, AND DETAILS

CHAPTER 1. A FIRE AND A STICK

EARLY HUMANS AND FIRE

Wrangham, Richard. *Catching Fire: How Cooking Made Us Human*. Basic Books, 2009.

Francesco, Berna, Paul Goldberg, Liora Kolska Horwitz, James Brink, Sharon Holt, Marion Bamford, and Michael Chazan. "Microstratigraphic evidence of in situ fire in the Acheulean strata of Wonderwerk Cave, Northern Cape province, South Africa." *Proceedings of the National Academy of Science of the United States of America* 109, no. 20 (2012): 1215–1220.

At present the earliest secure archaeological evidence for the use of human-controlled fire is "only" one million years old.

ASH-ROASTING POTATOES AND ONIONS

Leslie, Eliza. *Directions for Cookery, in Its Various Branches*, 10th ed. Philadelphia, 1840.

EGG-ROASTING IN LITERATURE

Old Peninsular. "My Peninsular Medal." *Blackwood's Edinburgh Magazine* 68, no. 417 (July 1850): 20–32.

Scott, Walter. *Waverly*. Vol. 1. James Ballantyne and Co., 1814.

BAKING FOWL AND FISH IN RAW CLAY

Shields, G. O. *Camping and Camp Outfits: A Manual of Instruction for Young and Old Sportsmen*. Rand, McNally & Co., 1890.

> Mix water and clay with your fingers into a stiff mud, and work until it is putty-like. Roll it out with a bottle to a half-inch in thickness, and large enough to entirely envelop the bird or fish. Draw your bird, wash, salt, and pepper inside, but leave the feathers on. Enclose it in this cake of mud, and smooth over the seams with your fingers. Dig a small hole in the ground in the edge of a wood-fire, place it in, and cover with hot ashes first; on the top of the hot ashes place live coals; replenish the coals now and then, and allow it to cook from one to two hours, according to age or size. When removed, you will find the clay cooked like potter's ware. Break the clay, and the feathers will come with it thus leaving the bird clean and white. Baste with butter, and eat while hot. Clean or remove entrails of a fish, wash, and season with salt and pepper; but leave the scales on, and treat as above. If not convenient to roll the clay out as above, it may be mixed thinner, and plastered into the feathers or scales.

BREAD BAKED UNDER ASHES

Bottéro, Jean. *The Oldest Cuisine in the World: Cooking in Mesopotamia*. University of Chicago Press, 2004.

Cotgrave, Randle, comp. *A Dictionarie of the French and English Tongues*. Adam Islip, 1611.

> *Fouace*: f. A thicke cake hastily baked, on a hot hearth, by hot imbers layed on it, and burning coals over them; . . . also *Fouasse*.

In the Book of Ezekiel (4:9-15), an angry Yahweh condemns his people to eat bread baked under ashes in the manner of barley bread, only with human excrement as the fuel. When the prophet exclaims how gross that is, Yahweh relents, saying, "Okay, you can use cow dung."

HEARTH BANNOCK RECIPE

White, John. *A Treatise on the Art of Baking, with a Preliminary Introduction*. Anderson & Bryce, 1828.

305

CHAPTER 2. A FEW SIMPLE TOOLS

SPIT-ROASTING EQUIPMENT
SpitJack

800-755-5509

www.spitjack.com

Geared specifically to the modes of cooking examined in this book, from fireplace cookery to large whole-animal roasting. Good source for the "meat forks" that clamp onto the spit and the "Tuscan" fireplace grill mentioned later in this chapter.

CORMARYE RECIPE
Pegge, Samuel. *The Forme of Cury.* 1780. First published in 1390.

[TO] ROSTE A CARPE RECIPE
Hess, Karen, ed. *Martha Washington's Booke of Cookery and Booke of Sweetmeats.* Columbia University Press, 1995.

DOUBLE STRING MEAT ROASTER
Hazard, Thomas Robinson. *The Jonny-Cake Papers of "Shepherd Tom."* Subscribers, 1915.

SALLET OF COLD CAPON ROSTED RECIPE
Stevenson, Jane and Peter Davidson, eds. *The Closet of Sir Kenelm Digby Knight Opened.* Prospect Books, 1997.

POSTWAR AMERICA AND BARBEQUE CULTURE
Hale, C. Clark. *The Great American Barbeque & Grilling Manual.* Abacus, 2000.

PLANKING
Orr, N. *De Witt's Connecticut Cook Book, and Housekeeper's Assistant.* Robert M. De Witt, 1871.

BROWNING AN OMELET WITH A SHOVEL
Kitchiner, William. *The Cook's Oracle.* Whittaker, Teacher and Co., 1829.

BURNT CREAM RECIPE
Nott, John. The Cooks and Confectioners Dictionary. C. Rivington, 1723.

FLIP PANCAKES
Child, Lydia Maria Francis. *The American Frugal Housewife*, 27th ed. Samuel S. & William Wood, 1841.

. . . Flip makes very nice pancakes. In this case, nothing is done but to sweeten your mug of beer with molasses; put in one glass of N. E. rum; heat it till it foams, by putting in a hot poker; and stir it up with flour as thick as other pancakes. [Then fry in bacon grease or other hot fat, and serve with molasses. To be honest, we did better adding a pinch of salt and an egg.]

HOT POKER MUSTARD RECIPE
Scammell, H. B., ed. *Scammell's Universal Treasure-House of Useful Knowledge.* H. A. Hess, 1885

PEBBLE SEARED SAUCES RECIPE
Ruperto de Nola. *Libre del Coch.* Translation by Robin Carroll-Mann, 1525. www.florilegium.org.

CHAPTER 3. POTS AND PANS

GRIDDLED BREADS OF CENTRAL ASIA
Perry, Charles. "The Taste for Layered Bread among the Nomadic Turks and the Central Asian Origins of Baklava." In *A Taste of Thyme: Culinary Cultures of the Middle East*, edited by Sami Zubaida and Richard Tapper, 87–92. Taurus Parke, 2000.

CHIVE PANCAKES RECIPE
Matthew Amster-Burton. "Scallion Pancakes." In Simple Cooking 72, edited by John and Matt Lewis Thorne, (January/February 2001).

SUPERIOR MASA HARINA
Bob's Red Mill

Milwaukie, Oregon

800-349-2173

www.bobsredmill.com

GEOLOGY AND BAKESTONES

Farey, John. *General View of the Agriculture and Minerals of Derbyshire.* Vol 1. McMillan, 1811.

ARCHAEOLOGY OF SCANDINAVIAN BRITAIN

Crawford, Barbara E. and Beverley Ballin Smith. *The Biggins, Papa Stour, Shetland: The History and Archaeology of a Royal Norwegian Farm.* Monograph Series 15. Society of Antiquaries of Scotland, 1999.

ORKNEY AND BERE

Birsay Heritage Trust

www.birsay.org.uk

FLATBREADS FROM SWEDISH CREMATION BURIALS

Hansson, Ann-Marie. "Pre- and Protohistoric Bread in Sweden: A Definition and a Review" *Civilisations* 49 (2002): 183–190.

MUFFINS RECIPE

Glasse, Hannah. *The Art of Cookery, Made Plain and Easy*, rev. ed. Strahan et al., 1774.

INFIERNILLO COOKING

Mallmann, Francis. *Seven Fires: Grilling the Argentine Way.* With Peter Kaminsky. Artisan, 2009.

EARLY CLAY POTS

Craig, O. E., H. Saul, A. Lucquin, Y. Nishida, et al. "Earliest evidence for the use of pottery" *Nature* 496 (18 April 2013): 351–354.

Wu, Xiaohong, Chi Zhang, Paul Goldberg, David Cohen, Yan Pam, Trina Arpin, and Ofer Bar-Yosef. "Early Pottery at 20,000 Years Ago in Xianrendong Cave, China." *Science* 336, no. 6089 (June 2012): 1696–1700.

Nieuwenhuyse, Olivier P., Peter M. M. G. Akkermans, and Johannes van der Plicht. "Not So Coarse, Nor Always Plain: The Earliest Pottery of Syria." *Antiquity* 84, no. 323 (2010): 71–85.

Akkermans, Peter M. M. G., Rene Cappers, Chiara Cavallo, Olivier Nieuwenhuyse, Bonne Nilhamn, and Iris N. Otte. "Investigating the Early Pottery Neolithic of Northern Syria: New Evidence from Tell Sabi Abyad." American Journal of Archaeology, (January 2006).

Lemme, Chuck. "The Ideal Pot." In *Oxford Symposium on Food & Cookery, 1988: The Cooking Pot*, edited by Tom Jaine, 82–98. Prospect Books, 1989.

The earliest use of pottery has long been believed a product of the Neolithic revolution, accompanying the domestication of plants and animals and many other sweeping cultural changes. But tantalizing new evidence from Japan and China pushes the ceramic horizon back significantly into late Ice Age hunter-gatherer days. Chemical analysis shows pots securely dating to 15,000 to 20,000 years before the present that had predominantly contained fish and been exposed to fire.

TO BUTTER GOOSEBERRIES RECIPE

Spurling, Hilary, ed. *Elinor Fettiplace's Receipt Book.* Viking, 1986.

CAST-IRON COOKWARE

Lodge Manufacturing Company
Multiple locations
423-837-7181
www.lodgemfg.com

CRACKERS, BISCUIT, AND HARDTACK

G. H. Bent Company
Milton, Massachusetts
617-698-5945
www.bentscookiefactory.com

PLYMOUTH FISH CHOWDER RECIPE

Archival recipe courtesy of the Plymouth Antiquarian Society, Plymouth, Massachusetts.

DOUGHNUTS FRIED IN WHALE OIL

Druett, Joan. *Petticoat Whalers: Whaling Wives at Sea, 1820-1920.* Harper Collins, 1991.

Aboard the whaleship Merlin in 1858 Henrietta Deblois wrote:

> Today has been our doughnut fare, the first we have ever had. The Steward, Boy and myself have been at work all the morning. We fried or boiled three tubs for the forecastle — one for the steerage. In the afternoon about one tub full for the cabin and right good were they too, not the least taste of oil — they came out the pots perfectly dry. The skimmer was so large that you could take out ½ of a peck at a time. I enjoyed it mightily.

OLIE-KOECKEN RECIPE

Groen, Jan de. *de Verstandige Kock, oft Sorghvuldige Huyshoudster.* M. Doornick, 1668.

BAKE-KETTLES

"A Letter from an Officer, Shewing How He Made His Own Bread in Scotland." *The Gentleman's Magazine and Historical Chronicle* 16 (1746): 374.

In America, the term "Dutch oven" was sometimes used for the bake-kettle, a usage which grew to be very common by the twentieth century. (When this denotation started and why is obscure. It is notable, but probably unrelated, that a 1667 Dutch cookbook did outline a couple of tarts "baked with fire below and on top," a rather unusual technique at the time.) In England, the term "Dutch oven" invariably referred to the reflecting roaster Americans often called "tin kitchen" or "Yankee baker"; many American cookbook authors followed the English usage. To add to the nomenclature confusion, some New Englanders called a masonry oven which protruded from a house and had its own roof a Dutch oven.

PHOTOS AND NARRATIVES OF BAKE-KETTLES IN ACTION

Tibbott, S. Minwel. *Baking in Wales.* National Museum of Wales, 1991.

———. *Welsh Fare: A Selection of Traditional Recipes.* National Museum of Wales, 1976.

CHAPTER 4. MORE GEAR

ROCKET STOVES

Aprovecho Research Center
541-767-0287
www.aprovecho.org

TANNURS

Tkačova, Lenka. "Near-Eastern Tannurs Now & Then: A Close-Up View of Bread Ovens with Respect to the Archaeological Evidence and Selected Ethnographical Examples from Khabur Region," Bachelor's Diploma Thesis. Masaryk University, 2013.

Bottéro, Jean. *The Oldest Cuisine in the World: Cooking in Mesopotamia.* University of Chicago Press, 2004.

POTAGERS AND PROTO-STOVES

Wheaton, Barbara Ketcham. *Savoring the Past: The French Kitchen and Table from 1300 to 1789.* Touchstone, 1996.

Moussette, Marcel. "Kitchen Stove or Potager?" *Bulletin of the Association for Preservation Technology* 8, no. 1 (1976). www.jstor.org/stable/1493561.

CAST-IRON COOKSTOVES

Brewer, Priscilla J. *From Fireplace to Cookstove: Technology and the Domestic Ideal in America.* University Press, 2000.

Cooper, Jane. *Woodstove Cookery: At Home on the Range.* Storey Publishing, 1977.
Practical advice about selecting, using, and maintaining a cookstove.

BUYING A COOKSTOVE

Restored Antiques
Antique Stove Hospital
Little Compton, Rhode Island
401-635-4896
www.stovehospital.com

Barnstable Stove Shop
West Barnstable, Massachusetts
508-362-9913
www.barnstablestove.com

Ginger Creek Antique Stoves
Taylorsville, North Carolina
828-632-2505
www.gingercreekstoves.com

The Love Barn
Orland, Maine
207-469-7420
www.antiquecookstove.com

Contemporary Manufacturers
Country Maid Stoves
Rosebush, Michigan
989-944-1492
www.countrymaidstoves.com

Elmira Stove Works
Elmira, Ontario
800-295-8498
www.elmirastoveworks.com

Heartland Appliances

Greenville, Michigan

800-223-3900

www.heartlandapp.com

Hearthstone Quality Home Heating Products, Inc.

Morrisville, Vermont

877-877-2113

www.hearthstonestoves.com

BARREL OVENS DIY

Edleson, Max and Eva Edleson. *A Guide for Making a Versatile, Efficient, and Easy to Use Wood-Fired Oven.* Hand Print Press, 2012.

Vogelzang International

Holland, Michigan

616-396-1911

www.vogelzang.com

PALEO-SMOKING

Wetterstrom, Wilma. "Foraging and Farming in Egypt." In *The Archaeology of Africa: Foods, Metals and Towns*, edited by Thurstan Shaw, Paul Sinclair, Bassey Andah, and Alex Okpoko, 165–226. Routledge, 1993.

WAMPANOAG SMOKING

Wood, William. *New England's Prospect.* Tho. Cotes, 1634.

> In summer these Indian women, when lobsters be in their plenty and prime, they dry them to keep for winter, erecting scaffolding in the hot sunshine, making fires likewise underneath them (by whose smoke the flies are expelled) till the substance remain hard and dry. In this manner they dry bass and other fishes without salt, cutting them very thin to dry suddenly before the flies spoil them or the rain moist them, having a special care to hang them in their smoking houses in the night and dankish weather.

MAYA SMOKE-ROASTING AND MARKETS

Coe, Sophie D. *America's First Cuisines.* University of Texas Press, 1994.

CHAPTER 5. RETAINED HEAT

KHORKHOG

Apparently, some fun-loving, non-risk-averse Mongols with an understanding of sous-vide cooking have recently kicked the knorkhog up a notch. Not content to use only retained heat, they set the steel or aluminum milk can — lid locked on! — directly on the fire. Aside from the occasional shrapnel, the resulting stew must be extraordinary. (Warning — trying this yourself will probably invalidate your homeowners' insurance.)

EARTH OVENS

Evans, Susan Toby and David L. Webster, eds. *Archaeology of Ancient Mexico and Central America: An Encyclopedia.* Garland, 2001.

Raab, L. Mark, Jim Cassidy, Andrew Yatsko, and William J. Howard. *California Maritime Archaeology: A San Clemente Island Perspective.* AltaMira Press, 2009.

Doerper, John and Alf Collins, eds. "Pacific Northwest Indian Cooking Vessels." In *Oxford Symposium on Food & Cookery, 1988: The Cooking Pot*, edited by Tom Jaine, 28–43. Prospect Books, 1989.

Hayward, Vicki. "False Traditions: Pots in the New Hebrides." In *Oxford Symposium on Food & Cookery, 1988: The Cooking Pot*, edited by Tom Jaine, 68–70. Prospect Books, 1989.

OVENS IN 17TH-CENTURY EUROPEAN COLONIES IN NORTH AMERICA

Marcoux, Paula. "Bread and Permanence." In *Exploring Atlantic Transitions: Archaeologies of Transience and Permanence in New Found Lands*, Peter E. Pope and Shannon Lewis-Simpson, eds. Mongograph no. 7. Society for Post-Medieval Archaeology. Boydell Press, 2013.

Resources, References, and Details

FINDING A MASON

Masonry Heater Association of North America
Tucson, Arizona
520-883-0191
www.mha-net.org

ONLINE OVEN-BUILDING RESOURCES

Brick-Oven
www.groups.yahoo.com/group/brick-oven

Forno Bravo
Salinas, California
800-407-5119
www.fornobravo.com

Traditional Oven
www.traditionaloven.com

SOME WOOD-FIRED OVEN MANUFACTURERS

Forno Bravo
Salinas, California
800-407-5119
www.fornobravo.com

Le Panyol
www.lepanyol.com

Maine Wood Heat Co., Inc.
207-474-7465
www.mainewoodheat.com

Mugnaini, Inc.
Watsonville, California
888-887-7206
www.mugnaini.com

BUILD YOUR OWN OVEN

Boily, Lise and Jean-François Blanchette. *The Bread Ovens of Quebec.* National Museum of Man, 1979.

Denzer, Kiko. *Build Your Own Earth Oven,* 3rd ed. With Hannah Field. Hand Print Press, 2007.

Jaine, Tom. *Building a Wood-Fired Oven for Bread and Pizza.* Prospect Books, 1997.

Wing, Daniel and Alan Scott. *The Bread Builders: Hearth Loaves and Masonry Ovens.* Chelsea Green, 1999.

17TH-CENTURY ILLUSTRATIONS OF ENGLISH BAKING TOOLS

Holme, Randle. *The Academy of Armory.* 1688.

PIZZA FAMILY TREE

Wright, Clifford A. *Cucina Paradiso: The Heavenly Food of Sicily.* Simon & Shuster, 1992.

KEEPING LEAVEN

Markham, Gervase. *The English Housewife.* Edited by Michael R. Best. McGill-Queen's University Press, 1986. First published in 1615.

ANCIENT SOURDOUGH CULTURES

Wood, Ed. *World Sourdoughs from Antiquity: Authentic Recipes for Modern Bakers.* Ten Speed Press, 1996.

GENERAL BAKING RESOURCES

The Fresh Loaf
www.thefreshloaf.com

The Kneading Conference
MAINE GRAIN ALLIANCE
www.kneadingconference.com

Chattman, Lauren. *Bread Making: A Home Course.* Storey Publishing, 2011.

Hamelman, Jeffrey. *Bread: A Baker's Book of Techniques and Recipes,* 2nd ed. John Wiley, 2013.

Miscovich, Richard. *From the Wood-Fired Oven: New and Traditional Techniques for Cooking and Baking with Fire.* Chelsea Green, 2013.

VIENNA BREAD

Hounihan, J.D. *J.D. Hounihan's Bakers' and Confectioners' Guide and Treasure.* 1877.

AUSTIN CAKE RECIPE

Archival recipe courtesy of the Plymouth Antiquarian Society, Plymouth, Massachusetts.

TABUN TECHNOLOGY

Turathuna Center
BETHLEHEM UNIVERSITY LIBRARY
http://library.bethlehem. edu/e-turathuna/tabun

A NOTE ABOUT MEASUREMENTS

With the influx of cheap, compact, easy-to-use kitchen scales on today's market, no cook embarking on a baking project need rely on imprecise measuring cups. That said, a volume cheat sheet for ingredients commonly rendered in ounces in this book may turn out handy on the occasion when the cook is working without a scale.

INGREDIENT	WEIGHT OF ONE CUP
Wheat or rye flour	4½ ounces
Cornmeal	5½ ounces
Sugar	7¼ ounces
Most liquids	8 ounces
Leaven	8 ounces

ACKNOWLEDGMENTS

A heartfelt thank-you is due to all the folks whose homes were invaded and lives disrupted during the photography for *Cooking with Fire*: Tim and Joy Csanadi, Eric and Christine Cody, Hannah Whipple and Justin Keegan, Julie and Michael Burrey, Stephen Feeney, Frank and Sally Albani, and Betsey Frawley and Jim Litton. Special thanks also to Brian Taylor and Cherie Mittenthal of the Truro Center for the Arts at Castle Hill for letting us photograph the construction of their oven — and the great good sportsmanship of all the workshop participants.

Thanks to Kofi Ingersoll and Erin Koh at Bay End Farm in Buzzards Bay, as well as Tammy and Mike Race, for coming up with beautiful ingredients at clutch moments. Also David Marsh, for catching the world's best scallops.

Thanks to Mark Atchison, Jack Pitney, Pret Woodburn, Martha Sulya, and especially, George Paré for forged iron cooking gear, and Bruce Frankel of SpitJack for other hearth-cooking equipment and pithy insider information.

I really lucked out the day Carleen Madigan called me out of the blue and introduced me to this book idea. She has been a good-humored and patient collaborator, as well as a champion daub-mixer at oven-building time. I am inutterably grateful to art director Alethea Morrison for her gorgeous and detailed work creating the physical artifact called *Cooking with Fire*. Joe Keller's outstanding photography speaks for itself but cannot communicate what a pleasure he and his assistant Jeffrey Stiles were to work with.

Thanks to Julie and Leo Marcoux — in general, for a lifetime of love and support, and in particular, for imparting to me their respective passions for cooking and history.

This book would have been inconceivable without the extraordinary skills, enthusiasm, and creativity of my husband, Pret Woodburn. The process confirmed that there's almost nothing he can't build or eat.

INDEX

Page references in italic indicate photos.